YALE STUDIES IN ECONOMICS, 14

PRICE FORMATION
IN NATURAL GAS FIELDS

A Study of Competition, Monopsony, and Regulation

BY PAUL W. MAC AVOY

New Haven and London, Yale University Press, 1962

Published with assistance from the foundation
established in memory of Calvin Chapin of the
class of 1788, Yale College.

For Louise, Katherine, and Libby

Preface

Because important and frequent changes in the national regulation of gas fields make it difficult to provide a study of economics and public policy that is up-to-date, it seems preferable in a study of this industry to concentrate upon long-standing assumptions and objectives of national regulatory policy. This study focuses on the economic reasons for regulation. Most discussions that preceded policy formation referred to the necessity of preventing monopoly pricing in gas fields (as outlined in Chapter 1). There were also statements that regulation was needed to prevent future price increases, since such increases would be derived at least in part from the use of monopoly power. Some factual basis for these assertions may be found in an analysis of field price formation before the advent of price regulation. The purpose of this study is to state the characteristics of monopoly price formation, and of competitive and monopsony price formation (in Chapters 2, 3, 4), in order to see which corresponds most closely to actual price formation in the 1950s (in Chapters 5, 6, 7).

Such a study, it is hoped, will provide new materials pertinent to policy formulation. The general conclusions of this economic analysis (Chapters 5–8) are that field markets in the 1950s were centers of highly competitive pricing, or were characterized generally by movement away from monopsony (buyer's monopoly) toward competition. The results suggest that monopoly pricing is not a substantive reason for regulation. They suggest that there is no urgent need to retain recent Federal Power Commission price controls (as is argued in Chapter 8).

The study benefited greatly, at three stages, from the counsel and assistance of many persons. Most of the structure of analysis, and a study of price formation during 1956 and 1957, were completed between March 1958 and July 1959, and were submitted as a Ph.D. thesis in economics at Yale University. The dissertation committee, Professors John Perry Miller and Charles H. Berry of the Economics Department and Professor Ward S. Bowman of the Yale Law School, commented upon an unduly large number of drafts at that stage. I am grateful to them for their patience, interest, and particularly for their suggestions.

The analysis was later modified and extended, while I was not otherwise engaged as an instructor at Yale, to include markets during the early 1950s. Discussions of the technical aspects of gas fields were carried on with people in most of the larger petroleum companies and pipelines in Texas and Oklahoma. Statistical computations were graciously provided by the Yale University Computing Center. I am indebted to personnel in these organizations for information obtained, to the James Morris Whiton Fund of the Yale Graduate School, and to the Ford Foundation Faculty Research Funds at Yale for funds making visits and computer use possible.

The third stage consisted of producing a manuscript from the materials of analysis. This has been done since I came to the University of Chicago in July 1960 as assistant professor of economics in the Graduate School of Business. I am grateful to Professor John Miller for continued attempts to clarify the analysis and to render the literary style more pleasing. Professors Charles Berry and Harold Watts (of the Cowles Foundation at Yale) provided criticisms of the analysis, and suggestions for continued further research, that added substantially to the results. Professor Alfred E. Kahn of Cornell University furnished criticisms of the first three, and the last, chapters which were the basis for substantial revision. Professor George J. Stigler of the University of Chicago succeeded in finding means by which to decrease the length of the early chapters by one-third, while increasing content by a similar fraction. This perceptive gentleman subsequently greatly reduced the irrelevancies and errors in the last four chapters, and suggested the basis for the last table in Chapter 5 (and subsequent similar tables). Professor Morris A. Adelman, of the Massachusetts Institute of Technology, provided discussions and written criticisms of inestimable value on each chapter. His understanding of the relationship of economic analysis to policy in the gas industry, and his knowledge of long-term supply of gas reserves, have been borrowed extensively. Also, Richard A. Miller of Wesleyan University, Victor Zarnowitz of the University of Chicago, and Osmon Abdel-Salam of the University of Khartoum have provided valuable page-by-page comments. Miss Muriel Snider, Miss Carol Lovrencic, and Mrs. Judith Jensen are responsible for producing a manuscript from my scribbled notes. Each of these individuals has my appreciation for their additions to this work. I remain responsible for all the subtractions.

Paul W. MacAvoy

University of Chicago
January 1962

Contents

xi

Tables, Figures, Maps

FIGURES

PRICE FORMATION IN NATURAL GAS FIELDS

1. Public Policy and a Study of Competition

The central question of public policy on natural gas in recent years has been whether producers' sales to interstate pipelines should be regulated. Before 1954, the producers were free of price control. In 1954 a Supreme Court decision, *Phillips Petroleum Company v. Wisconsin,* found that the Federal Power Commission had jurisdiction to determine whether prices and sales conditions were "reasonable" on gas sold in interstate commerce.[1] Since then, discussion on the necessity of price control has been continuous but inconclusive. In the United States Congress, representatives and senators have argued the case for and against legislation to exempt the producers from the *Phillips*-imposed regulation. The most successful bill was the Harris-Fulbright Bill which proposed to amend the Natural Gas Act so as to exempt producers from any regulation; it carried a majority of both houses but was vetoed by the President.[2] Meanwhile, the Commission has considered a method of regulation which itself questions the need for any regulation. In *Champlin Oil and Refining Co.,*

1. Cf. *Phillips Petroleum Co. v. Wisconsin,* 347 U.S. 622; jurisdiction followed under the Natural Gas Act, U.S.C. 717.52 Stat. 821 (1938).
2. The Harris-Fulbright Bill S. 1853 of the 84th Congress (1955) was vetoed because some industry personnel had exerted "extraordinary" pressure on some members of Congress. It was followed by the Harris-O'Hara "Compromise" Bill, and others that were not reported out of committee in 1956 and 1957.

et al.,[3] the gas producers proposed that only those prices which were not "fair field prices" be regulated. "Fair field prices" were defined as those following from competitive market forces. They would be allowed automatically; other prices would be regulated by the Commission. This meant that, if all prices were fair field prices, the Commission would do no price regulating. By considering this method of regulation, the Commission in effect considered the need and reasons for any regulation.

MONOPOLY AS THE REASON FOR REGULATION

In the *Phillips* case, in the congressional bills, and in the Commission hearings a number of reasons were presented for regulation of gas producers' prices. The most persistent, and effective, said that prices were not being determined in a competitive manner. It was argued that there was monopoly control of the in-ground gas, and that the pipeline buyer paid higher-than-competitive prices for restricted total amounts of gas. It was said that monopolistic pricing in gas fields should be controlled, as monopolistic electricity rates or rail freight rates were controlled.

Rationale for Regulation in the Phillips *Case.*   Testimony in *Phillips Petroleum Co. v. Wisconsin* (when not concerned with defining a "natural gas company") was concerned with producers' power to control prices. At one point, counsel for Wisconsin consumers stated: "We want to buy your gas, we want to pay a fair price, but we feel you have a monopoly . . . we don't think you are justified in assuming the Federal Power Commission will not give you a fair price and we don't think we should be subject to the arbitrary whim of some company not even subject to (state) Commission (control), as to the price at which it sells."[4] The Phillips Company disputed the assertion that prices were monopolistic. Its brief

3. Federal Power Commission Docket G-9277, the "Omnibus" hearings on regulatory methods, 1957–59.
4. 347 U.S. 672, Testimony, pp. 3667–70.

stated: "The advocates of federal regulation rely heavily upon the assertion that regulation is necessary to protect consumers against excessive prices. This assertion has no basis in fact. . . . There is sufficient evidence in the record to negate any assertion that Phillips' prices are now excessive or exorbitant. The nature of the business is such as to be carried on by a large number of business units. In 1946 and 1947 approximately 2,300 independent producers or gatherers sold gas directly to natural gas companies (pipelines)."[5] This implied that the monopoly power to set prices, so far from being used to set "excessive" prices, did not in fact exist. The Supreme Court ignored the Phillips' position and stated: "The rates charged (by producers) may have a direct and substantial effect upon the price paid by the ultimate consumers. Protection of consumers against exploitation at the hands of the natural gas companies was the primary aim of the *Natural Gas Act*."[6]

Rationale for Regulation in Senate Hearings. In the Senate hearings and debate on the Harris-Fulbright Bill, the economic reason given for exempting producers from regulation was that field gas markets were competitive.[7] After a lengthy analysis of current gas deliveries, Dr. John Boatwright, of Standard Oil of Indiana, concluded for the producers: "The producing phase of the industry represents over 8,000 operators. There is a wide diversification of ownership, with present producers daily inviting new men and capital to enter the field. There is no evidence of monopolistic control based on concentration of ownership on a national, regional, state, or producing area basis."[8] Dr. Boatwright found evidence for competition in market behavior as well as in structural conditions: "We have applied the normal tests of competitive

5. "Brief for Petitioner Phillips Petroleum Company," no. 280 *Records,* 347 U.S. 672 (1954), pp. 85, 89, 90–91.
6. 347 U.S. 672 (1954) at 685.
7. There were "noneconomic" reasons, of course, including political and legal considerations.
8. "Consumer Interest in Natural Gas Competition," statement of John W. Boatwright in support, cf. S. 1853 before the Senate Committee on Interstate and Foreign Commerce, p. 110.

behavior on the supply side of the market . . . prices vary through time, have the flexibility characteristic of lack of control . . . have not gone up with competitive fuels or with the general cost of living . . . prices vary among fields and react to variations of supply resulting from new discoveries. Each and every one of these tests has indicated price behavior typical of that expected in a competitive market. Therefore . . . there is no evidence to indicate monopolistic control on the part of producers." [9] His strongest conclusion was: "The facts here reviewed have established that the consumer inevitably receives his greatest protection from competitive activity . . . and (given the costs of regulation, expected inefficiencies, etc.) there can be no question but that under regulation the long-run prices paid by the consumer would be higher than if the producing phase were unregulated." [10]

Some members of Congress disagreed with Dr. Boatwright's analysis and conclusion. One in particular, Senator Paul H. Douglas of Illinois (formerly professor of economics at the University of Chicago) took issue with the analysis, point by point, in a lengthy speech on the pending Harris-Fulbright Bill. He said: "Competition is limited by the domination of supply and reserves by a very few major companies . . . by the need (of the pipelines) for huge long-term supplies which only dominant producers can provide . . . by the fact that pipelines can pass high prices on to the consumer . . . and the system of Favored Nations Clauses makes these artificially high prices the new dominant or average prices." [11] In other words, if the pipelines do not have the incentive to bargain for the lowest (or competitive) prices, and if the larger producers control the major part of the gas supply, then the producers control the price. Senator Douglas emphasized the "public utility" nature of gas pipelining, and the "large" relative shares of production he saw coming from a "few" sellers in some field areas. He concluded: "As the consumer

9. Ibid., p. 104.
10. Ibid., p. 110.
11. The speech has been summarized by Senator Douglas as "The Case for the Consumer of Natural Gas," 44 *Georgetown Law Journal* 566. The quotation is from page 589.

is the captive of the industry, he will get it in the neck if the Federal Power Commission is denied jurisdiction over the sales for resale of natural gas in interstate commerce." [12]

The differences between Dr. Boatwright and Senator Douglas were not resolved. The Harris-Fulbright Bill was voted by the Senate, so that Dr. Boatwright's arguments, and others like them, were apparently persuasive. But discussion of competition, its existence and effectiveness, continued nevertheless.

Rationale for Regulation in the Commission Hearings. In the *Champlin Oil* hearings, Professor M. A. Adelman testified: "Natural gas is produced under conditions of low concentration, lower than 75–85% of manufactured products. Buyers of gas operate in what is fast becoming a national market . . . they are large, able to review all offers, and have strong inducements to make even small savings." [13] Observation of price differences and price levels led Professor Adelman to conclude: "Variations in prices may be normally expected to exist . . . based on considerations above (i.e., differences in demand for different sales contracts) it is my conclusion that the production of gas is a competitive industry." [14] It was argued that, with the industry *generally* competitive, attention of the Federal Power Commission may be centered upon regulating only the few sales that might not be competitive because of isolated location, and the like. All competitive prices—fair field prices—should be allowed to stand. For "when regulation is based upon (competitive) market prices, the ends if not the means are simple, and they make economic sense." [15]

The proposal to regulate only those prices that were not fair field prices raised immediate objections. Witnesses for pipeline and retail gas distributors denied the proposal's usefulness since the industry was not "generally competitive." Pro-

12. Ibid., p. 577.
13. Before the Federal Power Commission, *Champlin Oil and Refining Co., et al.,* Docket G-9277, p. 458 L.C.
14. Ibid., p. 458 L.C.
15. Ibid., p. 461 L.C.

fessor Alfred E. Kahn presented a lengthy analysis of seller concentration, of price behavior over a period of time, and of prices from sale to sale at a given time. When asked, "Would you characterize the market for natural gas in the field as ineffectively competitive or monopolistic?" [16] he answered, "I have avoided reference to such characterizations thus far for two reasons. First of all . . . it is not the simple single firm monopoly you find in traditional public utilities. In my judgment however there are peculiar characteristics of these markets that make it impossible for me to call the industry workably competitive—characteristics indeed that introduce the possibility of significant monopoly exploitation." [17] Professor Kahn found that price behavior in existing markets had adverse effects upon income distribution, by favoring producers' returns while not providing incentives for further additions to the supply of reserves. This followed from the ineffectiveness of competition and from "questionable aspects having nothing to do with the effectiveness of competition . . . (but which) may justify price regulation." [18]

Professors Adelman and Kahn disagreed fundamentally upon the extent and effects of competition in gas markets. Their disagreement was similar to that found in the *Phillips* hearings and in the debate on the Harris-Fulbright Bill; it led to similarly contradictory proposals for regulatory policy. In each set of discussions, a conclusion that markets were competitive implied that regulation of gas field sales should be abandoned; a conclusion that markets exhibited monopoly-type behavior implied that prices should be controlled.

ADDITIONS TO THIS CONTROVERSY

A central consideration for regulatory policy is a thorough analysis of the roles of competition and monopoly in natural gas pricing. Such an analysis—involving a detailed study of individual gas markets and prices—seems to be the only method by which the issues sketched above may be resolved.

Competition is "explored" in the natural gas producing

16. Ibid., p. 4896 L.C.
17. Ibid., p. 4896 L.C.
18. Ibid., p. 4896 L.C.

areas of the southwest United States in the following chapters. Chapters 2 and 3 describe the product and the conditions of sale as involving commitments of long-term rights to take natural gas reserves out of the ground for interstate delivery. The production conditions, the producer's cost, and the pipeline buyer's demand under this type of sale are considered. The geography and time period of the "market" are defined.[19]

To find the extent of actual market competition, standards must be provided. Chapter 4 describes the structure of a "competitive" gas market in terms of the numbers and relative sizes of firms, and discusses the patterns of prices and sales expected under competitive conditions. In contrast, structural conditions and pricing characteristics for monopoly gas markets are described. In further contrast, behavior in a monopoly buyer's (i.e., monopsony) market is described.

These structure-performance criteria allow actual markets to be characterized as "competitive" or "monopolistic" or "monopsonistic." Chapters 5, 6, 7 contain such a classification of recent Southwest markets. Some of the markets are seen to exhibit price and sales behavior markedly similar to the theoretical competitive pattern, while some indicate behavior identical to the theoretical monopsony pattern, and none indicates behavior characteristic of the theoretical monopoly pattern.

The final chapter considers the implications for regulatory policy of mixed competition-monopsony. The findings allow some judgments on the arguments for or against regulation, and shed some light on the effects of continuing present regulations. Some part of the controversy concerning "the facts" on the state of competition and on the urgent need for regulation may end up being closer to resolution than previously.

19. Interest is confined to the "short-run" period and area within which it is not possible to establish an entirely new productive facility. Professor George Stigler, for one, has indicated the insight that can be gained into giant firm behavior by confining attention to the "short run." Cf. his "Monopoly and Oligopoly by Merger," 40 *American Economic Review* 23–24. Here the fixed production facility is the *volume of discovered reserves* from exploration up to a given point in time.

2. The Conditions of Supply of Natural Gas Reserves

Sales of volumes of gas in the field are determined in part by the "costs of production." These costs, following from the technology of gas recovery coupled with prevailing legal arrangements, are incurred at discrete stages. Production of the first cubic feet of gas in the reservoir requires a large initial expenditure. Production of additional volumes necessitates little additional expenditure until recovery nears the maximum amount in the "trap," when further very large expenditures are required. In other words, as "capacity" is approached, limits on even small additions to sales result in sharply rising costs.[1]

To explain the effect of "indivisible" production conditions upon costs and supply, the technology of gas withdrawal from a reservoir is outlined. The legal arrangements affecting the nature of costs are mentioned as well. Subsequently, the illustrative cost curves are drawn.

TECHNICAL CONDITIONS OF PRODUCTION

"Natural gas" is a simple hydrocarbon that is gaseous when surfaced from an underground reservoir. This hydrocarbon is composed of 85 to 95 per cent methane, and can be proc-

1. Price levels offered for the "capacity volume" can vary greatly, in this case, without affecting supply. The prices charged by the monopolist should theoretically differ from those expected from the monopoly buyer (the "monopsonist") or from competition, when supply is inelastic.

essed to provide 1,000 BTU per cubic foot energy content, usually at a pressure of 14.65 pounds pressure per square inch.[2] It is removed from reservoirs or "traps" that are porous, permeable rock formations in a surrounding seal of impermeable rock and water. The permeable rock may be sand, sandstone, limestone, dolomite, or chalk and may be found from 1,000 to 16,000 feet below surface. The reservoirs may contain not only gas of the requisite quality, but also crude oil (hexane with more complex forms of hydrocarbons of the paraffin series) and "liquid petroleum gas" (propane with the butanes that liquefy out of solution in the gas at lower surface pressures). Typically a number of traps occur close together—side by side or one above the other—so that they form a "field." [3]

Gas is sold while still in the reservoir on the assumption that it can be recovered by the producer. Recovery consists of delivering the gas into the pipeline of the buyer. Before the buyer agrees to purchase the gas, and before he constructs a gathering line to allow delivery, the producer must estimate how much gas is underground and how much can be recovered. Surface geological surveys and underground sounding techniques are employed to establish both the boundaries and the thickness of the (potential) gas-bearing formation. These dimensions are then used to estimate the volume of gas underground. It remains to estimate what portion is recoverable.

The recoverable reserve is the amount of trapped gas that can move to the well-base in the permeable rock, and then expand through the well piping to surface pipelines. Movement

2. This compares with manufactured coal gas that provides 500 BTU per cubic foot at similar pressures.

3. Dr. R. S. Knappan of Tulsa, Oklahoma, compares one type of field with "a stack of saucers turned upside down." There usually are a number of stacks close together as well. Conditions of temperature, pressure, and the presence of organic waste matter in an area over a number of centuries may have created anticline domes or "saucers,' containing oil and gas, in a "basin." A number of reservoirs or traps may be adjacent in a field area, and all the fields within a 1,000 to 10,000 square mile area may be in a "basin" because their geological ages, depths, and pressures are quite similar.

is made possible by a pressure differential between the sealed trap and the surface pipeline. In-ground pressures usually range from 500 to 10,000 pounds per square inch, while pipeline pressures range from 250 to 1,000 pounds. As long as a differential is maintained—either by the force of underground water in the trap, or by the gas itself expanding—delivery can take place.[4]

An estimate of the volume of recoverable gas can be obtained only by drilling preliminary producing wells. These so-called "step-out" wells, placed at intervals over the hypothesized producing reservoir, provide estimates of potential daily recovery of gas from each section of the trap, and an estimate of the total volume "in place."[5] Then, taking into account the buyer's insistence upon a uniform rate of production,[6] and upon a particular pipeline pressure, the producer can estimate the amount of in-place reserves he can recover. This figure is only an *estimate*, because further drilling may discover non-producing sectors of the trap. But it is an estimate the buyer is likely to accept, whereas one based upon forecasts from one "wildcat" well is not.

After the buyer agrees to take the estimated recoverable reserves over a ten to twenty-year period, preparation for production really begins. Only 20–40 per cent of the necessary

4. A trap with gas expansion and water encroachment may have recovery of 70–80 per cent of the gas volume "in place." Perhaps 50 per cent of reserves are recoverable as a result of the pressure differential created by gas expansion alone.

5. The estimates in practice follow from both the "volumetric" and "pressure-drop" calculations. The "volumetric" arrives at a figure for recoverable reserves by using samples of well-base rock and mobility of gas in tests, et al. to calculate the part of the trap volume that is not rock but gas. Recoverability is estimated from the type of pressure source: water drive vs. gas expansion. The pressure-drop calculation follows from plotting pressures and produced gas as a straight line on semilog paper, in accordance with Boyles' and Charles' Laws of gas expansion. By extrapolation, the gas "produced" (when well-base pressure falls to shutdown level) can be predicted. The prediction is quite accurate when wells have been operating for some period; it is not accurate when based on first tests of "step-out" wells, to any extent. The calculations are widely used for revising production forecasts after five years of operation.

6. The predominant requirement of buyers is for a contract of purchase that specifies or implies a uniform rate of delivery. Reasons for this are discussed in Chapter 3.

wells are usually drilled in stepping-out, so drilling must be completed and/or compression equipment installed. There must be enough wells and compression to produce, in the last year of delivery, the uniform annual volume requested by the buyer.

In technical terms, the number of wells to be drilled and the size of compressors installed depends upon "capacity" required. "Maximum capacity" is the percentage of total reserves recoverable from operating all wells to maximum flow (if the first year's maximum output is Q_1 cubic feet of gas and there are Q estimated cubic feet in the reservoir, then Q_1/Q is "maximum initial capacity"). Maximum capacity declines over the lifetime of the reservoir because pressure declines. In gas-expansion traps, maximum capacity declines proportionally with the amount of actual production, so that $Q_2/Q = [Q_1/Q] \ (1-R)$ where Q_2/Q is "maximum second year's capacity" and R is the rate of the first year's actual production.[7] Capacity in the *last* year of production, Q_T/Q, has to be equal to R (given the buyer's preference for a uniform annual amount of delivery). The producer is required to provide "maximum final capacity" $Q_T/Q = R = [Q_1/Q] \ (1-R)^{T-1}$, so that $Q_1/Q = \dfrac{R}{(1-R)^{T-1}}$. The required initial capacity to produce, Q_1/Q, depends upon the uniform rate of production, R, and the number of years of delivery, T.

Diminishing returns in production follow from providing additional capacity. If the required uniform rate of production is to be 2 per cent per annum for twenty-one years, a well pattern that can produce 2.97 per cent the first year is sufficient.[8] But if the production is to be at the rate of 4 per cent then required initial capacity is 8.76 per cent.[9] To double

7. That is, if first year's production is 10 per cent, while capacity is 40 per cent, then the second year's maximum capacity is only 36 per cent because of pressure (reserve) depletion.

8. $Q_1/Q = \dfrac{R}{(1-R)^{T-1}}$ with $T = 21$, $R = .02$, then $Q_1/Q = 2.97$ per cent.

9. With $Q_1/Q = \dfrac{R}{(1-R)^{T-1}}$ and $R = .04$, $T = 21$, $Q_1/Q = 8.87$ per cent.

recovered reserves takes *at least* four times as many wells. If an attempt is made to provide a 4.50 per cent rate of production each year, required initial capacity rises to 11.58 per cent (an increase of more than $\frac{1}{3}$ in required capacity and wells for a $\frac{1}{10}$th increase in recovery.)[10] Such sharply decreasing returns from providing more initial capacity implies sharply increasing expenditures for drilling in order to produce an additional amount of the estimated available reserves in the trap.[11]

Wells are drilled *capable* of producing Q_1/Q the first year, so as to be sufficient to produce Q_T/Q the last year. The larger the required initial capacity Q_1/Q, the greater the necessary number of wells. In gas traps, there are diminishing returns from increased drilling. The closer wells are to each other, the less the additions to capacity from drilling given the fixed volume of in-ground gas. Well-clogging and interwell pressure differentials lead to loss of reserves as wells overlap. Both the limit on volume and well-clogging result in diminishing additions to recovered volume from constant additions to compressor horsepower.[12]

In brief, technical conditions require a minimum number of wells and/or compressors. The required "capacity to produce" and the equipment for providing required capacity both increase more than proportionally with increased percentage recovery of the in-ground volume of gas.[13]

10. For a uniform rate of production of .045 and $T = 20$, required initial capacity is 11.588 per cent. This is approximately 35 per cent higher than for $R = .04$, and consequently requires at least a 35 per cent increase in wells. The real problem is to increase capacity by 35 per cent with an additional 35 per cent increase in numbers of wells.

11. That is, unless there are substitute methods of production (such as compression of the gas) diminishing returns to providing capacity imply rising marginal production costs. Cf. J. M. Cassels, "On the Law of Variable Proportions," reprinted by American Economic Association, *Readings in the Theory of Income Distribution* (Philadelphia, Blakiston, 1946); Tibor Scitovsky, *Welfare and Competition* (London, Allen & Unwin, 1952), pp. 113–34.

12. Compression equipment serves as a substitute for wells in providing capacity at high rates of recovery, because it can compensate for low pressures in the immediate vicinity of established wells.

13. There are some further incidental requirements from the producer. He must replace well tubing, operate a "work-over rig," scour well holes, and provide meter supervision during production.

LEGAL CONDITIONS AFFECTING PRODUCTION COSTS

Costs of recovered gas are strongly affected by legal requirements governing the drilling of wells. These legal requirements in effect build indivisibility into production by making
one drilling pattern mandatory for all rates of gas recovery.

State conservation commissions prescribe production methods because natural gas "fugaciousness" (high subsurface
mobility) makes it possible for one well-owner in a common
reservoir to produce gas from under another well-owner's
land. At the same time, landowners lease mineral rights on
terms that demand the maximum legal number of wells.

There are "conservation" rules covering all stages of production in most states. An attempt is made to prevent high rates
of production when the trap is discovered so that the first
producer does not deliver more gas than is under his leased
acreage. The state conservation commissions request adher-
ence to "Rule 25" requiring production at rates no more than
25 per cent of maximum initial capacity. High rates of production likely to result in well-clogging [14] or to drain another
producer's part of the reservoir continue to be prevented
throughout the lifetime of the trap. In practice, production is
"prorated" for each field separately by the state conservation
commission for each month during the reservoir's production
life. The state agency prorates on the basis of total "nominations" of the producers or buyers for the number of cubic feet
they wish delivered. The total is divided into producers'
shares, according to relative amounts of reserves estimated to
be located under the various land-leases, and according to the
relative holdings of surface acreage or of wells. The result is
a "legal share" for each owner in gas produced from a reservoir with many owners.

Proration affects the timing of production. It may not be
possible for a producer to "save" his proration shares, so that

14. Permanent loss of potentially recoverable reserves is possible in
water-drive traps when high rates of production suck the water seal
into the well, so as to cause pockets of gas to be isolated. It is not
usually possible in gas expansion traps, although in rare instances high
rates of production cause wells to become *sand*-clogged and gas is lost.

plans involving delivery over a thirty-year period or plans to begin delivery only after "shutting-in" for five years may not be feasible.[15] In most instances, plans to begin production farther in the future than two years have to be eliminated because they differ from those of others in the trap (and allow others to produce a shut-in firm's prorated shares).

Proration has an important effect upon the pattern of drilling. "Field spacing rules" limit producers to one well for each 300 to 700 acres (with minimum spacing in *any one field* being determined by the permeability of the sand). The rules require wells to be placed centrally within large blocks of land so that recovery can be limited generally to gas under that block, and so that full recovery can take place in that block utilizing natural expansion over a ten to twenty-year period. The rules may prevent drilling to provide capacity for differing rates of production.[16] The producer may have to forego intensive drilling for high rates of recovery in five years because well drilling would be "too close." He may also have to forego low rates of recovery because each landowner requires, in the lease, the drilling of any well that can legally be placed on his land.[17]

15. Oklahoma has procedures which protect "shut-in" producers from losing their shares and thus from being drained over any extended period of time. M. B. Murray, Oklahoma director of conservation, has suggested that other producers can be shut-in when their shares are depleted and short-term monthly "underproduction" can be made up. Texas has been applying such rules on a trial basis since 1957.

16. It should be remembered, now and later, that gas proration differs significantly from oil proration. Production limits on gas in any month come from buyer's nominations according to the sales contract. There is no method by which commissions can control the *amount* of gas promised by a seller over the contract period and thus the volume of supply in a gas market. Without control of market supply, practices complained of in oil proration by E. V. Rostow in *A National Policy for the Oil Industry* (New Haven, Yale University Press, 1949) and by M. de Chazeau and A. E. Kahn, *Integration and Competition in the Petroleum Industry* (New Haven, Yale University Press, 1959) are not possible. That is, there do not seem to be legal sanctions enforcing output restriction in a relevant market.

17. This is for the landowner's protection: he receives an initial lump-sum payment and an annual return equal to 12½ per cent of the value of the gas surfaced *on his land,* in return for granting "mining rights" to the producer. To receive the annual return, the landowner

Three decisions remain for the producer, within the technical and legal limitations upon production. He decides whether to carry out the original wildcat exploration and drill the exploratory step-out wells. He decides whether to drill the proration pattern of development wells. He also decides whether to use compression equipment to produce volumes that cannot be surfaced by gas expansion. The first decision involves "long-run" variation in the number of discovered reservoirs. The last two decisions are concerned with production in the "short run" since they center upon recovery of discovered in-ground reserves of gas (or production from a "fixed plant" of reserves and discovery wells).[18]

SHORT-RUN COSTS OF PRODUCTION

The measure of costs pertinent to supplying discovered gas is "marginal development costs"—the change in total costs over the production period following from recovery of small additional amounts of in-ground reserves.[19] Such costs include increased expenses for well drilling, well operation,

---

must have wells operating on his property. The "habendum" clause in the typical lease *requires* the drilling of all legal wells within a specified period of six months to three years (depending upon the extent of field development). The "unless" clause requires drilling *and* production from the allotted well within another specified period unless additional "delay rentals" are paid. Otherwise, the producer can be required to forfeit the lease (cf., *Romero v. Brown*, 132 F2d. 872 [1943]). Legally allotted wells determine the location of actual wells along with the timing of the drilling, unless the producer can convince the landowner with "delay rentals" to forego invoking the expressed covenants. The risks for landowners in accepting "delay rentals" are great, particularly if other owners are receiving production royalties (since ultimate royalties may be lost if drainage from another well has taken place). It is not likely that producers and landowners can agree to defer production or drilling.

18. The first decision involves a commitment to undertake building a "new plant." Volumes of gas at various locations that have not been "proven" by actual discovery have little direct effect upon supply and price offers of known volumes. The latter are those for which price formation is to be analyzed.

19. These are the analogy of marginal costs found in analyses of manufacturing costs, the change in total costs from increasing output by one (small) unit. In natural gas production, consider total development costs $C = f(V, R, T)$ from producing at various uniform rates R

interest, and royalties from increased volumes of delivered reserves.

Intensive use of *given* exploratory wells may enable the typical producer to supply small volumes at zero (short-run) cost (from utilization of discovery wells alone). However, to produce any appreciable part of estimated reserves over a twenty-year period, the entire pattern of "legally spaced" wells must be drilled.[20] Once this has been done the required capacity for higher uniform rates of recovery has been obtained.[21]

Operation expenses are small for low rates of recovery and large for high rates of recovery. In the first case, maintenance expenses—well-pipe cleaning and replacement—are the only costs of operation, and these vary with the number of wells. In the second case, where compression equipment is used to increase recovery from 80 to 90 per cent of in-ground reserves, costs rise as larger equipment and more fuel are required to counteract continually decreasing pressures in the trap.[22]

---

over the term-length of production T an amount V. Then, $V = \int_0^T R(t)dt$

for time t, and marginal development costs $MC = \dfrac{\partial C}{\partial V}$.

20. The entire pattern includes some nonproducing wells also. Even with the estimates of the extent of the trap obtained from the "step-out" wells, there is uncertainty as to locations for producing holes. The formation containing gas may be discontinuous at some locations, the actual producing strata may be a number of separate traps with sealing rock between so that some development wells turn out to be unsuccessful "dry" holes. Experience with development may eventually enable the producers to suggest "a chance for success" on each new development well in a new trap on the basis of the type of sealing rock, character of soundings, et al. The experimental probabilities of development drilling success are used in practice to find a priori the necessary pattern of drilling for a new, undeveloped trap. If each trap development well has a .75 probability of providing producing capacity, the producer can expect to have to redrill one out of four wells. Cost estimates include the expected expenditures on dry-hole development wells.

21. As one Richfield Oil Corporation executive said in private correspondence, "They [drilling costs] are incurred in practically the same amounts regardless of the percentage of a capacity utilized above zero," presumably because the one well pattern for minimum spacing is required by landowners for all rates of production.

22. Production engineers at Cities Service Gas Company of Oklahoma

Interest and royalty charges may also be included in marginal development costs. Under the typical sales agreement the producer receives payment only when the gas is surfaced so he incurs a mortgage-type interest charge on drilling expenditures either as interest on a gas development loan, or as opportunity costs of 10–20 per cent per annum on personal funds.[23] In either case, total interest costs increase with drilling costs, with the length of production period, and (given increased risk of default) with the proportion of the total estimated available reserve produced.

The lease-royalty cost to the producer normally consists of a lump-sum payment before exploration, plus $12\frac{1}{2}$ per cent of total revenue thereafter. In special circumstances the lump sum may vary with the extent of the development program. When production is deferred, "delay rentals" are paid to keep the lease in effect and to compensate the landowners for a longer investment period and for increased risk of drainage by producing wells. The increased royalty is an additional cost of the initial rates of recovery and implies higher marginal costs of initial recovery.

These characteristics of drilling, operation, interest, and royalty expenses result in marginal development costs that fall sharply for low relative volumes of recovery and rise sharply for production of 60–80 per cent of estimated reserves.

The marginal development cost curve is shown in Figure

estimate that the first 10 per cent beyond natural drive costs an *average* of 4–5 cents per thousand cubic feet (while drilling costs on the whole average 8–10 cents per thousand cubic feet). This is a rough estimate when pipeline pressures are 700–800 pounds per square inch.

23. Some of the larger producers consider the internal rate of return to be at least 18 per cent on development drilling. Since they are in competitive markets for development capital, this may be close to the prevailing interest rate. It would be surprising to find the rate any higher for small producers, given the number of sources of bank "oil loans." The reason for so high a rate may be the presence of risk in development drilling. The rate should reflect the "pure rate of interest" on riskless loans plus an addendum for the a priori risk of dry-hole drilling (or the variance in realized costs). For procedures seeking to evaluate risk, cf. C. E. Dodson, "Petroleum Engineering for Bank Loans" (mimeographed, First National City Bank of New York, 1958).

2:1.[24] Since legal conditions require drilling to be completed before the recovery program begins, the major expenditure is indivisible and attributable to low rates of recovery. Since compression is undertaken only when natural forces are insufficient, and provides only a small addition to production, the cost of compression is large relative to the last amounts of reserves recovered. Indivisibilities and diminishing returns in providing gas at a uniform rate give a U-shape to the curve.

The marginal and average development cost curves indicate expenses for recovering varying percentages of the available reserves in one trap. These curves shift with changes in the length of the delivery period. As the period lengthens, the marginal production cost curve shifts to a higher level.[25] Operation costs are larger because there are additional charges for supervisory labor and for tubing replacement each year. Drilling costs change not at all as term increases in most cases.[26] Interest charges on drilling costs and other

24. The curve is an indication that, if $C = f(V, R, T)$ and $V \leqq Q_0$, the estimated reserves in the trap, then $\dfrac{\partial C}{\partial V} > 0$ for V equal to the aggregate volume of recovered reserves during some term-length $T = T_0$ and for some rate of production R such that $V = \displaystyle\int_0^{T_0} R(T) dT$. The curve also indicates that $\dfrac{\partial^2 C}{\partial V^2} \leqq 0$ for $V < V_1$ where V_1 is that volume which is the maximum attainable from gas and water pressures; for $V > V_1$, $\dfrac{\partial^2 C}{\partial V^2} > 0$.

25. When total development costs $C = f(V, R, T)$ and the contract has *longer* term length of production, the MC curve $\dfrac{\partial V}{\partial C}$ shifts up. That is, $\dfrac{\partial^2 C}{\partial T \partial V} > 0$. This second derivative is interesting because term T does vary between contracts in actual markets.

26. Smaller capacity and fewer wells are necessary to produce any given percentage of reserves over a longer period (because the rate of production the last year needs to be less). For 80 per cent recovery and term of eleven years, $\dfrac{Q_1}{Q} = \dfrac{R}{(1-R)^{T-1}} = 18.40$ per cent rather than $\dfrac{Q_1}{Q} = 8.76$ per cent for a term of 21 years. If the number of wells increases proportionately with capacity, increasing the term to twenty-one years

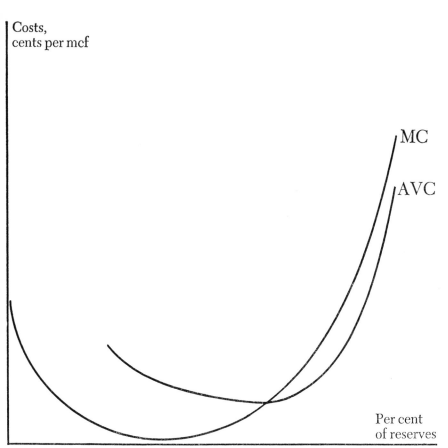

Costs,
cents per mcf

MC

AVC

Per cent
of reserves

FIGURE 2:1 Producer Development Costs

more than halves the required well drilling. But landowners in jointly
held fields incur much greater risk of drainage from having less wells
on *their* individual properties, so that wider spacing may not result.
The minimum spacing rules of the conservation commission determine
actual spacing, because individual landowners require that all their wells
be drilled or the lease be forfeited. The only alternative recourse is to
greatly increase delay rentals, which have effects on costs of longer term
similar to those from drilling all wells.

21

items increase as the production period is lengthened.[27]

This effect of longer term-length upon development cost is indicated in Figure 2:2. The curve $MC(10)$ indicates mar-

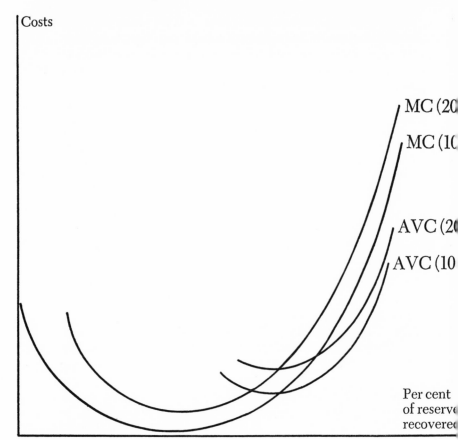

FIGURE 2:2 Producer Development Costs

ginal costs of recovering 0–100 per cent of estimated reserves over a ten-year period at a uniform per annum rate, and the curve $MC(20)$ indicates marginal costs of 0–100 per cent

27. Interest costs on drilling expenses per annum become smaller as term-length is extended, because principal is smaller in the last years of delivery. At the same time, deferred payment of capital increases

recovery over a twenty-year period. The second curve is considerably higher than the first at the lower levels of recovery because it is here that higher interest and operation costs of longer term are incurred. For higher levels of recovery, marginal development costs are the same for both production periods because compression costs are the same.[28] Average production costs are higher for longer term because of the higher operation and interest costs on initial volumes recovered.[29] The curve $AVC(20)$ for a twenty-year term, is higher than $AVC(10)$ for a ten-year production period by the increased interest and operation expenses.[30]

SHORT-RUN COSTS OF PRODUCTION IN DIFFERENT RESERVOIRS
AND FIELDS

Figures 2:1 and 2:2 indicate the effect of recovery rates and production periods on the costs of developing a reservoir of

---

interest charges in a longer-term delivery period. The result is total interest costs that, on balance, increase about the same amount for each additional year of term. The effects of longer term are the same on interest charges for exploratory and royalty expenses. That is, for $C = f(V, R, T)$ and $V = V_0$ (a given volume of recovered reserves), $\frac{\partial C}{\partial T} > 0$, $\frac{\partial^2 C}{\partial T^2} \cong 0$.

28. If operating costs increase proportionately to the increase in term and interest rates are the same for all term-lengths, then the shift from 10 to 15 years is the same as from 15 to 20 years. That is, with $C = f(V, R, T)$ if MC is $\frac{\partial C}{\partial V}$, the shift $\frac{\partial^2 C}{\partial T \partial V} = K$, with K the same for each term T (given V).

29. If relevant term-lengths are 10, 15, or 20 years and the interest charge is 18 per cent on drilling and deferred royalty expenses, an estimate can be made of the amount of increase in average costs. For each dollar of expenses, repayment at uniform rates with interest requires .2013 dollars per year for a ten-year term, or 2.013 for this period. The fifteen-year period requires .1930 dollars per year, or 2.895 for the entire period. The twenty-year period incurs costs of .1850 dollars per year, or 3.700 for the entire term. By increasing term from 10 to 15 years, the producer incurs (per dollar, per unit volume recovered) additional costs of .882 dollars.

30. To anticipate what follows, the question of whether to develop a trap or shut-in is decided by comparing price to average production costs, at least in competitive markets and in markets where *buyers* have price-setting power. The producer in theory undertakes development

dry gas. The depth of the reservoir can also affect costs. In the Texas and Louisiana gas fields, for instance, costs vary from producer to producer in one reservoir with the advantage going to those who drill on the upper side of a slanting trap, or at the point of least depth on the trap dome. Similarly, developmental drilling may be cheaper in one field than the others because the field is closer to the surface. Other natural factors like the absence of gas impurities or the presence of higher pressures can result in advantages in maintenance and compression costs.

There are also reasons for production conditions to be quite similar in neighboring producing facilities. Reservoirs in adjoining fields usually share a "basin" where gas is found under uniform temperature and pressure. For example, a series of traps in the Anadarko Basin of North Texas are found at depths less than 8,000 feet with uniform low pressure whereas most of the traps in the San Juan Basin of New Mexico are deeper and exhibit well-head pressures greater than 1,000 pounds per square inch. Traps in the same basin and at the same level can be expected to have similar development costs.

Two traps in the same basin, actually should have "similar" cost curves regardless of the estimated reserves in place in each. The costs of additional *percentage recovery* are the same, since these follow from providing capacity and from well operation. But if one firm has twice the in-ground reserves of the other it can attain any given level of marginal costs at twice the level of output. Consider marginal costs MC in Figure 2:3 to indicate expenses of development in a reservoir estimated to contain 100 billion cubic feet of gas, and marginal costs MC_2 to indicate costs in a 200 billion cubic foot reservoir with the same physical characteristics. The marginal costs of producing 70 billion cubic feet from the first trap are the same as for recovering 140 billion from the second trap, because the *percentage rate of recovery* is the same

of that percentage of reserves for which marginal production costs are equal to price, but only as long as average costs are less than price. The higher marginal and average costs of longer term may reduce the supply of reserves for twenty-year delivery, by making it necessary for some traps to shut-in or to promise production only for shorter term.

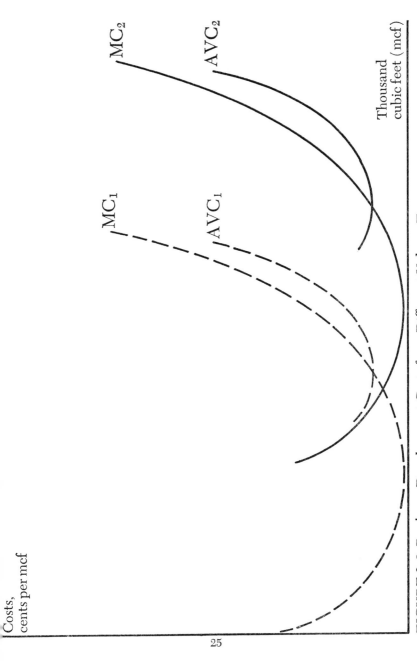

FIGURE 2:3 Producer Development Costs from Different Volume Traps

for each. Marginal costs MC_2 are the same as MC_1 for a volume of reserves twice as large.[31]

SUMMARY

The major reservoirs are those in which hydrocarbons are primarily "dry gas."[32] The producers have marginal development costs as shown in Figure 2:1.[33] The cost of *additional*

31. In anticipation of the discussion of costs and supply in Chapter 4, it can be noticed that series of traps with uniform physical characteristics have particular conditions of supply. If the quantity promised for delivery is that at which marginal production costs are equal to (competitive) price per mcf, a higher price will result in slightly larger volumes recovered from each trap. The volumes added to recovery are *slight,* since the marginal production cost curve rises sharply. There are some exceptions: large-volumed traps off the Louisiana Gulf Coast can be developed only with significantly higher average production costs, for all rates of recovery, because of adverse drilling conditions. A higher Gulf Coast price can induce a supply of gas from these traps that would otherwise be undeveloped. In the Anadarko Basin, during the middle 1950s, a price increase from 7.5 cents per mcf to 11.0 cents induced the development of two trillion cubic feet from reservoirs previously shut-in. It is presumed that, at the lower price, returns were less than variable production costs while at the higher price this was not the case.

32. In certain fields, the producers together may be able to complete development that prevents drainage of each other's property. They may "unit-operate" and be allowed flexibility in well spacing by convincing landowners to permit drilling over a number of years *to obtain only the minimum* necessary capacity. In this instance, the marginal production cost curve is lower for low rates of recovery and rises gradually throughout the range of 0–80 per cent recoverability (as compared to the U-shaped cost curve for single operations in a common reservoir). In such a unit operation, the producer may consider shutting-in and developing in the future. This is profitable if future (expected) price is higher than the present price by a sufficient amount to result in net returns over the additional expenditures on delay rental and interest charges. These marginal costs (including the opportunity costs of not deferring production) are in striking contrast to the costs incurred in production from jointly owned reservoirs.

33. Other exceptions to the cost conditions of Figures 2:1, 2:2, 2:3 occur in fields in which gas is produced with oil and liquid petroleum gas (LPG). In "oil" fields it is possible to produce gas at uniform rates only by violating oil conservation laws. Gas produced according to a technical gas/oil ratio requires crude oil production at an unchanging rate, but proration "allowables" of crude oil vary from month to month "according to market demand." The gas cap is available for long-term

recovery declines when total production is a small proportion of the volume in place; it rises sharply when total recovery is a large proportion of the reserves in place.

The level of marginal development costs may differ from reservoir to reservoir. Production under a fifteen-year development program results in lower costs than under a twenty-year program because of lower interest and operation expenses. Those firms with reserves in deep, low-pressure traps have higher costs than firms with shallow, high-pressure traps. But common geophysical conditions in traps in the same basin suggest that producers there all have similar marginal and average costs.[34] The actual volume of production per se should not affect costs (Figure 2:3).

The implications for supply depend partly upon the extent of competition in area markets. Producers encountering competition with marginal costs, as in Figure 2:1, can be expected either to recover most of their reserves or to "shut-in" production entirely (if price is less than average development costs). Noncompetitive price and production should differ. The theory to explain the differences between competitive and noncompetitive price formation, with such production conditions, will be developed here after some discussion of the conditions of "demand."

recovery only *after* the oil has been produced, and, for sale at that time marginal costs of joint recovery can be considered. Volumes of gas from traps also containing heavier liquids (LPG) are recovered under orthodox development programs. The drilling and operation costs of development result in marginal *joint* costs that are similar in appearance to the marginal gas costs of Figure 2:1. Technically it is impossible to produce gas in other than fixed proportions with the liquids (unless pressures are so dissipated that there is complete physical loss of the LPG) so that marginal costs for each cannot be determined.

34. As far as actual levels of costs are concerned, all that can be extracted from present data is an indication of equilibrium levels of *average* development costs. Taking the estimate of S. P. Porter as to direct "production and development costs," per thousand cubic feet, for 17 gas producers in 1955, the average at actual levels of recovery was 9.963 cents. This would be an average in many diverse traps for recoveries of 60–90 per cent of estimated reserves. Cf. S. P. Porter, "Determining the Cost of Finding and Producing Gas under Federal Power Commission Regulation" (Address before F.P.C. hearing, July 17, 1958, reprint).

3. *The Demand for Natural Gas Reserves*

Companies purchasing natural gas in the field are engaged in transporting it to retail utilities and manufacturing firms. These pipeline companies "buy" volumes of gas by contracting with field producers for exclusive surface rights to reserves recovered from some portion of a reservoir. Desirable contracts usually specify that the production of in-ground reserves will be at a uniform rate over an extended period.

Demands for new volumes occur continuously, as established pipelines seek to continue their delivery of gas and new transporters seek to begin operations. Each pipeline demands a different quantity of gas at any price per thousand cubic feet because of differences in final consumer demand, transportation costs, or regulatory requirements. In general, each pipeline's demand for reserves can best be represented by a declining demand curve. Price elasticity of demand in the prevailing range of prices should differ greatly from buyer to buyer. It seems likely that any pipeline's demand for new reserves *from one field to another* follows a distinct pattern, however. In fact, the maximum price the potential buyer can offer should be *relatively greater* where there is a larger volume of reserves, where the volume is nearer to gas delivery locations, and when the volume is to be produced over a longer period.

Competition among buyers should result in actual prices resembling this pattern of "maximum offer prices." Where buyer's competition is absent, the purchaser would *not* offer maximum prices. Consequently, the pattern of "maximum prices" forms the basis for contrast between competition and buyer's monopoly. Similarly, competition among sellers should ensure uniform prices on all comparable sales, and not discrimination according to differing elasticities of demand. An extended discussion of the characteristics of "maximum demand price" is necessary for contrasting competition, monopsony, and monopoly.

THE PURCHASE CONTRACT

The largest buyers of natural gas are interstate pipeline companies whose main occupation is delivering gas to consumers.[1] These companies obtain reserves by signing contracts with producers that delegate ownership rights to "produced" gas. They are induced to purchase in this manner partly as a result of the thrust of Federal Power Commission regulation,[2] partly in order to ensure security holders of future revenues.[3]

1. Approximately 50 per cent of total *production* of gas is transported across state lines by pipelines; cf. *Gas Facts* (New York, American Gas Association, 1958) pp. 26, 68. Neglecting oil-well gas, and that not for sale but for field uses, the percentage of *marketed* gas that goes into interstate commerce is probably 60–70 per cent. Since the percentage of production has been rising, the percentage of *sales of new reserves* in interstate commerce is probably 70–80 per cent.

2. The *Natural Gas Act* [15 U.S.C. 9171 (1938)] required regulation of interstate pipelines by the Federal Power Commission. The transporting companies are required under section 7c to obtain a "certificate of public convenience and necessity" before constructing any transmission facilities. If the certificate is to be issued, the company must establish to the satisfaction of the Federal Power Commission that there is a demand for volumes of gas, that there are financial resources sufficient to cover the costs of construction, and that there are enough new reserves to satisfy the demand for a reasonable period. To establish "adequacy of reserves," the pipeline has to have "a firmly committed natural gas supply to provide the full requirements of this project for the definite term of fifteen years." Cf. *Transcontinental Gas Pipeline, et al.,* F.P.C. Docket G-704 (1948). This is obtained by signing contracts for gas for uniform delivery per annum for fifteen to twenty years.

3. The pipeline's major source of funds for construction of new lines is bond issues. Customary issues are completed following agreements to make sinking fund payments from depreciation. The extent of the sinking fund payments depends upon gas reserve depletion: if "reserves" of gas under signed contracts become depleted, additions to the fund

The contracts are designed to provide gas over long periods with some certainty, and also to protect the interests of the producer. The main provisions affecting price formation are those involving "term," "volume," and "price." The "term-length" of production is stated explicitly in the contract (usually as 15 to 20 years).[4] The volume, or quantity of reserves consigned for future delivery, is assumed to be "reserves in place" at a given location. The buyer and seller have estimates of the amount of produced gas from the relevant location, but neither wishes to be committed to a particular volume of production.[5] They agree to a per diem "take or pay" amount of production (usually equal to 80 per cent of the expected uniform rate) for which the transporter is obliged to reimburse the producer even if actual production is smaller. "Price" in the contract is a schedule of prices beginning with an "initial price" for the first years of production and continuing with a series of higher "base prices" at later intervals.[6] These prices can be overruled by the operation of

---

to retire bonds are usually required to be increased. If "reserves" of gas remain at a level allowing 15–20 years of continuing operation, then bond retirement may be foregone and depreciation funds used for capital expansion. In periods of rising interest rates, it may be to the distinct advantage of the pipeline to prove to the bond trustee that there is available 15–20 years of production of firmly committed reserves so that capital can be prevented from going into sinking funds.

4. In a sample of 997 contracts of interstate pipelines signed for production to begin in 1956 and 1957, 874 had terms of twenty years or longer. The sample consists of new 1956 and 1957 contracts submitted by producers to the Federal Power Commission in Form 301. It was compiled by Foster Associates of Washington, D.C. for presentation in F.P.C. Docket G-9277 and contains further information to be described below.

5. There are reasons of strategy for not acknowledging volume in the contract. From the buyer's point of view, the higher the estimate presented to the Commission, the better the chance of certification. If the "maximum estimate" is entered in the contract, however, the price is likely to have to be higher and the "take or pay" rate of production greater. From the seller's view, it is best to have high estimates in unregulated markets, but if future markets are to be regulated on a cost basis, the low estimates result in higher "full cost" prices (including exploratory fixed expenses). Discretion may result in notations of only "reserves in place."

6. The "base" prices are higher in almost all cases. Of the 1956–57 sample mentioned on the previous page only 4.4 per cent of the contracts had the same initial and average base price.

"Favored Nation" or "Renegotiation" clauses. The Favored Nations clause requires that scheduled price be raised to equal any higher initial price on any new contract of the purchaser in the surrounding field area. The Renegotiation clause allows the parties to the contract to agree to a higher price than the scheduled price, at some specified time, without canceling the original agreement as to "volume" or "term." [7]

PIPELINE DEMAND FOR NEW CONTRACT RESERVES

The pipelines purchase reserves under contracts in order to satisfy home and industrial demands for gas over extended periods. Of course, final consumers will seek somewhat less gas over the lifetime of their burner equipment if the resale price is increased. Less resale demand implies lower aggregate pipeline demand in the producing regions; that is, the field demand of any pipeline is derived from resale demand. Field demand is also affected by pipeline transmission costs and by requirements of interstate regulatory authorities.

Determinants of field demand can be seen in the demand of any pipeline company about to construct a new transporting system.[8] Before construction begins, the company seeks reserves of gas in order to obtain a certificate of "convenience and necessity" (see footnote 2 of this chapter). The pipeline's

7. Renegotiation is obviously completed *while* the producer cannot vary quantity dedicated. In such a bargaining situation, an increase in price from the pipeline can only follow from the producer invoking some concept of "fairness" or, more likely, from the producer promising to dedicate further volumes in a *separate, new* contract for a higher price on an old contract. In the latter case, the Renegotiated increase should be attributed to the new contract.

A majority of 1956–57 contracts in the above sample had either Favored Nations or Renegotiation clauses. The short-term contracts of 1–9 years term included 14 per cent with clauses, while 34 per cent of the 10 to 19-year contracts had them, and 69 per cent of the contracts of 20-year or more terms had them.

8. The pipeline can be assumed not to construct gathering lines, but rather to purchase reserves that are delivered to the main line by producers. This restrictive assumption is relaxed below in the discussion of different offer prices in different fields. At this point, it allows attention to be centered upon a uniform price for each different total volume of new reserves.

maximum possible price for any total volume of reserves is
equal to the price that can be obtained for that volume at
some point of resale, minus the average cost of transporting

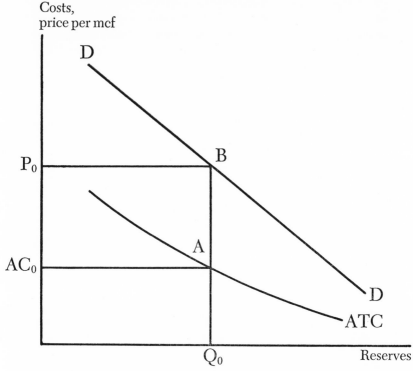

FIGURE 3:1 Pipeline Existing Costs and Resale Price

that volume. Prices in resale to industrial users [9] and to gas
utility companies [10] are indicated by the demand curve *DD*
in Figure 3:1. Average transportation costs for the expected

9. The prices on industrial sales in the North and Midwest are probably
greater than on home sales, as indicated in Dr. Boatwright's unique study
of 14 pipelines in these areas. The lines in these areas delivered approximately 10 per cent of 1953 sales to industrial consumers at an average
price of 28.1 cents per mcf and sold the other 90 per cent to utilities at
an average (regulated) price of 26.5 cents per mcf. Cf. Boatwright's
speech, p. 22.

10. Gas utilities, in turn, resell heating and cooking gas to households
and gas boiler fuel to commercial and industrial firms.

volumes of annual production are shown by the curve ATC.[11] With such demand for resale and unit transmission costs, the maximum offer price for total reserves Q_0 is AB, the greatest possible difference between resale price P_0 and average costs AC_0.[12] The quantity of reserves purchased probably becomes larger with prices lower than AB, given the probable nature of resale demand DD and costs ATC.

Resale Demand as a Factor Affecting the Pipelines' Demand for Reserves of Gas. The nature of the resale demand for gas (such as DD) has scarcely been investigated, even by the transporters. Most purchasers from pipelines seem to be gas retail utility companies seeking volumes under long-term "firm" contracts. (Some buyers are industrial firms seeking gas as a raw material or as boiler fuel, and they are sometimes induced to take a particular volume for immediate delivery.) There is indication that *resale purchasers* have demand schedules of varying elasticity—that is, the quantity demand of the pipeline in a long-term agreement is to varying degrees sensitive to changes in the price of delivered gas.[13]

The retail utility buys volumes of gas to be received "at the city gate" from the pipeline over a 15 to 25-year period. The gas is for resale to householders, for cooking and heating,

11. This cost curve falls throughout most of the range of alternative total volumes of reserves, given that there are economies of large-scale transmission. Included in costs is the (regulated) cost of capital for the line.

12. Of course, the pipeline is able to increase profits by paying less than $\{P_0 - AC_0\}$ for Q_0 new reserves and reselling these reserves at P_0—if regulation allows. Given less than "ideal" regulation, the pipeline can obtain *some* portion of the difference between P_0 and AC_0 not paid to the producer. The pipeline cannot increase profits, moreover, by offering a price *greater* than $\{P_0 - AC_0\}$. Since regulation of pipelines is *designed* to provide average returns to the pipeline equal to field gas price *plus* AC_0, there are neither pressures nor incentives for the transporter to earn less than "normal profits" by increasing field price so that average costs are not covered by receipts.

13. Demand is "elastic" when the percentage change in quantity resold is greater than any percentage change in prices, and inversely related to a change in price. That is, if quantity $Q = f(P)$, price for new volumes of gas delivered over a twenty-year period, then "elasticity" $= \left/ \dfrac{P \, dQ}{Q \, dP} \right/ > 1.$

and to industry for boiler fuel. The price the utility can pay the pipeline for any volume of gas depends upon opportunities to resell the gas to home users *for twenty years,* and such opportunities would seem to depend upon the availability of substitute fuels for home users. There are a priori reasons for believing that home users in some communities have extensive opportunities to substitute other sources of heat for gas during this period.[14] In other communities, lack of low-priced substitute fuels should prevent substantial changes in the consumption of gas as a result of changes in the price of gas.[15]

Statistical analysis of total gas sales in a number of cities indicates that demand elasticity varies over the range of relevant prices. An approximation of a city's demand is shown in Table 3:1, where "quantity" is the city-wide purchase of gas from the retail utility, and "price" is the retail delivered price. The estimate of a demand equation is arrived at by considering actual deliveries of gas in a number of United States cities to be representative of deliveries in any one city at the actual (different) prices prevailing.[16] The resulting equation,

14. To be able to resell any volume of gas taken from the pipeline transporter, the retail utility must be able to offer the gas at such a price that gas is expected to be preferred over electricity for twenty years. The lower the relative price of fuel oil, the less likely gas resale takes place at any price—or the more likely is demand to be elastic.

15. That is, individual buyers may have demand curves (for twenty-year supplies of gas) that are quite flat at the price at which gas stoves are displaced. This displacement price differs in different locations because prices of alternative fuels differ.

16. For cross-section data to be representative of per capita demand at any one city, a large number of restrictive assumptions have to be valid. The "tastes" and income of all consumers in the various cities have to be the same, the number of heating days should be similar, and the heating value of gas should be similar. Prices of substitute fuels have to be the same. If these assumptions are justified, demand at various cities should provide an estimate of points on the aggregate demand curve in each city. Given that long-run adjustments of price changes are the same in each city, prices and quantities are representative of points on the demand schedule *in one city.* To justify the assumptions, the equation $\{Q = \alpha + \beta_1 P + \beta_2 P_0 + \beta_3 T + \beta_4 N + \beta_5 Y + v\}$ was computed, where P_0 = price of fuel oil, T = temperature degree days, N = number of buyers, Y = median income in each city for a sample of 52 United States cities. (The computations are discussed in the Appendix.) By inserting values for P_0, T, N, Y in the computed equation, a demand equation may result for which "other things" are constant.

a rough indication of "long-run" demand, points to different elasticity for different prices throughout the middle of the pricing range. When resale price is $1.20 per mcf., elasticity can be higher than -1.00; when price is as low as $.75 per mcf, as in southern cities, elasticity is likely to be less than $-.450$ (as shown in Table 3:1).

TABLE 3:1. *City Gas Purchases and Prices*

Given that $Q = \alpha + \beta P + v$ describes demand for home use in any city and that the computed demand is: $\{Q = 27,390.820-66.359 \ P + u\}$, $Q =$ millions of cu. ft. of gas, $P =$ price in cents per mcf, standard deviation of residuals $S_u = 11,406.30$, standard deviation of computed coefficient $S_b = 54.792$.

Quantity of gas (millions of cu. ft.)	Price of gas (cents per mcf)	Elasticity of demand $\frac{P}{Q} \cdot \frac{\partial Q}{\partial P}$ (with Q equal to computed $Q \pm S_u$)
19,327.74	120.000	from -0.259 to -1.005
21,112.22	93.108 *	from -0.190 to -0.637
22,313.90	75.000	from -0.148 to -0.456

* Equals mean price.

Source. Computed demand is from the least-squares calculations, for data for 52 United States cities, of the expanded equation: $Q = \alpha + \beta_1 P + \beta_2 P_0 + \beta_3 T + \beta_4 N + \beta_5 Y + v$. The average values of P_0(price of fuel oil), T(temperature degree days), N(city population), and Y(city median income) were inserted in this expanded equation to obtain the "typical" quantity-price relation. The computations are discussed in the Appendix.

The extent of demand at each price varies from city to city as well, so that demand can be said to be less elastic at some locations than at others. Gas demand is more extensive (and inelastic, as a result), in cities with larger numbers of consumers. Consumers in cities with lower temperatures have greater need for gas as a fuel and, consequently, should have less elastic demand at each price.[17] Wide variations in popu-

17. The estimated values for coefficient in $\{Q = \alpha + \beta_1 P + \beta_2 P_0 + \beta_3 N + \beta_4 T + \beta_5 Y + v\}$ include $b_2 = 806.597$, $b_3 = +.0307$, $b_4 = 2.242$, $b_5 = 19.613$ (from the statistical analysis described in the Appendix). The values of the coefficients suggest that gas demand is approximately 818 million cubic feet greater in any city experiencing temperature one degree per day below the average (or 365 temperature degree days), and that gas demand is 31 million cubic feet greater in the city with

lation and climate between state regions should result in different resale demand curves for pipelines serving different regions.

Sales of gas directly to industry account for five to thirty-five per cent of any pipeline's deliveries. In the Midwest and North, the cement, steel, and chemical industries and other manufacturers purchase gas if it has a price advantage over fuel oil or coal. The industrial firm may sign a long-term agreement to purchase gas if its price is expected to be lower than the price of other fuels, or the firm may take gas during short periods of low household demand when there is an "off-peak" price advantage. A few plants have boiler facilities that can be switched from gas to oil or coal if the price of gas increases slightly, and the purchaser may be able to alternate fuels for other industrial uses where technology allows.[18] A priori, the demand for industrial gas under long-term contract should have varying price elasticities according to the extent of fuel substitutability.

Statistical analysis of industrial gas demand indicates that price elasticity varies greatly from industry to industry. Purchases by firms (at different locations and at different prices) may approximate an aggregate demand schedule in one state for each industry.[19] This demand schedule in the Meat Proc-

1,000 more consumers than the average. Lower temperature and greater population decrease considerably the elasticity estimates (of the last columns in Table 3:1).

18. There has been some question as to whether the F.P.C. has controlled industrial sales by refusing to certify extensions of lines to purchase or sell gas destined for boiler fuel use. There seems little evidence of this effect; the Commission requires a *positive* showing of public convenience (in the form of lower transportation costs for all gas) before certification. It has not yet refused certification on the grounds that gas was replacing "superior" uses of coal, or on the grounds that some industrial sales were "inferior" uses of gas. Investigations of industrial sales involve more intensive examination of "public convenience" than for home sales, but that is perhaps all. Cf. *Commonwealth Gas Company*, F.P.C. Docket G-963 (1950), *Mississippi River Fuel Corp.*, F.P.C. Docket G-1945 (1953), *Northern Natural Gas Corp.*, F.P.C. Docket G-2409 (1955), *Cities Service Gas Company*, F.P.C. Docket G-10458 (1957).

19. The assumptions are the same as for the cross-section analysis of home consumer demand. The series of buyers in one industry at different locations have to be assumed to operate in a manner similar to buyers at *one* location over a long-term period. If all buyers in the

essing or Bakery Products industries seems quite inelastic at average price. The demand schedules in the Structural Clay Products industry and Iron and Steel industry are even less elastic at average prices. But the demand schedules in both the Motor Vehicle and the Beverage industries are highly elastic, as shown in Table 3:2.

The industrial demand equations and the home-consumption demand equation all exhibit some decrease in quantities purchased when the price increases. Demand is most elastic in certain industrial gas uses and least elastic at low prices for home use, and there is great variation in elasticity, even given users that are the same in most respects.[20] As a result, demand of purchasers from pipelines (curve DD in Figure 3:1) is likely to vary from pipeline to pipeline.

Transmission Costs as a Factor Affecting Field Demand for Gas Reserves. Transportation costs from the trap to the final buyer also affect pipeline offer prices for new reserves of gas. Economies of scale in transmission indicate that there are cost savings in delivering larger volumes of reserves to the final buyers. With lower transport costs for larger delivery, pipelines can offer prices for large volumes that are higher than otherwise possible. Thus, the extent of falling average transportation costs also influences the price elasticity of demand of gas in the field.

Economies of scale are inherent in the technology of transmission. Prevailing construction techniques and costs result

---

industry have the same production functions, have the opportunity to have installed alternative fuel burning equipment, and all react to fuel price changes in a uniform manner, then the study indicates demand at one location for *new volumes* to be delivered over a twenty-year interval. It is not possible to determine whether these assumptions apply in the industries examined. There is little reason for there to have been differences in production functions, but "reactions" to fuel price changes may not have been uniform, because price may have changed *more* recently in *some* cases. Some sales are according to "short-run" demand (because the purchaser has not been able to consider relocation as one response to a price change), while other sales are according to "long-run" demand since these are according to long-established prices. Information on price change frequency in the industry samples is not available.

20. This is indicated by the large standard errors of estimate in the computed demand equations.

in total expenses for a pipeline that vary slightly more than proportionally to the diameter and the length of the pipeline.[21]

TABLE 3:2. *Industrial Demand for Gas*

$$\left[Q_{gas} = \alpha + \beta P_{gas} + v \atop (\sigma_\beta) \right]$$ Q_{gas} = quantity of gas sold to an industry in one state, millions of cu. ft.

P_{gas} = average price per thousand cu. ft. (cents per mcf) in the state for the industry being considered

σ_β = standard error of coefficient.

Industry	Computed demand curve	Elasticity of demand at average price
Meat Processing	$Q_{gas} = 1527.56 - 16.496 P_{gas}$ (12.90)	— .259 to — .593
Bakery Products	$Q_{gas} = 1169.17 - 9.348 P_{gas}$ (4.657)	— .262 to — .893
Structural Clay Products	$Q_{gas} = 5696.03 - 43.155 P_{gas}$ (27.81)	— .196 to — .650
Motor Vehicles and Equipment	$Q_{gas} = 2089.39 - 30.685 P_{gas}$ (17.29)	—0.648 to — 2.269
Beverage Manufacturing	$Q_{gas} = 433.26 - 8.711 P_{gas}$ (3.062)	—0.710 to —48.347
Iron and Steel Foundries	$Q_{gas} = 1937.73 - 14.639 P_{gas}$ (7.219)	—0.199 to — .509

Source. The equations are derived from the least-squares regression calculations for $[Q_{gas} = \alpha + \beta_1 P_{gas} + \beta_2 P_{oil} + \beta_3 P_{coal} + \beta_4 P_{electricity} + \beta_5(\text{Scale}) + \beta_6(\text{Consumers})]$ where the independent variables include the prices of fuel oil, coal, electricity, the average "scale" of output of the plant in the state, and the number of industrial consumers in the state. Average values have been inserted into the original equations for all variables except P_{gas} to obtain the equations above. The calculations of the full equations and the data, from the 1948 census of manufacturers, are described in detail in the Appendix.

21. This is shown in a 1947 study of operating lines of the Federal Power Commission. Cf. *Natural Gas Company Unit Costs*, F.P.C., s-54 (Washington D.C., 1947). It is assumed throughout this chapter that costs are proportional to distance but are more than proportional to line diameter.

Operation costs for the line are the same for each thousand cubic feet of gas delivered.[22] But the volume of gas transported is proportional to the square of the diameter of the line.[23] The transporter can double the diameter of the pipeline (and the costs of construction) while increasing the volume delivered by a multiple of four.

The extent of economies of scale may be indicated by the changes in average costs of a "typical" pipeline which follow changes in line size. Suppose the transporter is seeking reserves for delivery over a twenty-year period to gas companies in a city 1,000 miles north and he has yet to construct a pipeline. What would be his costs of transmission per mcf for different volumes in different-sized lines? He contemplates operating with 1,000 pounds (psia) inlet pressure and with intermediate compression so as to allow delivery "at the city gate" at 600 pounds pressure. Construction costs per mile are, roughly, $27,825 for a 16-inch diameter pipe (the average for country-wide construction) and $55,971 per mile for a 36-inch diameter pipe.[24] Additional costs include investment expenses incurred on installed equipment over a twenty-year period (presumably at the rate of 10 per cent per annum before taxes, or 6 per cent per annum after taxes). Construction and operating expenses of pumping stations for the entire twenty-year transmission period vary from approximately $17,994 per mile for the 16-inch line to approximately $136,621 per mile

22. Obtaining horsepower involves the paramount operation cost. The turbine required for pumping (for 28.8 horsepower per 1,000 mcf of annual gas delivery) does not appear to be obtainable only in indivisible sizes. With varying-sized turbines, costs can be made proportional to mcf of gas delivered, if price per h.p. is constant.

23. In the Johnson-Berwald equation for high pressure and long distance pipelines, quantity of gas delivered per hour $Q = 28.7417$ $\left[2D^5 \left(\int_0^{P_0} P dP - \int_0^{P_2} P dP \right) \right]^{1/2}$ where D is inside diameter of the line, P_0 is inlet pressure, P_2 is outlet line pressure, and L is length of the pipeline. Cf. R. V. Smith, J. S. Miller, J. W. Ferguson, "Flow of Gas through Transmission Lines," *Bureau of Mines Monograph 9* (1956), p. 72.

24. Based upon 1955 revisions of the "Nelson Construction Index" of per mile and per inch diameter pipeline construction costs. Cf. 54 *Oil and Gas Journal* (Dec. 6, 1956).

TABLE 3:3. *Transportation Costs in a Natural Gas High Pressure Transmission System 1,000 Miles Long*

1	2	3	4	5	6	7	8	9
						MAINTENANCE COSTS		
Diameter of pipe line (in inches)	Throughput 20 years, billions of cu. ft.	Initial construction costs (Nelson Index + 2.790 % for land rights), in dollars	Pumping station costs [= mmcf (28.8) · (15) · ($250)], in dollars	Interest charges, in dollars	Pumping (present value, uniform costs of $30 per horsepower per year), in dollars	Line maintenance $25 per inch mile per annum (present value uniform annual charge), in dollars	Total costs in dollars	Average costs (cents per mcf)
16	1216.04	27,824,777	17,993,750	49,828,492	22,875,029	4,237,604	122,759,604	10.095
20	2124.38	35,688,187	31,429,288	69,447,827	39,955,308	5,297,005	181,817,614	8.558
24	3351.04	43,852,823	49,577,373	90,830,091	63,026,549	6,356,406	247,286,836	7.379
26	4093.39	48,114,865	60,558,309	107,687,037	76,986,352	6,886,757	300,233,320	7.334
30	5854.10	48,782,414	86,608,613	129,103,554	110,103,494	7,945,478	382,543,553	6.535
36	9234.36	55,971,150	136,621,633	175,576,992	173,683,848	9,534,573	551,388,196	5.971

Source. Assume inlet pressure = 1,000 psia,
outlet pressure = 600 psia,
that it is necessary to step up pressure to 1,000 only after first 100 miles, so that roughly 15 compression stations are required.

The result is throughput of reserves delivered in twenty years $Q = 1.6156N \dfrac{T_b}{P_b} \sqrt{1/f} \sqrt{1/z} \left[\dfrac{(P_1^2 - P_2^2)d^5}{GTL} \right]^{1/2}$

where:

T_b = temperature base defining cubic feet of gas, °F absolute (519.7)
P_b = pressure base defining cubic feet of gas, (psia = 14.73)
$\sqrt{1/f}$ = transmission factor, dimensionless (18.0)
$\sqrt{1/z}$ = average compressibility factor, dimensionless ($\sqrt{1/0.87}$)
P_1, P_2 = inlet and outlet pressure
d = internal diameter of pipe in inches (as in column 1)
G = specific gravity of the gas (0.6)
T = temperature of flowing gas (529.7)
L = length of pipe between compression stations (60 miles).

To obtain estimates of compression costs, it is assumed that there is a requirement of 28.8 horsepower per mmcf transported per day per year, investment costs are $250 per horsepower, and operating costs are $25 per inch mile, $30 per compressor horsepower per year. "Interest charges" are the present value of annual 10 per cent returns on undepreciated capital (given that 10 per cent is the rate "before taxes," and there is twenty year straight

40

for the 36-inch line.[25] Total costs for this transporting company would rise as the size of the contemplated pipeline increases, but only slightly more than proportionally to the increase in line size (as shown by columns 3 to 8 in Table 3:3). Quantity of gas transported increases more than proportionally to line size, however (as shown in column 1 of Table 3:3).[26] Consequently, unit costs of transmission fall from 10.095 cents per mcf, for throughput of slightly more than one trillion cubic feet in a 16-inch line, to 5.971 cents per mcf for transmission of more than nine trillion cubic feet in a 36-inch line. Transmission cost savings of more than 5.0 cents per mcf could be realized by purchasing large volumes of gas and constructing a large transmission line. With such cost savings for transporting larger volumes, maximum offer prices should reflect the premium value to the purchaser of large total amounts of reserves.

Elasticities of Demand for New Contract Reserves. Each transporting company at some time has undertaken to obtain reserves in some field area in order to fill a proposed long-distance transmission line. In order to secure the reserves for resale over a twenty-year period, these companies have been prepared to pay, at most, the difference between resale price and unit transport costs (and less if possible). As has been mentioned, the maximum offer price of one of the prospective buyers for one total amount of new reserves is equal to the difference between P_0 and AC_0 in Figure 3:1. The buyer's maximum prices for other total amounts of gas are equal to resale price minus unit transportation costs. Each such price is shown as a point on the curve $D'D'$ in Figure 3:2—Price θ_i is the pipeline buyer's maximum for total quantity Q_i of new reserves to be produced over twenty years (as derived from subtracting AC from P for each quantity in Figure 3:1).

25. Based upon $250 per horsepower for construction, $30 per horsepower for station maintenance, $25 per inch diameter, per mile for line maintenance, as of 1955. These are estimates of the average for all pipelines over normal terrain.

26. The quantity is maximum throughput according to the Johnson-Berwald formula. Average per annum throughput, in most cases, is 70–95 per cent of this for long-distance transporters.

The elasticity of demand for transporter at price θ_i is likely to be different from that of each other transporter. Resale home demand in different cities is likely to differ because of variations in temperature, the number of customers, the prices of competing fuels. Consequently, resale demands should ex-

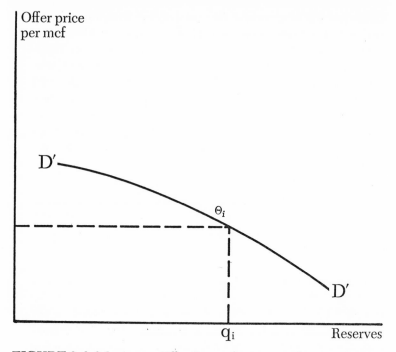

FIGURE 3:2 Maximum Offer Prices for New Volumes of Reserves

hibit varying price elasticities. Resale industrial demands seem to have different elasticities from industry to industry, so that field demands for gas volumes for industrial resale should differ from pipeline to pipeline, depending upon the industries to be served. Lower long-run unit transport costs for larger volumes of gas have an effect upon θ_i for large q_i.[27] The transporter with the most extensive economies of scale

27. Since the steeper the slope of ATC, in Figure 3:1, the greater is θ_i for each succeeding value of q_i.

should have the more elastic demands.[28] All three factors—home resale demand, industrial resale demand, and economies of large scale transmission—have the effect of producing variations in the price elasticity of pipelines' field demands.

Differences in field demand between pipelines may follow also from differences in regulatory requirements. The established line may not face delays and difficulties of "certification" so that transport costs would be lower, and field demand

28. Conditions of elasticity of field demand are concerned with the slope of the cost curve ATC and the elasticity of resale demand DD in Figure 3:1. Define *field price* $\theta = P - AC$, where $P =$ resale price (cents per mcf), $AC =$ average transport costs (cents per mcf). Elasticity of field demand

$$\eta_\theta = \frac{\theta}{q} \cdot \frac{dq}{d\theta} = \theta \bigg/ q \frac{d\theta}{dq}. \text{ Since } \theta = P - AC, \frac{d\theta}{dq} = \frac{dP}{dq} - \frac{dAC}{dq}. \text{ Then } \eta_\theta =$$

$$\theta \bigg/ q \left[\frac{dP}{dq} - \frac{dAC}{dq}\right].$$

It is possible to rewrite this last definition in terms of variables mentioned in Tables 3:1, 3:2, and 3:3. The slope of the resale demand curve

$$\frac{dP}{dq} = \left[\frac{q}{P} \frac{dP}{dq}\right] \frac{P}{q} = \frac{P}{q} \cdot \frac{1}{\eta_D}$$

where η_D is the elasticity of resale demand. The slope of the average cost curve

$$\frac{dAC}{dq} = \frac{1}{q} \frac{d(AC \cdot q)}{dq} - \frac{AC}{q} \text{ or } \frac{dAC}{dq} = \frac{MC - AC}{q}$$

where MC is marginal transport costs. Elasticity of field demand

$$\eta_\theta = P - AC \bigg/ \left[\frac{P}{\eta_D} - (MC - AC)\right].$$ In some one resale area 1,000 miles north, average resale price might be 60.0 cents per mcf (for both home and industrial use). Elasticity of resale demand might be -1.50, primarily because of extensive industrial purchases. Unit transport costs from the 16″ pipeline might be 10.0 cents per mcf (and marginal costs 6.0 cents per mcf, as a rough approximation to the change in total costs shown in Table 3:3, for volumes slightly larger than 1.2 trillion cubic

feet). In this case, $\eta_\theta = \dfrac{60.0 - 10.0}{\dfrac{60.0}{-1.50} + 4.0} = -1.14.$ This is without taking

account of gathering costs in the field and particularly, retail transmission costs. If these are included in $(MC - AC)$ and in θ, it is likely that η_θ would be much larger. If any of these values for elasticity of demand or for the level of costs are changed, elasticity of field demand changes.

more elastic than for the new line.[29] Field demands may differ because the costs of building and operating the various pipelines differ. For instance, lines going west from Texas and some of those in South Louisiana pass through mountainous or swampy terrain where construction is difficult. As a result, they have higher unit costs than lines built through less obstinate country—and presumably they have a more elastic demand (*ceteris paribus*). Most important, the transporters traversing the longest distance have the highest unit transport costs. Construction costs increase proportionately with the miles of entrenched steel pipe, so that 1,000-mile pipelines have twice the transport costs per mcf, for any given volume of gas, of the 500-mile pipeline.[30] Higher transport costs, for any of these reasons, result in smaller field purchases for any offer price θ_i. (This would result in curve $D'D'$ being lower and more elastic than for the transporters with less transport costs.)

Clearly, resale demand conditions and the costs of transmission cause significant variation in the demand curves of individual buyers. If a number of lines are competing for reserves, then the lines with the higher resale demand prices or lower transport costs in the given market period might obtain most of the reserves.[31]

29. The level of prevailing regulated price for old transporters may set a "ceiling" on resale prices for new reserves, however. The "ceiling" sometimes can be removed only by instituting (costly) rate-increase procedures for all sales, so that the older transporters may have a "flat" resale demand curve.

30. The dispersion in unit transportation costs in reality is quite large. For the line 1,000 miles longer, the average costs are almost a cent higher per mcf per hundred miles. This amount is based on technology of full flow transmission (as outlined in Table 3:3), and it is only approximated by lines built under a variety of conditions. For varying construction costs on specific projects, cf. G. Kinney, "What It Costs To Build and Operate Gas Pipelines," 58 *Oil and Gas Journal*, no. 26 (June 29, 1960), 99. The dispersion on South Louisiana costs, in particular, is great; but at the same time, Kinney's *average* construction costs per mile lead to per mcf transportation costs close to those in Table 3:2.

31. There might be a number of lines with "excess demand" at any price slightly below the existing price. The unsuccessful bidders would be the large buyers in future market periods, or in any situation where buyers attempt to offer prices below the maximum level. Highly varied field demands may imply competitive purchasing by a few buyers able to offer slightly higher prices. Such demands, if realized, imply a large

VARIATION IN PRICES OFFERED BY ANY ONE
PIPELINE BUYER

Maximum offer prices from any one buyer should vary between spatially separated fields. Pipelines usually agree to construct gathering lines into the fields in their general supply areas, and to purchase reserves at the well-head. The maximum offer prices for gas at various wells differ because gathering costs differ, or because conditions of the contract differ. In effect, variations in buyer's costs result in higher (maximum) offer prices on longer-term contracts, for larger volumes, from those traps closest to resale locations.

The pipeline gathering new reserves in a number of fields can make substantial savings by gathering large volumes in large lateral lines. The unit gathering costs for any volume of reserves from one trap are considerably less than for the same volume gathered piecemeal from many traps. There are savings on rights-of-way costs and there are savings on construction-operation costs per thousand cubic feet of gathered gas.

The extent of cost savings on gathering gas from "advantageous" reservoirs can be illustrated by considering a transporter seeking reserves from a trap that lies thirty miles distant from his main line. Volumes are sufficient at this location to build lines from 2 to 12 inches diameter (the common range of gathering line size). Construction costs increase with pipeline diameter—the 2-inch line costs approximately $3,677 per mile, and the 12-inch line $20,067 per mile.[32] Operating costs increase proportionally with line diameter,[33] and interest costs for the investment period increase according to the size of undepreciated construction expenses. As a result, total costs

"turnover" in successful buyers over any extended time period. This would be the case if all demand curves were flat over the relevant range of prices, but some few being higher than others. If all demand curves are inelastic and reserves are relatively large, then concentration of purchases would be low.

   Noncompetitive purchasing is likely to be different, as shall be seen in the next chapter.

   32. As quoted from the "Nelson Construction Index" of average construction costs in 1955. Cf. 54 *Oil and Gas Journal* 101 (Dec. 3, 1956).

   33. Estimate of S. P. Ford in 53 *Oil and Gas Journal* 109 (Dec. 12, 1955). It is assumed that natural pressures in the trap are sufficient so that compression expenses are not incurred.

for gathering enough gas to fill the larger lines are proportionately larger than for gathering in small lines, as shown in
column 6 of Table 3:4. The volume of gas that can be transported increases more than proportionately with the diameter
of the line, however. More than five times as much can be
transported in the 12-inch line than the 6-inch line, as shown
in column 2 of Table 3:4. With total costs proportional and
"throughput" more than proportional to line diameter, the per-
unit costs for gathering a larger volume are much lower than
those for a smaller volume. Estimates of per-unit costs (as
shown in column 7 of Table 3:4) indicate savings of up to 3.0
cents per mcf, in the extreme, from transporting 500 billion
cubic feet in one 12-inch gathering line rather than 6 billion in
a 2-inch line.[34]

Maximum offer prices for volumes in various fields depend
upon these gathering costs and upon the general price level θ
offered by the buyer for all reserves (shown in Figure 3:2).
In the simplest case, the transporter might consider constructing a feeder line to distant reservoirs, rather than purchasing
from a reservoir located directly on the transmission line.[35]
His alternatives are shown in Figure 3:3A: He can offer to pay
prevailing maximum price θ for reserves from the trap on the
transmission line, or offer this price minus the unit costs AGC
of gathering gas in the field some thirty miles distant. There
is no need to offer more than $(\theta - AGC)$ for reserves in the
distant trap because equal reserves are available for θ at the
main line (and the price is not less than $[\theta - AGC]$ for any
amount of reserves in the distant trap if it is the defined "maximum offer price").[36]

34. The extent of actual savings, of course, depends upon other factors such as P_1, P_2 (the inlet and delivery pressures).

35. Actual alternatives may be to purchase in the field thirty miles
from the line or in a number of others at varying distances. The relevant
comparison is then between maximum offer prices of Figure 3:2, minus
additional transportation costs in this field, and minus additional costs
elsewhere. But this is the second stage of complexity of the analysis.

36. To be exact, prices θ and $(\theta - AGC)$ are *offer* prices at the main
transmission line. Whether purchases are made depends upon not only
demand prices, but the conditions of supply and competition. Price θ,
here, is some *one maximum offer price* of one successful or unsuccessful
potential buyer.

TABLE 3:4. *Unit Costs of Gathering Gas in Various-Sized Lateral Pipelines*

1	2	3	4	5	6	7
Inside diameter of the pipeline (in inches)	Q, Millions of cubic feet of delivered gas in twenty years	Construction costs, in dollars	Interest costs (present value), in dollars	Line maintenance costs (present value), in dollars	Total costs (6 = 3 + 4 + 5), in dollars	Unit cost, cents per thousand cubic feet delivered 7 = 6/2
2	6,131	110,916	70,071	12,770	193,757	3.160
4	34,656	190,097	120,093	25,540	335,730	0.969
6	95,569	287,785	181,795	38,310	507,870	0.531
8	196,014	397,757	251,282	51,081	700,120	0.357
10	342,475	497,581	314,346	63,851	875,778	0.256
12	540,716	602,027	380,330	76,621	1,058,978	0.196

Source. From the Johnson-Berwald Formula: $Q = 1.6156 \frac{T_b}{P_b} \sqrt{1/f} \sqrt{1/z} \left[\frac{(P_1^2 - P_2^2) d^{5}}{GTL} \right]^{\frac{1}{2}}$

Q = throughput, cubic feet per hour · (24 hours) (7300) = reserves delivered
d = line diameter, etc. (as in Table 3:3)
P_1 = 1200 psia
P_2 = 1000 psia
"Construction costs" estimates were obtained from the "Nelson Construction Index" in 54 *Oil and Gas Journal* (Dec. 6, 1956). "Interest costs" were derived from considering the present value of uniform 10 per cent charges on undepreciated construction expenditures for twenty years (with twenty-year straight-line depreciation). "Line maintenance costs" were estimated as the present value of the uniform annual expense of $25 per mile, per inch of line diameter.

47

The maximum field price is greater for larger volumes because of savings in gathering costs. Savings from transporting reserves sufficient for capacity of a 12-inch feeder line vary from .05 to 3.00 cents per mcf (according to the size of the feeder lines considered in Table 3:4). Maximum prices on the large amount of reserves should be from .05 to 3.00 cents per mcf greater than on smaller amounts, as indicated in Figure 3:3B,[37] because field gathering costs are lower for the larger volumes.[38]

Offer prices should be higher for reserves in traps closer to the point of final resale. Gas volumes located at the main pipeline should have maximum price θ, while equal-sized volumes thirty miles from the main pipeline should have the price $(\theta - AGC)$.[39] Volumes of reserves located farther from resale cities would have lower maximum prices because of greater transmission and gathering costs. Gathering from the field 100 miles farther away requires the construction of thirty miles of gathering pipeline and seventy miles of higher pressure "lateral" pipeline.[40] Average gathering costs of roughly 60 cents and transmission costs of 70 cents per mcf increase costs for the purchaser in this field by 1.30 cents per mcf. Given that

37. The curve *FP* is in no sense a demand curve since it *assumes* aggregate price and quantity demanded. It represents relative offer prices for a small portion of total reserves *given* price θ from the firms aggregate demand $D'D'$, and the relative gathering costs AGC: $FP = \theta - AGC$.

38. This is true for volumes up to that amount sufficient to operate a 12″ line to full capacity. There are not likely to be further savings from transporting even larger volumes, however, because transportation to the main line of larger volumes involves two 8″–12″ feeder lines or a 16″ transmission "lateral" with compression. These alternatives involve duplication of one gathering line or operation of the *transmission* line at less-than-full capacity. There is no obvious further cost saving from line duplication or from underutilizing the small *transmission* lines. Operating thirty miles of 16″ line at ⅓–⅔ capacity involves average costs of .99 to .65 cents per mcf according to the construction costs (and ⅓–⅔ volumes) of Table 3:3.

39. With costs proportional to distance, offer price should be .323 cents higher for 34,656 mcf of gas, and .085 cents higher per mcf for 342,475 mcf (Table 3:4).

40. The lateral transmission line may be constructed for transmission from a number of fields, however.

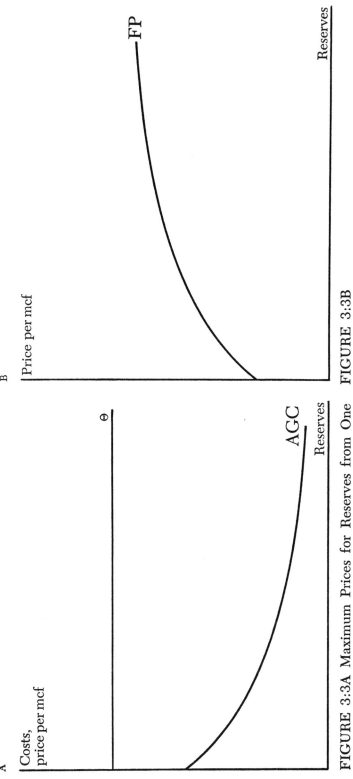

FIGURE 3:3A Maximum Prices for Reserves from One Trap

FIGURE 3:3B

the buyer can take gas elsewhere at price θ, the maximum offer price should be somewhere near 1.30 cents per mcf less in this reservoir 100 miles farther.[41]

Maximum offer prices for reserves should increase with the length of the proposed production period. Gas delivered over ten years, and the same reserves delivered over twenty years, are not of "equal quality" to the buyer. Gas volumes under short-term contract do not provide the basis for resale to retail gas companies seeking long-term commitments. Short-term contracts are disadvantageous to the pipeline when obtaining capital, because the "number of year's reserves" is smaller and because Federal Power Commission certification is more difficult to obtain for resale of reserves *not* contributing to "a twenty year index of deliverability." Therefore, the buyer should be willing to pay a higher maximum price for volumes on long term rather than short term (the extent of the premium in maximum offer price cannot be predicted easily, however, since it is not based upon equipment and operation cost savings).

There are other aspects of contracts that may make for differences in a pipeline's maximum offer prices—Favored Nations or Renegotiation clauses, for instance.[42] It is evident that a Favored Nations agreement is disadvantageous for the purchaser. The expected price increase from the clause should be zero when maximum price is being offered, but the risk of having to pay a higher price is increased.[43] If there is substantial risk that the clause will "trigger" the prevailing contract price, then the Favored Nations contract is substantially

41. But when all traps require thirty miles of gathering line, maximum offer price in the trap 100 miles farther should be approximately .70 cents per mcf less than in a trap 30 miles from the main pipeline. The differential in costs *between fields* is only 70 cents so that the price differential should be 70 cents.

42. Cf. discussion of the nature of these clauses, pp. 30–31 above.

43. The quoted contract price would not be a maximum if, on the average, returns are expected from the contract clauses. The risk of price increase is increased from zero to that indicated by the probability of new contract price being greater than "base price" on the existing Favored Nations contract.

less desirable to the buyer than the contract without the clause, and the maximum price offered for a Favored Nations contract should be less than for the same reserves purchased without Favored Nations.[44] The maximum price for a contract with Renegotiation should be less for the same reason.[45]

DEMAND PRICES IN GENERAL

This is to suggest that there are a number of factors affecting the maximum prices offered by any pipeline buyer for new reserves. Resale demand conditions and pipeline transport costs probably result in demand curves for each pipeline that are quite different. Also, each pipeline's offer prices in different reservoirs should be greater for larger volumes of reserves sold as a unit at one location, and should be greater for volumes closer to resale locations. Offer prices should be greater for volumes sold under longer-term contract, and under contracts that do not have Favored Nations or Renegotiation clauses.

The question for analysis is whether this pattern of *maximum prices* for one buyer emerges from a market for new reserves. It is expected that, if the market is competitive, buyers are forced to pay maximum prices, and thus are required to follow a pattern of price variation according to contract volume, to the trap-distance from points of resale, and to the term-length of the contract. Under competition, different pipelines' demand curves at prevailing prices should result in fluctuating concentration in the actual purchase of reserves from market period to market period. In noncompetitive mar-

44. Given that the buyer has an "aversion" to accepting such a risk of upward price change. It is difficult to evaluate the monetary equivalent of this risk since "cost" to the purchaser is subjective. There should be a slight, or great, decrease in price θ for reserves sold under Favored Nations contracts depending upon the buyer's evaluation of risk.

45. The "risk" of price change from Renegotiation should be less than from Favored Nations, however, since there is no *requirement* that price be increased because of higher newer contract prices elsewhere. If the risk of loss for the buyer is less under Renegotiation, then the discount in offer price should be less.

kets, *patterns of purchase price* should be in contrast to these theoretical competitive maximum offer prices (and in some cases should be related to each pipeline's demand elasticity). Explaining the nature of the contrasts in the competitive and noncompetitive pricing patterns is the task of the next chapter.

4. Markets and Market Prices

Prices for gas volumes in new contracts are related to the transporter's maximum offer prices and to the marginal costs of producing reserves. The exact nature of the relationship depends, however, upon the competitiveness of the relevant markets. When there is buyer and seller competition, prices should closely follow the pattern of maximum offer prices and marginal development costs (with the two tending toward equality). When markets are monopolized by one or a few producers, prices should be higher than marginal production costs and should vary from buyer to buyer (with the higher prices being paid by those with the more inelastic demands). When markets are monopolized by one buyer, prices should be below maximum offer prices and should vary only according to differences in development costs.

Patterns of price formation depend upon the extent of control of the "relevant market" by producers or pipelines. This chapter outlines the characteristics of markets that result in control or lack of control of sales prices. For each set of market conditions, theoretical pricing patterns are developed in detail. These theoretical prices will be compared with market prices during the 1950s in the subsequent chapters.

MARKETS

Unfortunately for the ease of this study, volumes of new reserves are not sold at specified central clearing houses under conditions that allow perfect knowledge for all buyers and sellers.[1] The gas reserve markets do not strongly resemble those for corporate stock or even those for grain "futures." Rather, they are spread over various production regions— because of lack of information, gas quality differences, etc., and they do not include all firms located in the region. More- over, markets in which buyers purchase reserves do not have the same geographical boundaries as markets in which pro- ducers sell reserves.

Each seller's market is the area of demand for his in-ground reserves. This geographical region (containing all relevant buyers of reserves) is limited to the producer's field area in most cases. The field or reservoir is the region within which the buyer must be located because gas cannot be taken to another field (without the seller becoming a pipeline).[2] Pro- ducers have confined themselves to selling in the fields in which they have had gas reserves: the overwhelming majority of contracts in the 1950s have been for gas volumes in a given field going to a pipeline buyer located in, or about to enter, that field.

The relevant time-length of the producer's market is the period during which he can consider alternative sources of demand. Before a certain number of "step-out" wells have been drilled, the producer has very little to sell and probably would not consider offers at all. He can consider alternative offers after drilling has proceeded to the point where a volume estimate can be substantiated by initial open-flow capacity. He cannot consider further offers after the time when deferral of sale leads to surrender of the lease. In most cases, there seems to be a one or two-year maximum interval between "step-out" discovery drilling and the lapse of the lease. The market period consists of this one or two-year span.

With hundreds of separated fields passing through the pre-

1. For the "perfect" market, cf. G. S. Shepherd, *Marketing Farm Products* (Ames, the Collegiate Press, 1946), appendix A: "The Perfect Market in Time, Place, and Form," pp. 399–409.

2. The seller becomes, in effect, an (integrated) buyer if he trans- ports gas out of the field. This may increase the number of effective alternative demanders but only by providing a new pipeline *into the field area*. The actual purchase area continues to be limited to the field with the producer-pipeline now encountering all the entry considera- tions on the buying side of the market.

development stage in the 1950s, there must have been hundreds of separate producer's markets. Many oil and gas companies with reserves in more than one reservoir operated in numerous two-year markets. A few, with unit-operations, were able to consider alternative offers over a longer period.[3] A few with small portions of a trap in which production had begun were forced to sell within less than two years or lose reserves to drainage. But in the typical case, the producer had the opportunity to sell reserves to any pipeline that was in the reservoir within about two years of reserve discovery.

The buyers purchase in markets that are much larger in every respect. As purchaser-transporters, they are technically capable of moving large gas volumes more than 2,000 miles after gathering gas over a 60,000 square mile area. The limits to particular supply areas for each line are determined by the costs of gathering and the price for gas in prevailing contracts. But the extent of any supply market at any time is no less than the *current* gathering area of the pipeline, which is typically thirty miles wide on each side of each established transmission line, and some 500–1,000 miles long.[4] All new reserves within this region can usually be considered alternative supplies within the buyer's market.[5]

Moreover, the time-length of the market is longer for the buyer than for the seller. A new pipeline usually obtains the reserves necessary for certification within one to four years (while engineering and financing of transmission are planned). Once the original reserves are obtained, there is no urgent need for a transporter to purchase replacement reserves until twenty years have passed. Actually, it may be least costly for the buyer to purchase *reserves* equal to five year's *produc-*

3. On the assumption that most unit development took place on large-acre ranches. The producers there may have been able to convince one or few ranchers that it was in their interest to "shut-in" for the present in order to consider future buyers.

4. For new lines or expansions of old lines, the relevant supply area includes fields within the region of *any* planned area for the new facilities.

5. Some Gulf Coast pipelines, such as Tennessee Gas Transmission, United Gas Pipeline Company, and Texas Eastern Transmission, have more than one main transmission line. They have supply areas inclusive of territory around all their lateral lines.

tion every five years.[6] (A pipeline usually has the opportunity to take fully explored reserves in its gathering region immediately, or to wait five years for newly discovered reserves to be ready for sale.)

The buyer's market includes most reserves offered in a five-year period in the established gathering region. Gas need not be of uniform quality. If low-pressure gas can be compressed at a cost to the transporter of ½ cent per mcf, then this gas can be considered at a price ½ cent per mcf less than for gas at 1,000 pounds per square inch. Similarly, gas requiring gathering can be considered identical to gas located at the end of the transmission line if prices are reduced by the cost of gathering. In effect, all gas volumes for which there are price differentials to compensate for physical or locational disadvantages are in the same market for the buyer.[7]

Thus the market is of greater extent for the buyer than for the seller. The supply area for the buyer is composed of a number of fields and extends over approximately five years. The selling area for the producer is usually limited to the field in which the new reserves are located and to a two-year period. Particular limits to markets differ for each pipeline and each producer. It is apparent only that the large number of markets gives rise to the possibility of great diversity of behavior.

CONDITIONS NECESSARY FOR CONTROL OF MARKET PRICE

If any buyer is to control prices on new contracts, he must control the demand for new reserves in the producer's market

6. This span of years is no more than a "rule of thumb" quoted quite frequently by gas buyers for the larger interstate pipelines. The reason for purchasing replacement reserves in this period is to forego adding capital to the fund for retirement of corporate bonds (as mentioned in Chapter 3) or to forego Federal Power Commission review of continued "feasibility of service."

7. This is to say that all gas volumes for which the cross-elasticity of demand is high are considered effective alternatives. Where gas can be graded and transportation volume or distance costs are measurable, there seem to be no reasons for $\dfrac{\partial Q_1/Q_1}{\partial P_2/P_2}$ to be less than infinite for reserves in field 1 and reserve price in field 2.

area. This monopoly buyer, or monopsonist, must be the only source of a price offer in the field during a period of about two years.[8] The relevant geographical region for measuring the extent of monopsony is the producer's selling market as indicated by any *one* of the black dots in Figure 4:1.

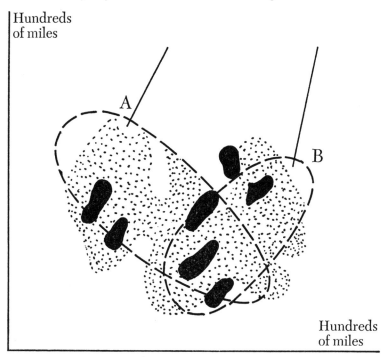

FIGURE 4:1 Geographical Representation of Markets

To set price, the producer (or seller) must control the supply of new reserves over the pipeline's supply area. In order to set price above the competitive level, the monopoly seller must have lease-rights to all new volumes of gas in the transporter's market area.[9] Pipeline A, for example, may have

8. Actually this is a short-run view. It is argued below that exploration should be influenced by the prospect of a monopsony price, and that long-run control of demand over larger regions (or pipeline exploration) may be necessary to set price below a competitive level.

9. An emphasis upon control of supply as the key to power over price

gathering facilities within the area encompassed by the dotted lines (in Figure 4:1). To be able to dictate price to A, the monopolist would have to be the only source of new reserves in all the fields in the encompassed area, and would have to control lease-rights for all immediate exploration in the area. Pipeline A must not be able to postpone present purchasing in order to obtain newly discovered reserves from other producers in the future, nor be able to turn to inferior quality gas owned by other producers. It follows that, for there to be monopoly in the (overlapping) markets of pipeline A and pipeline B there must be single control of new reserves throughout the areas A and B for a five-year period.[10]

If monopoly control is not present, there might be market control by a *few* producers acting together. Four or five sellers of equal size, holding some 80 per cent of uncommitted reserves can control price to transporters if they agree to sell for the same price and on the same terms.[11] The buyers would then have to accept the new contract prices suggested by the few producers. The possibility of a few producers cooperating in this fashion must be considered in any attempt to evaluate the extent of control over prices.[12]

is necessary for understanding "partial monopoly" situations to be described. Cf. W. D. Arant, "Competition of the Few among Many," *Quarterly Journal of Economy* (August 1956), pp. 339–45.

10. The "monopolist" would have to be the *same firm* if the market areas A and B overlap (as shown) so as to prevent the pipelines from concentrating purchases in the overlapping portion of the supply regions with the alternative source of supply.

11. The percentage is somewhat arbitrary but must be close to that necessary for control. If an attempt should be made to raise price above any given level, and 80 per cent of the reserves are found in the acreage of the suppliers seeking to raise price, then the buyer has to seek additional reserves from others controlling the remaining 20 per cent. Their opportunity to expand sales is limited by that amount of the 20 per cent that would not be sold at the competitive price. This would seem to be strictly limited given the limits on production (in Chapter 2). The buyer has little recourse but to deal with the large producers when they control this percentage, at least. But if their control extended only to 50 per cent, then *perhaps* control is limited. This can be examined in detail.

12. It is equally possible for a few large *buyers* to act in concert and control demand in any (producer's) market. These possibilities for oligopoly *buying* power will also be examined

THE COMPETITIVE PRICE LEVEL IN NEW CONTRACTS

If there are large numbers of producers in pipeline purchase regions and also large numbers of pipelines with gathering facilities in each field, neither the buyer nor the seller can control contract prices. Competition among buyers in (overlapping) supply markets requires the successful bidder to pay *maximum* offer prices for new contract reserves. Competition among producers results in supply at prices no higher than marginal production costs.

One result of competition is illustrated in Figure 4:2 by price P_0, the market clearing price given "demand" and "supply" of new reserves. Demand for new reserves DD indicates the maximum price (offered by a number of lines) for total volumes of new reserves at some common "end of transmis-

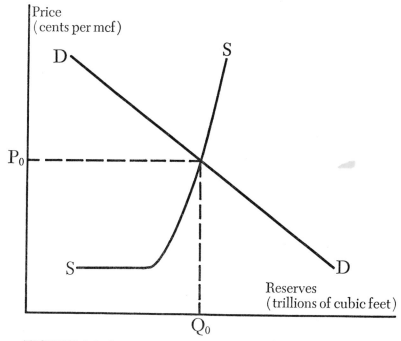

FIGURE 4:2 Competitive Supply Area Price

sion." [13] Supply of new reserves SS indicates volumes for sale "at the common point of transmission" for prices no higher than the marginal development costs. No producer would supply additional reserves for less than marginal costs, nor could he expect a higher price (given many alternative sources). The total new reserves that producers provide at a given level of price and marginal cost is the market supply at that price. It is to be expected that the quantity of new reserves which can be supplied at higher prices is only slightly larger than the amount supplied at lower prices because of the sharp rise in marginal development costs at capacity rates of recovery. However, at prices lower than average development costs no reserves would be offered since it would be less costly to "shut-in" the reservoir.[14] The aggregate supply curve should be horizontal for a range and then rise sharply, as shown.[15] Given such supply and demand the market for reserves should be cleared at price P_0, for aggregate sales of new reserves Q_0.[16]

13. The myth of a common point of purchase is maintained to predict the *average* level of area prices. The variation around the average is considered henceforth in the discussion of the competitive *pattern* of prices in different fields where there are additional gathering costs, etc.

14. Price is *given*, for all volumes, for the competitive supplier. When the given price is less than marginal costs for all amounts of recovered reserves, there is zero amount and no contract. This is the case, as well, for price less than average development costs because the per-unit loss (equal to the difference between price and the average development costs) can be avoided by "shutting-in." But when price is *greater* than average development costs, the producer can maximize revenues by committing to production that volume for which marginal costs equal price.

15. Supply would be *much* greater at a higher price if (a) there were substantial new recovery from compression or (b) there were a number of fields with higher average costs from which new reserves would be forthcoming at higher price. Neither is likely since compression is not usually highly productive and basin development costs are generally the same for each field.

16. A larger volume of reserves in new contracts can follow only from some producers receiving less than marginal production costs for additional units, which is not profitable. A smaller volume would have a maximum offer price greater than marginal costs, so that producers would have a tendency to increase individual volumes. Only for the amount P_0 is "maximum offer price" equal to the "marginal development costs," and is price at an equilibrium level.

Price P_0 is a per-unit return for new gas reserves to be delivered at "the common point of transmission," according to contracts signed within any two to five-year period. This price indicates the theoretical level of competitive area prices. In actual competitive sales and purchase markets there is no such uniform level, but rather there exists a number of different prices following from competitive demand for, and supply of, differing contracts.

VARIATIONS IN COMPETITIVE PRICES

Competitive prices for gas should vary among fields within a supply area. The price in each field contract can be expected to equal marginal costs and the maximum offer price of the successful bidder. Marginal production costs have a pattern of variation (as outlined in Chapter 2) and maximum offer prices vary from contract to contract (as outlined in Chapter 3). There should be a *pattern* of competitive prices according to variations in marginal production costs and in offer prices from reservoir to reservoir.

Higher Prices in Larger-Volume Reservoirs. Prices should be higher for contracts calling for production of larger volumes of reserves. Since the pipeline purchaser incurs lower transportation costs in taking any given volume from one location via one gathering line, the maximum offer price can be greater for the large "package of reserves." Relative offer prices for large and small volumes are shown as FP in Figure 4:3, given relative gathering costs and the area price level P_0. Production costs associated with large-volume traps may be equal to those associated with small-volume traps (for the same percentage recovery).[17] Development of the smaller reserve results in marginal and average costs MC_1 and AC_1 in Figure 4:3 (from Figure 2:1) while that from the larger trap results in marginal and average costs MC_2 and AC_2.[18] The producers,

17. The discussion in Chapter 2 led to the conclusion that the *percentage* recovered determined the level of marginal and average costs. For a trap with *twice the reserves* the marginal cost curve rose sharply for *twice the volume recovered,* given identical depth, pressure, etc.

18. The costs of developing the larger trap are double those of the smaller, as required drilling on the larger acreage, et al., increase, but

as a result of competition (and the lure of profits), can be
expected to contract the amount of reserves for which *MC*
equals price. The successful buyer is forced, by the bids of

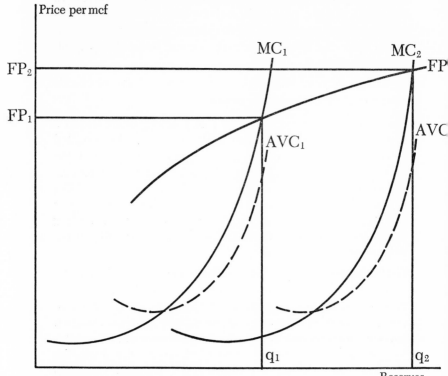

FIGURE 4:3 Competitive Field Prices

other transporters, to pay maximum prices *FP*. The price for
the larger volume of reserves q_2 is FP_2, while the price for the
smaller volume q_1 is at the lower level FP_1.[19] The purchaser

volume of reserves recoverable at 60 per cent also doubles. Both marginal cost curves increase sharply for recovery of 60–80 per cent of
in-ground reserves.

19. This difference is due to savings in the costs of gathering from
the *field area*, as well as savings in gathering from any part of the single
trap. The first cost saving should result in higher prices on *all* contracts
from the large field, the second cost saving should result in higher prices
on the *larger* contracts within *the field*. Given average costs of gathering

in competition pays a higher price for the larger volume because it is less costly to transport.[20]

Higher Prices in Closer Reservoirs. The farther traps are from the "end of transmission," the higher are gathering and transmission costs incurred by the purchaser. Given the opportunity to take reserves at closer points, the buyer's maximum offer price in the farther field is lower. As indicated by curve *FP'* compared to *FP* in Figure 4:4, the relative offer price for reserves 100 miles away is lower than for similar amounts at the "end of transmission." [21] The costs of producing reserves from both traps can be assumed to be equal, so that marginal development costs *MC* in Figure 4:4 indicate expenses of various rates of recovery from two identical but separate reservoirs. Competition among pipelines requires successful buyers to pay price FP_0 in the closer trap, and price FP_0' in the farther trap for substantially the same amount of reserves. A pattern follows of higher prices in fields closer to resale areas (and of economic rents to the nearer producer).[22]

Higher Prices for Longer-Term Contracts. Competition among transporters should result in higher prices for more "advantageous" contracts—those having longer production periods, for example. A longer production period allows the

within the field in 2″, 4″, 6″ lines (as shown in Chapter 3), the second source of cost (and price) differences seems more substantial.

20. In this example there is little difference in percentage recovery as a result of the higher price. Because of the almost vertical section of MC_1, MC_2, the increase in price for q_2 over q_1 adds insignificantly to the amount dedicated. Full recovery is substantially complete at price P_1 so that the producer receiving P_2 earns an economic rent or a return greater than that strictly necessary to elicit supply. The chief cause for the rent is the high level of *FP* and the high level of P_0 in Figure 4:2 (i.e., the high level of uniform area price).

21. On the average, each line may save .70–1.00 cents per mcf from purchasing in the trap 100 miles closer. If the successful bidder has "average" cost savings, the *FP* curve should be .70–1.00 cents higher for each volume than *FP'*.

22. The producer in both traps is required by competition to dedicate that volume for which marginal production cost equals price. Given that the volume is all that can be produced from natural expansion, the producer in the closer trap receives a higher return for about the same amount of gas (or an "economic rent" from superior location).

pipeline to build up required reserves, so that purchasers should be willing to pay more for a volume of gas to be produced over twenty years than for one to be produced over ten years. Greater demand for longer-term contracts can be indi-

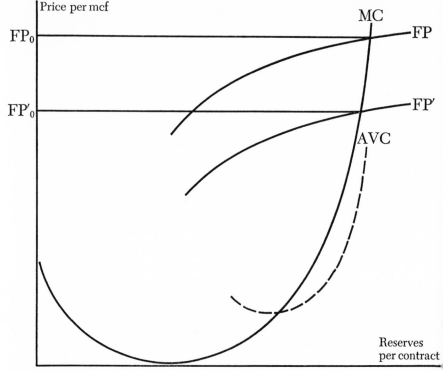

FIGURE 4:4 Competitive Prices in Spatially Separated Fields

cated by *FP''* maximum offer prices, compared to *FP* for shorter-term contracts (in Figure 4:5).[23] At the same time there are increased costs for longer-term contracts. The unit

23. Location and volume offer prices may differ by given amounts for each pipeline because they are based upon general differences in the costs of transportation. Differences between *FP* and *FP'* are not predictable on a cost basis, however. To predict the difference between *FP* and *FP''* in Figure 4:5, the *value* of longer term to the pipeline buyer has to be known.

costs of longer production periods are considerably greater because of greater interest expenses on original drilling costs, so that average costs AC'' for twenty years are higher than average costs AC for fifteen years (in Figure 4:5). The mar-

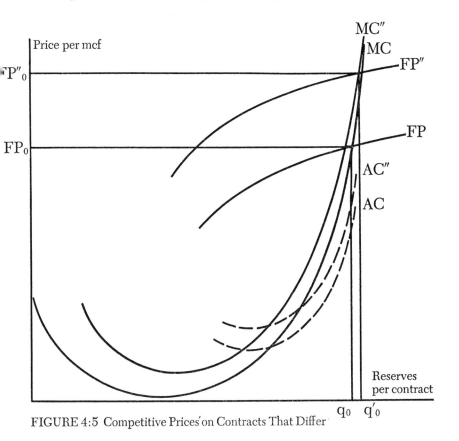

FIGURE 4:5 Competitive Prices on Contracts That Differ

ginal costs over different production periods are much the same since operation and compression expenses for additions to the initial volume are not affected by term-length. With these offer price and marginal cost curves, contract price equals FP_0 for production of q_0 reserves over ten years and FP_0'' for production of the same volume over twenty years.

Competition among buyers requires the purchaser to pay the premium indicated by the difference between FP_0'' and FP_0.[24]

Higher Prices for Contracts without Favored Nations Clauses. Other aspects of the contract may be "disadvantageous" enough to affect the competitive pricing pattern. Purchasers may include Favored Nations and/or Renegotiation clauses in new contracts, or they may seek contracts without such clauses. According to the theory espoused in the industry, the presence of either clause makes it probable, to some extent, that future delivery prices will be greater than those specified in the contract. If there is a buyer's "cost equivalence" to this risk of price increase, then maximum offer prices have to be lower in contracts with the clause than in those without. The highest bidder would have offer prices FP rather than FP'' (in Figure 4:5) for contracts with clauses. At the same time, the producers are relieved of contracting reserves immediately at the risk of missing higher prices in the future.[25] The pro-

24. This premium results in the entire volume of reserves being dedicated for production over the longer term (since the producers increase profits on each cubic foot of gas by incurring costs equal only to $\{AC'' - AC\}$ but receiving returns equal to $\{FP'' - FP\}$). To the other extreme a smaller premium would result in the dedication of all gas reserves under short-term contract (when $\{FP'' - FP\}$ is less than $\{AC'' - AC\}$). There may be both long and short-term contracts, however, if producers have varying costs of capital $\{AC'' - AC\}$.

25. The theory is part of the oral tradition in the industry communicated by gas purchasers and sellers in Texas and Oklahoma. The best written expressions are found in the Federal Power Commission testimony of Drs. J. R. Foster, H. B. Poran in *Pure Oil Co., et al.,* Docket G-17930, "Limited Issues Hearings," July 1959; and of Mr. J. R. McChesney, manager of the Pure Oil Co. Gas Department, in the same hearings. The most comprehensive explanation is found in Foster Associates, "Flexible Pricing Provisions in Natural Gas Markets," Special Study A-43 (Foster Associates, Washington, D.C., October 1959, 39 pp.). This study provides an outline of the above explanation and includes others. One other reason given for Favored Nations clauses is buyer's "lesser ability to pay in the earlier years" (p. 6) which is price behavior consistent only with monopoly price discrimination. A low present price and high future price for uniform deliveries would not continue on an informal basis under competition—either price would finally prevail where demand dictates. Another reason for *upward* "triggering" of price by the clauses is given to be "buyers and sellers have not expected that the value of gas would move downward (p. 9)." This is inconsistent with the "risk" reason since, regardless of expectations

ducer's marginal costs may be decreased by an amount "equivalent" to the risk of contracting too soon.[26] Prices for contracts with clauses are lower if the risk placed on the buyer results in a difference between curves FP'' and FP which is less than the differences in costs for at least some producers.[27]

A Review of Variations in Competitive Contract Prices. An examination of prices under competitive conditions of supply and demand should reveal a systematic pattern of variation. Prices on new contracts should be higher when larger volumes of reserves are committed and when the location of the reserves is closer to resale markets. Prices should be higher on new contracts for twenty-year delivery than on contracts with shorter term-lengths. In some cases, prices should be higher in contracts without Favored Nations and Renegotiation clauses.[28]

MONOPOLY PRICE LEVELS IN NEW CONTRACTS

The monopolist with control of the supply of new reserves within some gathering area can require any arbitrary pattern

---

held concerning future price, downward revision would *impose* risk on the producer. If upward revision is designed to remove producer's risk, then it is consistent not to allow downward revision.

26. This risk is likely to be small because the market period is little more than two years.

27. It is probable that the reduction in producer's costs (from "removal of risk") as a result of including a Renegotiation clause would be less than with Favored Nations. This is because Renegotiation does little more than allow for reappraisal of price in the operating contract, while Favored Nations changes price according to the standard of "prices on later contracts."

28. There are further "reasons" for price variation, of course. Quality of the gas in different traps may differ, ability and interest of the producers in considering relevant alternatives may differ, or "mistakes" may be made in the sense that the producers and buyers agree to contracts for what appears to be the area price (with corrections for location, volume, et al.) but turns out to be too high or low given prices on subsequent contracts. The variations in the competitive patterns mentioned should result in predictable variations in prices. The producer that signs without seeking the best alternative, or after making "a mistake," contributes to the divergence of prices from any systematic pattern. Over the market period of two to five years, for a large number of competitive contract sales, the predicted pattern should be observable within this dispersion following from "irrationality."

and level of contract prices. In order to maximize his returns, he would restrict the aggregate volume of reserves committed, thus raising the price above the competitive level. He could also increase his returns by setting different prices for different pipeline purchasers "at the end of the transmission line." Each prospective buyer has a different elasticity of demand in the relevant range of prices. By setting his prices accordingly, the monopolist can increase revenue through higher margins on sales to buyers with less elastic demand and through increased sales at low margins to buyers with more elastic demand. He can make further gains by varying field prices according to field location, the volume of reserves, the term-length of the contract, once the price level has been set for each purchaser.

The monopoly prices charged two buyers in one common supply area are illustrated in Figure 4:6. Pipeline A is seeking to purchase new reserves for resale to industrial consumers with highly elastic resale demands, so that its field demand curve D_A is highly elastic. Pipeline B is seeking to purchase new reserves for resale to home consumers and has a more inelastic field demand curve D_B. The monopoly producer first determines the marginal cost of supplying both, then sets the shares and prices for each.[29] Pipelines A and B are provided Q_a and Q_b reserves because additions to producer's revenues equal aggregate marginal costs for these volumes.[30] The prices for the two volumes are P_A and P_B, indicating a higher price for the pipeline with the less elastic demand.

When a number of pipelines make independent purchases, the one producer benefits from setting a separate price level for each line assuming that those with less elastic demands do not have the opportunity to repurchase from those buyers

29. The relevant level of marginal cost is that at which marginal costs for aggregate new contract reserves equal the additions to total sales revenues.

30. The marginal cost curve is not shown, but rather the level of MC for $Q_a + Q_b + Q_i$ for i further sales is indicated. For a complete discussion of the profit advantages and mechanics of price discrimination, cf. Joan Robinson, *The Economics of Imperfect Competition* (London, Macmillan, 1954), chap. 15.

with more elastic demands. Given different demand elasticities "at the end of the transmission line," as mentioned in Chapter 3, a number of discriminatory price levels could be expected.

VARIATION IN MONOPOLY CONTRACT PRICES

The monopoly producer sets different prices for reserves in different fields. Again, the variations could be wholly capri-

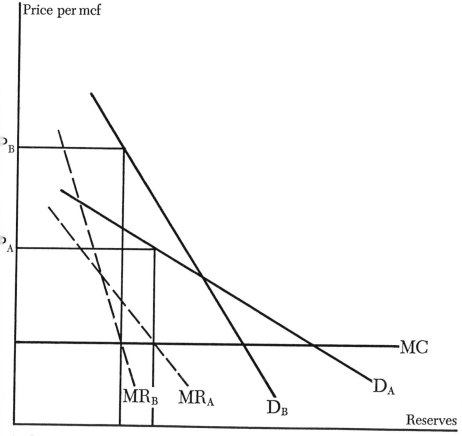

FIGURE 4:6 Monopoly Prices

cious as well as arbitrary, but they should be designed to take
advantage of all maximum offer prices. Prices should be
higher for contracts that are "more advantageous" for the
transporter. Prices charged pipelines A and B should be relatively greater for reserves in closer fields, or for larger volumes
at one location. The offer prices of pipeline A for various volumes from a field close to the main transmission line are indicated by curve FP_a in Figure 4:7 (equal to P_A in Figure 4:6
minus gathering costs) while offer prices in a trap 100 miles
farther are shown by curve FP_a''. Maximum offer prices of
pipeline B for reserves located near the transmission line are

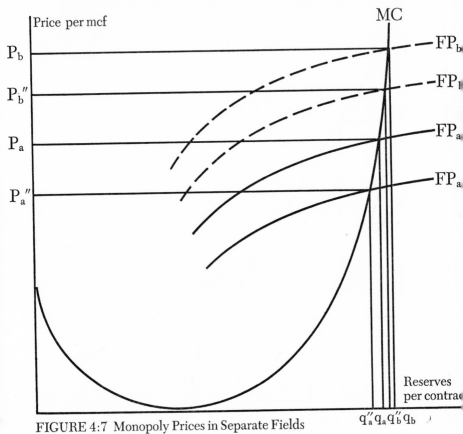

FIGURE 4:7 Monopoly Prices in Separate Fields

shown by curve FP_b and prices 100 miles farther from this buyer's transmission facilities are indicated by curve FP_b''. Demand prices of transporter B are considerably higher because this company (with the less elastic field demand) is being charged a higher *level* of prices (cf. P_B as compared to P_A, in Figure 4:6). Marginal production costs may be similar for all four volumes of gas and may be essentially vertical at full capacity recovery q_i.[31] The one seller in the four fields should set prices P_a and P_b in the two nearby fields, and P_a'', P_b'' in the fields 100 miles away, since these are maximum buyer's prices.[32]

Such prices result in an interesting over-all pattern. They vary with location for each buyer at the same time that they vary between buyers. Consequently, price in the nearer field for the pipeline with the more elastic demand (P_a) may be lower than price in the field 100 miles distant for the pipeline with the less elastic demand (P_b''). The pattern of price variation with distance becomes diffuse because of monopoly discrimination between purchasers.[33]

The monopolist can profitably set higher relative prices on larger volumes of reserves for each transporter. The result may not be an apparent price-volume relationship, however, because of the variation in prices between transporters. The curve FP_a in Figure 4:8 may indicate pipeline A's demand for reserves in some field and the curve FP_b may indicate pipeline B's demand at a location the same distance. Development costs in two reservoirs are shown by MC_1 for the small volume, and MC_2 for the volume twice as large (from Figure 4:3). The producer, for maximum profits, sets price FP_a'' for the smaller reserves and price FP_a for the larger reserves sold to

31. So that monopoly output restriction takes place only by "shutting-in" some of the traps.

32. That is, marginal revenue (not shown) equals marginal cost MC at q_i in all four fields. This level of sales q_i is consequently the most profitable level for the producer and can take place for the prices indicated.

33. With systematic dispersion between FP_a, FP_b as compared to FP_a'', FP_b'' as a result of discrimination between buyers, it is difficult to *distinguish* variation of price-with-distance from the lack of such variation.

pipeline A. Concurrently he makes the price FP_b'' for the smaller volume and FP_b for the larger volume sold to pipeline B. Price for the large volume to A is less than for the small volume to B, because A pays a lower level of price *for all reserves*

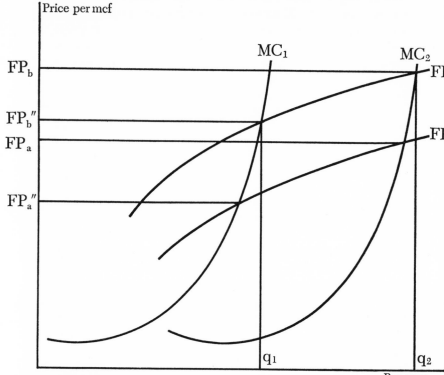

FIGURE 4:8 Monopoly Prices for Different Contract Volumes

(as shown by the price P_A for the aggregate volume of new purchases in Figure 4:6). Discrimination between buyers has the effect of disrupting a pattern of systematically higher prices on all larger-volume contracts.

Monopoly price variations associated with contract differences should be of a similar nature. Prices in long-term contracts should be higher than in short-term contracts for any one pipeline, because maximum offer prices and production costs both are higher over a longer term. Prices also vary from buyer to buyer, however, so that some pipelines may pay higher prices for ten-year contracts than others do for twenty-year contracts.[34] Therefore, there may be no discernable pattern of higher prices for the longer term. Prices offered by any one pipeline should differ according to the presence or absence of contingency clauses (Favored Nations and/or Renegotiation clauses). They should be lower in contracts with these clauses, because of reduced risk for the producer and increased probability of a price increase for the buyer. However, a pattern of lower prices for contracts with clauses may not be obvious when all contracts are considered together, because of deviations due to *different price levels* for different buyers.

VARIATION IN OLIGOPOLY PRICES IN DIFFERENT CONTRACTS

The monopoly pricing pattern may or may not appear when there is less than complete monopoly. A few producers may control a sufficient amount of unconsigned reserves to affect the level of contract prices in pipeline supply markets. An agreement to "separate" supply areas or to have each oligopolist offer reserves to only one line at any one location might result in the pattern of discrimination among buyers and of pricing according to distance, volume, term, etc. expected from monopoly.[35] On the other hand, an agreement among

34. Any diagrammatic illustration would utilize the same reasoning as provides the basis for Figures 4:7 and 4:8. The curves in Figure 4:7 can be taken to indicate demands and cost for long-term and short-term contracts. The offer price curves FP_b and FP_a are for twenty-year contracts, while FP_b'' and FP_a'' are for contracts with a ten-year production period. The monopoly price FP_a for longer-term for pipeline A is less than FP_b'', that for shorter-term for pipeline B.

35. A market-sharing agreement results in maximum profits for the group of producers if there are no *further* advantages in consolidating all firms in one unit. This is true when all firms with the same capacity have the same MC curves and markets are divided proportionate to capacity. Cf. W. Fellner, *Competition among the Few* (New York, Knopf, 1949) pp. 128–36. In gas supply areas, gas traps in the same basin have similar marginal production costs, and it might be possible for the producer with twice the reserves to be assigned the pipeline with twice the demand.

producers to follow the pricing pattern of one large producer might lead to significant deviations from this monopoly pattern. Discrimination between pipelines probably could not be maintained under this type of price leadership because the individual producer would be tempted to increase his sales and profits by offering reserves at slightly lower prices to those transporters who are being discriminated against. There would be equal difficulty in maintaining higher prices for larger volumes of reserves, from closer traps, etc., because any producer could increase his market share by offering larger-volume sales at a slightly lower premium (until all variation according to volume disappeared). Recognizing the probability of such "cheating," the price leader may simply have to set a uniform price at all locations for all volumes. This price would be higher than the competitive level, but maximum profits from discrimination would be foregone in the hope that the uniform price could be maintained.[36]

In other words, any pattern of noncompetitive prices depends upon the ability of the group to make each firm accept its predetermined share. When there is strict control, prices can be expected to vary with volume, trap location, the conditions in the reserve contract, and with each buyer's elasticity of demand. When there is a lack of complete control, the group probably would have to set prices that are relatively more uniform so that "cheating" would be apparent. If discipline in the group breaks down, competition should break out and prices should move to the competitive pattern.

36. Actual oligopoly pricing in a similar spatially-large market occurred in Connecticut in the late 1930s. Price control of milk was being practiced by organized producers over the area from Bridgeport to Hartford. Differences in prices over this retail area should have been "equal to differences between radii of the supply area multiplied by cents/ hundred weight transportation costs . . . and equal to approximately 45 cents in this case from the farthest to the closest locations." The actual differences were much smaller and did not reflect these costs, but rather reflected lack of control of producers in *part of the area* and complete price control in others. See D. O. Hammerberg, "Allocation of Milk Supplies among Contiguous Markets," 22 *Journal Farm Economics* 215 (1940). Cf. also F. A. Fetter, *Masquerade of Monopoly* (New York, Harcourt, Brace, 1931), p. 50, for the pattern of "nonsystematic" pricing following from oligopoly in petroleum sales at (closer) points and from competition at (farther) points.

MONOPSONY PRICE LEVELS IN NEW CONTRACTS

An entirely different set of prices should follow when there is only one purchaser. This "monopsonist" pipeline may have an exclusive supply area for any two-year period so that he can set price in each of several *producer's* markets. The price most advantageous to him (i.e., that minimizes purchase costs) is lower than the competitive price, and is most likely the same in each field.

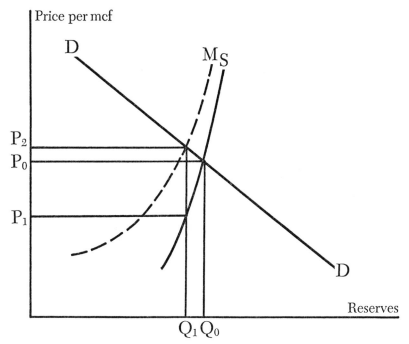

FIGURE 4:9 The Monopsony Price Level over the Supply Area

At most, the transporter offers prices such as are indicated by *DD* in Figure 4:9. It is to the advantage of the pipeline to pay less than these maximum prices whenever possible because the difference between maximum and actual price is additional profit for the pipeline for as long as regulation al-

lows.[37] The supply curve SS indicates the total volumes of
new reserves available for dedication to this purchaser at different prices (based upon sharply rising marginal development costs in each trap, as in Figure 4:2). Marginal purchase
costs to the buyer are greater than the supply price, however;
they include both an increase to induce consignment of marginal units and a concomitant increase in the price for all new
reserves. Marginal purchase costs for this one transporter are
shown by the "marginal outlay" curve M.[38] That level of purchases Q_1 is best for the buyer, since it is the level for which
the marginal costs to the purchaser are equal to maximum
possible additions to revenue from resale.[39] The transporter
purchases Q_1 new reserves at price P_1, which is below the
competitive price level P_0.[40]

The results of monopsony pricing are a lower price level
and higher (potential) pipeline profits. The extent of the
latter is indicated by the difference between the level of maximum offer price P_2 for Q_1, and the level of actual price P_1.
The enforcement of regulation on resale prices removes only
part of this profit [41] and even then only after a complete rate
investigation has taken place. Since the regulatory commission
is not likely to institute proceedings in each case or successfully terminate all rate investigations, the pipeline pursuing a

37. Or, in a world of uncertainty, the margin between actual and
maximum price increases the probability of receiving the "allowed"
rate of return.

38. Cf. Scitovsky, *Welfare and Competition*, pp. 261–63.

39. DD indicates maximum returns from resale since it is derived
from resale price minus unit transmission costs. The purchase of Q_1
maximizes net returns because there is no greater volume which adds
as much to revenue (shown in DD) as to purchase costs (shown by M).

40. Also quantity is decreased, but there is liable to be little difference
in the amount of reserves because of the steepness of the marginal cost
(and supply) curves.

41. By lowering resale price, the curve DD is lowered and flattened.
It is possible to lower DD (which indicates marginal returns from reselling more reserves) so that *per-unit profits* are less than previously.
It is *not* possible to remove *all* the excess profit. Since the "marginal"
curve M is always higher than SS, and since (in equilibrium) purchase
price is determined by SS while output is set so that resale price follows
from M there is *always* excess profit regardless of regulatory control of
demand price.

policy of setting price level P_1 probably can retain some of this excess profit.[42]

VARIATIONS IN MONOPSONY PRICES IN DIFFERENT CONTRACTS

Not only is the price level lower under monopsony, but variation in prices from field to field is likely to be less than under competition. Maximum offer prices vary between fields according to contract volume, production location, and the term-length of the production period. The monopsonist need *not* pay maximum offer prices, however, and it is to his benefit not to pay them (thus not allowing locational rents to producers). The only reason for the buyer to set different prices is to compensate producers for increases in development costs. This is not an extensive source of variation.

The monopsonist may, for example, be contemplating purchasing reserves in a number of different field locations. Maximum offer prices in those reservoirs located the same distance from the "end of transmission" are indicated by FP in Figure 4:10. Development costs of "small" traps, regardless of location, are shown by MC_1, and those of "larger" traps by MC_2. The pipeline buyer also has to consider his marginal purchase costs for various volumes (as indicated by M' for MC_1 and M'' for MC_2). This transporter should offer to purchase amounts q_1 and q_2, for which marginal purchase costs (M' and M'') are equal to maximum net resale value. The minimum prices necessary to obtain volumes q_1 and q_2 are FP_1 and FP_2. These prices are quite similar, since marginal costs of producing q_1 and q_2 from reservoirs in the same basin are quite similar. The only difference between prices is due to slightly larger development costs from greater percentage recovery in the large reservoir.[43]

42. To follow any *other* policy would be to give some of the excess return to the producer. Charity carries with it no opportunity whatsoever for greater returns, only some chance of severe criticism by the regulatory authorities and investors on the grounds of "irresponsible" management.

43. Prices are identical only when MC curves are *vertical* and AC curves are the same in all traps. It was the task of Chapter 2 to demonstrate that the relevant MC curve is *sharply* rising and that traps in the

Prices offered by the monopsonist should be similar in traps some distance apart as well. Maximum offer prices are greater at closer locations (as shown by FP' rather than FP, in Figure 4:11, for reserves closer to points of resale) but these do not determine the offered price. Rather, the monopsonist should

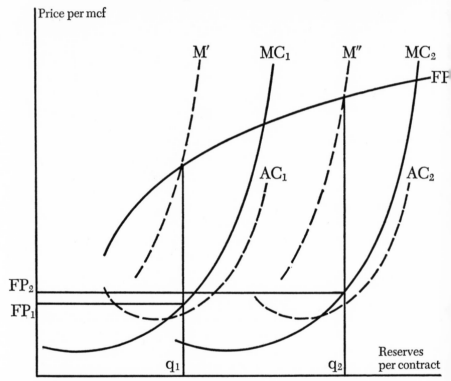

FIGURE 4:10 Monopsony Field Prices

purchase the amounts q and q' for which buyer's marginal outlay M' equals the maximum prices. The offered prices FP_1 and FP_2 are designed to cover no more than marginal development costs for these amounts of reserves.

same basin have *highly similar* unit production costs AC. In Figure 4:10 price is greater than AC_1, AC_2 so that these curves are not directly relevant. If the buyer makes an *all-or-nothing* offer, he may be able to lower price to the level of $AC_1 = AC_2$ however. Whether or not all-or-nothing offers are made, price differences should be negligible.

Similarly, price variations with the presence or absence of contingency clauses, or with variations in term-lengths of production, should be small. There should be some variation because marginal increases in term-length and the absence of

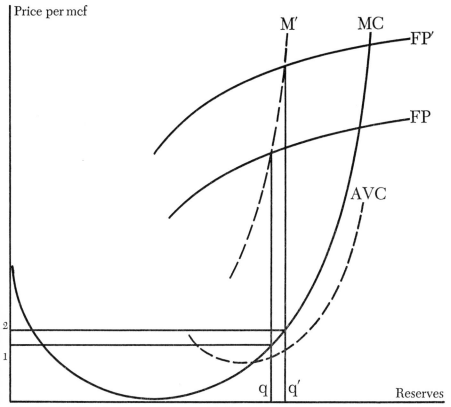

FIGURE 4:11 Monopsony Prices at Different Locations

Favored Nations may imply higher production costs. And higher production costs require higher prices, if reserves are to be forthcoming (given that monopsony prices for the most favorable contracts have been set equal to marginal costs). But these variations should be smaller than observed under competition.[44]

44. It can be demonstrated mathematically that price differences

The prices the monopsonist pays for contracts at different term-lengths are shown in Figure 4:12. Maximum offer prices FP' for reserves under a twenty-year contract are greater than maximum offer prices FP for volumes to be produced over fifteen years. The production costs MC_1 for the twenty-year term-length are not greatly different from costs MC_2 for the fifteen-year term on additions to the volume from initial recovery.[45] Consequently, marginal purchase costs M'' of longer term are greater than M' of short term for initial volumes, but similar for additional volumes up to full recovery. With maximum offer prices equal to marginal purchase costs, actual prices are set at minimum levels FP_1 for fifteen-year delivery and FP_2 for twenty-year delivery. These prices are minimum prices because marginal development costs are equal to FP_1 (for reserves q_1) and to FP_2 (for q_2). The difference between prices FP_1 and FP_2 is likely to be considerably less than the difference between the two curves FP and FP'.[46] That is, the monopsony price premium for longer term should be equal only to the (small) additional production costs for q_2 under

---

should be equal to differences in marginal transportation costs times the factor $\dfrac{E}{E-1}$ where E is the elasticity of supply to the pipeline. When the pipeline is competing for reserves, E is infinitely large, the factor $\dfrac{E}{E-1} = 1$, and the difference in prices is equal to the difference in transmission costs. When the pipeline is a monopsonist, E is the elasticity of the MC curve which, in the rising range, approaches zero. The factor $\dfrac{E}{E-1}$ approaches zero, so that the difference in prices under monopsony approaches zero. Cf. C. G. F. Simkin, "Aspects of Discrimination," 15 *Review of Economics Studies* 1–15. The Appendix to this chapter provides a similar analysis in some detail.

45. As mentioned in Chapter 2, increased investment expenses result in higher marginal costs for recovery of the first cubic feet, but not in an appreciably higher marginal cost curve for additional reserves thereafter.

46. The difference between prices under monopsony is due only to differences in marginal development costs from slightly varying rates of recovery. If prices are set at the level for which marginal costs equal average costs, however, the higher average costs of longer term probably dictate a differential close to 2.0 cents per mcf for each additional five years of term. This has to be the *minimum* difference between the FP curves if longer-term contracts are to be purchased.

longer term, and not equal to the *maximum* offer price premium.

The monopsonist has to "permit" some price variation because of producer cost variation. The buyer may have to pay a slightly higher price to cover higher producer costs for contracts without contingency clauses (the burden of the risk of underestimating future price may be so great that a producer without a Favored Nations clause may "shut-in" reserves unless a price premium is allowed). Also, there are cost differences from production in deeper reservoirs or in those without water drive, so that one producer may have considerably

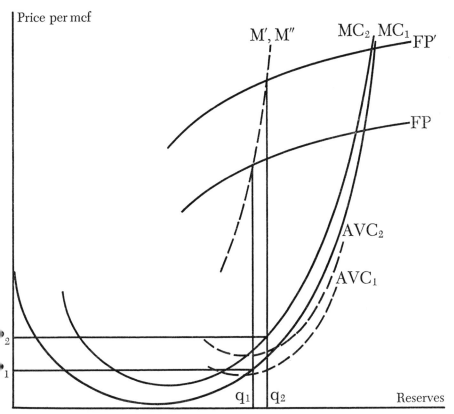

FIGURE 4:12 Monopsony Prices for Different Term-Lengths

greater unit production costs than another (larger than the difference between MC_1 and MC_2 in Figure 4:12). Rather than have high cost reserves "shut-in," the pipeline may set a higher price only for the high cost reserves. With monopsony control of demand in a number of basins, there may be general "basin prices" which differ because production costs differ. These pricing patterns (linked to regional development costs) should be observably different from the pattern corresponding to "maximum offer prices."

CONTRASTS BETWEEN PRICING PATTERNS UNDER COMPETITION, MONOPOLY, AND MONOPSONY

Characteristics of price formation differ when there are differences in the extent of power to control price. When there is such concentrated ownership of uncommitted reserves that a producer has monopoly power, prices should be set individually for each purchaser. Higher prices should be paid for all new reserves by pipelines with the more inelastic field demands. This should disrupt any variation in prices according to conditions of field location, the volume of committed reserves, or some other aspect of a particular type of contract.

When there is such extensive competition among producers and buyers of new reserves that there is no power for any firm to control price, a contrasting (competitive) pricing pattern should follow. Price levels should be uniform for all purchasers. There should be distinct price variation with contract volume, the location of the trap, and the term-length of production from contract to contract. There might possibly be price differences between contracts that do and do not have contingency clauses.

When there is one buyer in the relevant region, monopsony prices should be set lower than the competitive level and should exhibit little or no variation from contract to contract. Contract volume, distance to points of resale, or the term-length of contract, should have relatively little effect upon any contract price (since such would involve payments of unnecessary rental returns to producers). Actual prices should be so uniform as to indicate a *lack* of a pattern similar to that expected from competition.

To observe contrasts between competition and monopoly or monopsony, there is need for an examination of numbers of firms in markets and of actual market price formation. The market has to be defined, concentration has to be examined, and actual price behavior compared with the relevant theoretical patterns. From this sequence, and conclusions at each stage, an over-all conclusion can be formulated about whether the "market is competitive" or "not competitive."

Limits on information, and on human endeavor, do not permit examination of each gas field market from Pennsylvania to California between 1910 and 1960. The interstate pipeline's markets for new reserves in the 1950s have been selected as most relevant here, since these are the markets to be regulated through the 1960s. Available information on some thirty of the supply markets before 1960 can be analyzed for the presence of monopoly presumed in policy formulation (and for the presence of *contrasting* market behavior). This is the task of the following three chapters.

Appendix to Chapter 4. A Summary of Contrasts between Competitive and Noncompetitive Patterns of Price Formation

The differences in theoretical pricing patterns, for competition versus monopoly or monopsony markets, can be traced to particular conditions of development costs and of maximum offer prices. These conditions can be pointed out again in the process of restating the theory of price formation in mathematical terms.

For all markets, it is posited that pipeline n offers maximum prices $P = f(Q_n, Q_g, q_i, a)$ where Q_n is total purchases of reserves of that transporter, Q_g is the purchase from producer g, q_i is the volume purchased in field i, and a is some condition of the contracts (such as term-length or the presence of contingency clauses) that affects price. This offer price can be no greater than:

$$R(Q_n, Q_g, a) - \frac{\partial C_T(Q_n, q_i)}{\partial Q_n} - \frac{\partial C_T(Q_n, q_i)}{\partial q_i} \quad \text{where } R(Q_n, Q_g, a) \text{ is the}$$

pipeline's resale price for these reserves and $\dfrac{\partial C_T}{\partial Q_n}, \dfrac{\partial C_T}{\partial q_i}$ are marginal costs of transmitting and gathering the gas, respectively.

For the producer of gas g, it is posited that net returns G equal quantity of reserves Q_g times price P minus the total development costs $C = C(Q_g, q_i, a)$. This producer is assumed to seek greatest possible returns from new contract sales, or to maximize $(Q_g \cdot P - C)$ subject to constraints on total volumes for sale. (It is given that $Q = \displaystyle\sum_{i=1}^{M} q_i$, $Q = \displaystyle\sum_{n=1}^{N} Q_n$, $Q = \displaystyle\sum_{g=1}^{G} Q_g$ for total sales Q in the market region).

This requires that the partial derivatives of

$$G = Q_g P(Q_n, Q_g, q_i, a) - C(Q_g, q_i, a) + \lambda[\Sigma q_i - Q] + \gamma[\Sigma Q_n - Q] + \Delta[\Sigma Q_g - Q]$$

be equal to zero, where λ, γ, Δ are Lagrange Multipliers. That is,

$$\frac{\partial G}{\partial Q_g} = Q_g \frac{\partial P}{\partial Q_g} + P(Q_n, Q_g, q_i, a) - \frac{\partial C}{\partial Q_g} + \Delta = 0$$

$$\frac{\partial G}{\partial Q_n} = Q_g \cdot \frac{\partial P}{\partial Q_n} + \gamma = 0; \quad \frac{\partial G}{\partial q_i} = Q_g \frac{\partial P}{\partial q_i} - \frac{\partial C}{\partial q_i} + \lambda = 0$$

$$\frac{\partial G}{\partial Q} = -\lambda - \gamma - \Delta = 0$$

$$\frac{\partial G}{\partial a} = Q_g \frac{\partial P}{\partial a} - \frac{\partial C}{\partial a} = 0.$$

Combining these conditions, the *general* requirements for maximum profit are:

$$Q_g \frac{\partial P}{\partial Q_g} + Q_g \frac{\partial P}{\partial Q_n} + Q_g \frac{\partial P}{\partial q_i} + P(Q_n, Q_g, q_i, a) = \frac{\partial C}{\partial Q_g} + \frac{\partial C}{\partial q_i}$$

$$Q_g \frac{\partial P}{\partial a} = \frac{\partial C}{\partial a}$$

marginal revenue from any resale equals marginal development costs. The conditions for maximum profit also require that $Q_g \dfrac{\partial P}{\partial a} = \dfrac{\partial C}{\partial a}$, additional returns from changes in the contract have to equal costs from such.

Perfect Competition: When there are large numbers of buyers and sellers in some supply region, a number of limitations are placed upon price formation. No buyer need pay more for reserves than does any other buyer, nor can any purchaser have an effect upon field price $\left(\text{so that } Q_g \dfrac{\partial P}{\partial Q_n} = 0,\ Q_g \dfrac{\partial P}{\partial q_i} = 0\right)$. No producer, on the other hand, can have any effect upon pipelines' offer prices so that $Q_g \dfrac{\partial P}{\partial Q_g} = 0$. Assuming that $\dfrac{\partial C}{\partial Q_g}$ (marginal joint costs for sales from all fields) are minor, then conditions of maximum profit for the seller are:

$$\frac{\partial C}{\partial q_i} = P(Q_n, Q_g, q_i, a) = P(Q_1, Q_g, Q_i, a)$$

$$\frac{\partial C}{\partial Q_i} = \left[R(Q_n, \ \cdot\ ,) - \frac{\partial C_T}{\partial Q_n} - \frac{\partial C_T}{\partial q_i}\right] = \left[R(Q_1, \ \cdot\ ,) - \frac{\partial C_T}{\partial Q_1} - \frac{\partial C_T}{\partial q_i}\right]$$

as marginal development costs in field i should be equal to the uniform maximum offer price of pipelines n and 1. Also, in a common (competitive) market area, the marginal gathering costs $\partial C_T / \partial q_i$ should be the same for each transporter.

When any one producer in fields 3 and 4 has different volumes of available reserves such that $q_3 > q_4$, then sales to pipeline n should result in:

$$\frac{\partial C}{\partial q_3} = R[Q_n, \ \ldots,] - \frac{\partial C_T}{\partial Q_n} - \frac{\partial C_T}{\partial q_3} = p_{(3)}$$

$$\frac{\partial C}{\partial q_4} = R[Q, \ \ldots,] - \frac{\partial C_T}{\partial Q_n} - \frac{\partial C_T}{\partial q_4} = p_{(4)}$$

and given the common "end of transmission" price $(R[Q_n, \ \ldots,] - \dfrac{\partial C_T}{\partial Q_n})$ the differences in prices $p_{(3)} - p_{(4)} = \dfrac{\partial C_T}{\partial q_4} - \dfrac{\partial C_T}{\partial q_3}$. With equal *gathering* costs for all transporters in the region (and consequently $R[Q_1, \ \ldots,] - \dfrac{\partial C_T}{\partial Q_1} = R[Q_n, \ \ldots,] - \dfrac{\partial C_T}{\partial Q_n}$ for any two transporters included), then the difference in field prices is equal to the common difference in gathering costs. It has been indicated in Chapter 3 that, with $q_3 > q_4$, $\dfrac{\partial C_T}{\partial q_4} > \dfrac{\partial C_T}{\partial q_3}$ so that $p_{(3)} - p_{(4)} > 0$. Price is higher on the sale of the larger volume of reserves.

When field 4 is located farther from the end of transmission than is field 3, so that $\dfrac{\partial C_T}{\partial q_4} > \dfrac{\partial C_T}{\partial q_3}$, given the equilibrium conditions

$$\frac{\partial C}{\partial q_3} - \frac{\partial C}{\partial q_4} = p_{(3)} - p_{(4)} = \frac{\partial C_T}{\partial q_4} - \frac{\partial C_T}{\partial q_3}$$

it follows that $p(3) > p(4)$. This is to conclude that prices should be lower, as a result of competition, in the farther fields.[1]

Contracts may differ on sales in the same field. When differences cause $\frac{\partial p}{\partial a} > 0$ for the buyer all contracts include the change until $\frac{\partial C}{\partial a} = q_i \frac{\partial P}{\partial a}$ for the marginal "changed" contract (given that q_i is the quantity of reserves affected by the contract change). A contract with longer term-length has greater resale value (as seen in Chapter 3). This is to say that $\frac{\partial P}{\partial T} > 0$ (for T = term-length of production) and that all contracts will have longer term as long as $\frac{\partial P}{\partial T} > \frac{\partial C}{\partial T}/q_i$, or as long as the per-unit addition to price is greater than the per-unit addition to cost. Longer term contracts are required by buyer's competition to have higher field prices.

Similarly, the presence of a Favored Nations or Renegotiation clause in a contract has some impact upon buyer's demand. It is expected that these clauses result in $\frac{\partial P}{\partial a} < 0$, or in lower offer prices (lower because of additional "risk" for the buyer). With $\frac{\partial C}{\partial a} < 0$ (because of decreased risk for the producer) then contracts with clauses will be signed if $\frac{\partial C}{\partial a}/q_i \geqq \frac{\partial P}{\partial a}$. The producer will seek lower-priced contracts with clauses as long as the decrease in price is less than the per-unit decrease in costs.

Taking account of variation in prices between fields according to all of these factors, competitive pricing patterns should conform to the equation

$$[p = \alpha + \beta_1 q_i + \beta_2 D + \beta_3 T + \beta_5 CL_{(1)} + \beta_6 CL_{(2)} + v],$$

where D is distance from the end of transmission to the field, T is contract term-length, CL_1 is the presence of a Favored Nations clause, CL_2 is the presence of Renegotiation. When dif-

---

1. Regulation may require all purchasers to offer prices according to average transport costs C_T/q_i rather than marginal costs $\frac{\partial C_T}{\partial q_i}$. If average gathering costs have to be used as a basis for price formation, then price differences between fields are larger. This follows from $\frac{C_T}{q_i} > \frac{\partial C_T}{\partial q_i}$, $\frac{C_T}{q_i} > \frac{\partial C}{\partial q_i}$.

ferences in transport costs from different fields amount to a large percentage of field prices, and when there is greater value of longer term and (supposed) lower value of contingency contracts, it follows that $\beta_1 > 0$; $\beta_2 < 0$; $\beta_3 > 0$; β_5, $\beta_6 < 0$.

Monopoly: The constraints in competitive markets are not present when one producer has monopoly power. This seller has an effect upon area and field prices so that $Q_g \dfrac{\partial P}{\partial Q_g} \neq 0$ (while pipeline buyers continue to have no effect upon field price, and $Q_g \dfrac{\partial P}{\partial Q_n} = 0$, $Q_g \dfrac{\partial P}{\partial q_i} = 0$). Since $P(Q_n,Q_g,q_i,a) = \left[R(Q_n,Q_g,a) - \dfrac{\partial C_T}{\partial Q_n} - \dfrac{\partial C_T}{\partial q_i} \right]$ the one producer's sales of reserves affect resale prices for pipeline n; the effect upon field price $Q_g \dfrac{\partial P}{\partial Q_g} = Q_g \dfrac{\partial R}{\partial Q_g}$. The equilibrium conditions for maximum monopoly profit are:

$$Q_g \frac{\partial R}{\partial Q_g} + R(Q_n,Q_g,a) - \left[\frac{\partial C_T}{\partial Q_n} + \frac{\partial C_T}{\partial q_i} \right] = \frac{\partial C}{\partial Q_g} + \frac{\partial C}{\partial q_i}$$

$$R(Q_n, \ldots ,) \, [1 + 1/\eta_{D_n}] - \left[\frac{\partial C_T}{\partial Q_n} + \frac{\partial C_T}{\partial q_i} \right] = \frac{\partial C}{\partial Q_g} + \frac{\partial C}{\partial q_i}$$

where R is resale price and η_{D_n} is the resale price elasticity for pipeline n. Also, the conditions of the contract should be such that $Q_g \dfrac{\partial P}{\partial a} = \dfrac{\partial C}{\partial a}$. The price P charged pipeline n at the end of transmission is higher under monopoly conditions by the factor R/η_{Dn}. Since $\eta_{Dn} < 0$, this difference between monopoly and competitive price levels is positive.

For the particular pipeline n, the pattern of prices between fields is similar to that from competition. For this pipeline, Prices $P(1)$ and $P(2)$ in fields 1 and 2 are equal to: $P(1) = R(Q_n,Q_g,a) - \dfrac{\partial C_T}{\partial Q_n} - \dfrac{\partial C_T}{\partial q_1}$; $P(2) = R(Q_n,Q_g,a) - \dfrac{\partial C_T}{\partial Q_n} - \dfrac{\partial C_T}{\partial q_2}$.
It follows that

$$P(2) - P(1) = R - \frac{\partial C_T}{\partial Q_n} - \frac{\partial C_T}{\partial q_2} - \left(R - \frac{\partial C_T}{\partial Q_n} - \frac{\partial C_T}{\partial q_1} \right) \text{ or}$$

$$P(2) - P(1) = \frac{\partial C_T}{\partial q_1} - \frac{\partial C_T}{\partial q_2}.$$

When $q_2 > q_1$ so that $\dfrac{\partial C_T}{\partial q_1} > \dfrac{\partial C_T}{\partial q_2}$ it follows that $P(2) > P(1)$.

When the distance to q_1 is greater so that $\dfrac{\partial C_T}{\partial q_1} > \dfrac{\partial C_T}{\partial q_2}$ then $P(2) >$

$P(1)$ as well. When changes are made in the basic contract, for particular sales, so that $\dfrac{\partial C}{\partial a} \gtrless 0$, it should follow that $\dfrac{\partial P}{\partial a} \gtrless 0$ as in competitive markets.

Even though the pattern for one pipeline duplicates the competitive pattern, the over-all pattern of prices on all sales does not. Different purchasers in the same field are charged different levels of price. In field i, for pipelines 1 and 2,

$$\frac{\partial C}{\partial q_i} = R_1(1 + 1/\eta_{D1}) - \left[\frac{\partial C_T}{\partial Q_1} + \frac{\partial C_T}{\partial q_i} \right] = R_2(1 + 1/\eta_{D2}) - \frac{\partial C_T}{\partial Q_2}$$
$$+ \frac{\partial C_T}{\partial q_i}.$$

The maximum offer prices in field i for these two buyers, $P(i)$ for 1 and $P(i)'$ for 2, equal the difference between resale prices and marginal transport costs (as above). It follows that:

$$\frac{\partial C}{\partial q_i} = P(i) + \frac{R_1}{\eta_{D1}} = P'(i) + \frac{R_2}{\eta_{D2}}$$
$$\frac{\partial C}{\partial q_i} = P(i) - P(i)' = \frac{R_2}{\eta_{D2}} - \frac{R_1}{\eta_{D1}}.$$

With equal resale prices and $\eta_{D1} > \eta_{D2}$ then $p(i)' > p(i)$; the pipeline with the more inelastic demand is charged the higher field price. With some buyers paying higher field prices than others, it is likely that the pattern for all sales to one line would be obscured by differences $p(i)' > p(i)$ between buyers in any one field. The pattern may well be

$$[P = \alpha + \beta_1 q_i + \beta_2 D + \beta_3 T + \beta_5 CL(1) + \beta_6 CL(2) + v]$$
with $B_1, B_2, B_3 = 0$

or, more accurately,

$$p = \alpha + \beta_1 q_i + \beta_2 D + \beta_3 T + \beta_5 C_1 + \beta_6 C_2 + \sum_{i=1}^{n} \beta_1 X_1 \text{ with}$$
$$\beta_1 > 0, \ \beta_2 < 0, \ \beta_3 > 0$$

where X_n is a designation of sales to pipeline n. The last equation separates the effects on the pattern of contract prices of monopoly discrimination from the effects of variations *between* conditions of contracts for one buyer.

Monopsony: In supply regions where there is only one purchaser, and many producers with uncommitted reserves, the pattern of new contract prices should be in sharp contrast to that from monopoly *or* competition. The monopsonist, in offering prices according to his marginal costs of purchase, deviates sharply from the competitve pattern of variation with contract volume, term-length, etc.

Net returns $\{M = R(Q_X, a) \cdot Q_X - C_T(q_i, Q_X) - K(q_i, a) + \lambda(\Sigma q_i - Q_X)\}$ for Q_n total purchases and resales of the one pipeline X. For this transporter, $K = K(q_i, a)$ are purchase costs, of gas in field i, and $C_T(q_i, Q_1)$ are total gathering and transmission costs. To maximize total net revenue M, these equilibrium conditions are necessary:

$$\frac{\partial M}{\partial q_i} = -\frac{\partial C_T}{\partial q_i} - \frac{\partial K}{\partial q_i} + \lambda = 0$$

$$\frac{\partial M}{\partial Q_X} = R(Q_X, a) + Q_X \frac{\partial R}{\partial Q_X} - \frac{\partial C_T}{\partial Q_X} - \lambda = 0$$

$$\frac{\partial M}{\partial a} = Q \frac{\partial R}{\partial a} - \frac{\partial K}{\partial a} = 0$$

The pipeline sets prices such that:

$$\frac{\partial (Q \cdot R)}{\partial Q_X} = \frac{\partial C_T}{\partial Q_X} + \frac{\partial C_T}{\partial q_i} + \frac{\partial K}{\partial q_i},$$

the marginal returns from resale equal marginal transmission, gathering, and gas purchase costs; also $Q \dfrac{\partial R}{\partial a} = \dfrac{\partial K}{\partial a}$, the marginal returns from a variation in conditions in the field contract equal additional field purchase costs associated with varying the contract.

Purchase costs in field i equal $[q_i \cdot p(i)]$ for this one buyer.[2]

Marginal purchase costs $\dfrac{\partial K}{\partial q_i} = \dfrac{\partial [q_i \cdot p(i)]}{\partial q_i} = p(i) + q_i \dfrac{\partial p(i)}{\partial q_i}$

With elasticity of field supply of reserves defined as $E_i = \dfrac{p(i)\partial q_i}{q_i \partial p(i)}$, it follows that marginal purchase costs

$$\frac{\partial K}{\partial q_i} = p(i) + q_i \frac{\partial p(i)}{\partial q_i} = p(i)\left[1 + \frac{1}{E_i}\right].$$

These marginal purchase costs determine the pattern of prices in contrast with the competitive pattern. For fields 1 and i,

$$\frac{\partial (Q \cdot R)}{\partial Q_X} = \frac{\partial C_T}{\partial Q_X} + \frac{\partial C_T}{\partial q_i} + \frac{\partial K}{\partial q_i} = \frac{\partial C_T}{\partial Q_X} + \frac{\partial C_T}{\partial q_1} + \frac{\partial K}{\partial q_1}.$$

2. Price $p(i)$ is the minimum possible price to obtain the reserves, and is not defined as the "maximum offer" of above.

This is to require that:

$\frac{\partial C_T}{\partial q_i} + p(i)\,[1 + 1/E_i] = \frac{\partial C_T}{\partial q_1} + p(1)\,[1 + 1/E_1]$. With equal supply elasticity in the two fields, the differences in prices

$$p(i) - p(1) = \frac{\dfrac{\partial C_T}{\partial q_1} - \dfrac{\partial C_T}{\partial q_i}}{[1 + 1/E_i]}.$$

This price difference is not equal to the difference in gathering costs (as when there is buyer's competition) but to the gathering cost difference divided by a factor dependent upon the elasticity of the supply of uncommitted reserves.

When there are more uncommitted reserves in field i than in field 1, so that $q_i > q_1$, then $\frac{\partial C_T}{\partial q_1} > \frac{\partial C_T}{\partial q_i}$ and $p(q_i) - p(q_1) > 0$. The larger volume of reserves is sold for the higher price, but the price differential may be quite small. It is argued in Chapter 2 that marginal development costs rise sharply at rates of recovery close to full recovery (so that $\frac{p\partial q}{q\partial P_i}$ is quite small); as a result it is likely that $(1 + 1/E_i)$ is large. This should result in $\left(\frac{\partial C_T}{\partial q_1} - \frac{\partial C_T}{\partial q_i}\right) \Big/$ $(1 + 1/E_i)$ being quite small so that there would be little variation in monopsony prices between fields with different volumes.

For the same reason, there should be little price variation because of distances between fields. When the distance to field 1 is greater, so that

$\frac{\partial C_T}{\partial q_1} > \frac{\partial C_T}{\partial q_i}$ then $p(q_i) - p(q_1) = \left\{\left(\frac{\partial C_T}{\partial q_1} - \frac{\partial C_T}{\partial q_i}\right)\Big/ (1 + 1/E_i)\right\}$ > 0.

Here again the differential in price depends both upon the differential in marginal development costs and the elasticity of supply; with the latter quite small, the price differential corresponding to cost differences is quite small.

Variations in conditions of the contract result in some monopsony price variations, however. The one purchaser is willing to offer higher prices for "more advantageous" contracts as long as $\frac{\partial K}{\partial a}\Big/ Q = \frac{\partial R}{\partial a}$, or as long as additions to per unit purchase costs are less than or equal to per unit returns from the contract change.

Additions to purchase costs $\frac{\partial K}{\partial a}\Big/ Q = \frac{\partial[p \cdot q_i]}{\partial a}\Big/ Q$ for new contracts in field i with conditions or clauses a. The offer price $p(i)$, moreover, is set by the buyer at a level no greater than producers' marginal costs, $\dfrac{\partial C}{\partial q_i}$. These additional purchase costs equal

$$\frac{\partial \left[\dfrac{\partial C}{\partial q_i} \cdot q_i \right]}{\partial a} \bigg/ Q \quad \text{or} \quad \left\{ \frac{\partial C}{\partial q_i} \cdot \frac{\partial q_i}{\partial a} + q_i \frac{\partial^2 C}{\partial a\, \partial q_i} \right\} \text{ divided by } Q.$$

Then,

$$\frac{\partial R}{\partial a} = \frac{\partial C}{\partial a} \bigg/ Q + \frac{q_i}{Q} \frac{\partial^2 C}{\partial a\, \partial q_i}.$$ The buyer's addition to "maximum offer price" in the field is $\dfrac{\partial R}{\partial a}$, since this is the maximum addition to resale revenues. The buyer's change in actual offer price, when there is competition among sellers, is $\dfrac{\partial P}{\partial a} = \dfrac{\partial C}{\partial a} \bigg/ Q$ as concluded above. Consequently, $\dfrac{\partial P}{\partial a} = \dfrac{\partial R}{\partial a} - \dfrac{q_i}{Q} \cdot \dfrac{\partial^2 C}{\partial a\, \partial q_i}$ when there is monopsony.

When the condition in the contract is term of production T, the requirement for additions to term is that

$$\frac{\partial P}{\partial T} = \frac{\partial R}{\partial T} - \frac{q_i}{Q} \frac{\partial^2 C}{\partial T\, \partial q_i}.$$

Longer production terms require a longer investment period, so that $\dfrac{\partial C}{\partial T} \bigg/ Q > 0$. Also, maintenance costs at various rates of production increase somewhat, so that $\dfrac{\partial^2 C}{\partial T\, \partial q_i} > 0$. Longer terms decrease *pipeline* investment expenses, and resale demand, with the result that $\dfrac{\partial R}{\partial T} > 0$. Consequently, monopsony price $p(i)$ should be greater with longer term (that is, $\dfrac{\partial p(i)}{\partial T} > 0$). But the increase should not be as great as when there is buyer's competition: rather than

$$\frac{\partial P}{\partial T} = \frac{\partial C}{\partial T} \bigg/ Q = \frac{\partial R}{\partial T} \text{ for competition,} \quad \frac{\partial P}{\partial T} = \frac{\partial R}{\partial T} - \frac{q_i}{Q} \cdot \frac{\partial^2 C}{\partial T\, \partial q_i} \text{ and}$$
$$\frac{\partial^2 C}{\partial T\, \partial q_i} > 0.$$

The addition of a Favored Nation or Renegotiation clause to a contract is expected to lower costs for the producer (if such clauses decrease "risk" of committing reserves too soon). It follows that $\frac{\partial p \cdot q_i}{\partial a} \leqq 0$ when a indicates the presence of one of these clauses. If the negative value to the purchaser is equal to or less than this decrease, so that $\frac{\partial R}{\partial a} < 0 \geqq \frac{\partial p}{\partial a} + \frac{q_i}{Q} \frac{\partial^2 C}{\partial a \, \partial q_i}$, then price $p(i)$ for the contract with the clause should be somewhat lower than for the contract without the clause. Both the variations in price due to longer term-length and to the presence or absence of contingency clauses should be limited to smaller amounts than realized under buyer's competition (by the factor $\frac{\partial^2 C}{\partial a \, \partial q_i} \cdot \frac{q_i}{Q}$).

On the whole, monopsony prices should be quite uniform. There should be little variation in field prices because of contract volume, or the distance of the reservoir from points of resale; there may be some variation if the buyer is willing to compensate the producer for higher costs of longer term or of a contract without one or both contingency clauses. The extent of systematic variation should be similar to

$$\{ p = \alpha + \beta_1 q_i + \beta_2 D + \beta_3 T + \beta_5 C_1 + \beta_6 C_2 + v \} \text{ with}$$
$$\beta_1, \ \beta_2 = 0; \ \beta_3 \geqq 0; \ \beta_5, \ \beta_6 \leqq 0.$$

Monopsony prices also should be lower than those from competition. As seen above, the pipeline sets prices such that: $\frac{\partial (Q \cdot R)}{\partial Q_X} = \frac{\partial C_T}{\partial Q_X} + \frac{\partial C_T}{\partial q_i} + \frac{\partial K}{\partial q_i}$.

Marginal purchase costs in field i for the monopsonist $\frac{\partial K}{\partial q_i} = \frac{\partial (p \cdot q_i)}{\partial q_i} = p + q_i \frac{\partial p}{\partial q_i}$. The level of price p is set so that:

$$p + q_i \frac{\partial p}{\partial q_i} = \frac{\partial (Q \cdot R)}{\partial Q_X} - \frac{\partial C_T}{\partial Q_X} - \frac{\partial C_T}{\partial q_i} \text{ (rather than } \mathrm{p} = \frac{\partial (Q \cdot R)}{\partial Q_1} -$$

$\frac{\partial C_T}{\partial Q_1} - \frac{\partial C_T}{\partial q_i}$ in competitive supply areas). Price from monopsony is lower because $q_i \frac{\partial p}{\partial q_i} > 0$ (and quite significantly lower, since $\frac{\partial p}{\partial q_i}$ is quite large, according to the discussion of "inelastic" trap supply in Chapter 2).

5. *The Sale of Reserves in West Texas and New Mexico*

Most reserves sold for transportation to home and industrial consumers have come from Texas, Louisiana, Oklahoma, Kansas, and New Mexico. As expected, the reserve sources have not been spread evenly throughout these states, but instead have been clustered in three semi-isolated areas.

One area encompasses the state of Louisiana, adjoining regions of Texas, and the region along the Texas Gulf Coast as far south as Mexico. Gas traps of relatively small geographical extent are found in large numbers throughout this region. The traps are at many different levels in various producing strata, but almost all of them are located within 100 miles of the coast or the Louisiana border. There is a "Gulf Coast" concentration of fields containing reserves.

There is a second concentration of fields at least 350 miles away in Oklahoma, Kansas, and northern Texas known as the "Mid-Continent" region. Most volumes of reserves in this second area have been in the Panhandle and Hugoton fields that extend along the western borders of Oklahoma and Kansas down into Texas. Since the mid-1950s, large volumes of new reserves also have become available in traps throughout central Kansas and Oklahoma. The distance between these two sections of the "Mid-Continent" is not great so that the Panhandle-Hugoton and central Kansas-Oklahoma fields have formed a general supply source for new reserves.

The third group of fields is found in West Texas and New

Mexico. There are two basins there, the "Permian Basin" extending throughout southwest Texas-southeast New Mexico, and the "San Juan Basin" in northwest New Mexico-southwest Colorado. The Permian Basin contains a number of gas traps at depths from 3,000 to 6,000 feet and also contains large volumes of gas in oil traps in diverse strata from 3,000 feet down to 12,000 feet. Sales of reserves in this basin promise production of at least 14.9 trillion cubic feet—12.9 trillion cubic feet of residue oil-well gas to be produced at varying rates per annum and the remainder to be "packages" of dry gas reserves produced under long-term contract.[1] The San Juan Basin contains at least a dozen traps in shallow formations from 1,800 to 5,000 feet. Sales of reserves there have been for at least 14.4 trillion cubic feet, all from dry gas traps.[2] Sales and purchases from the Permian and San Juan Basins will be discussed in this chapter, and transactions in the Gulf Coast and Mid-Continent areas will be reviewed in the following two chapters.

THE PERMIAN AND SAN JUAN BASINS

The two basins in West Texas-New Mexico provide a common source of gas for the West Coast of the United States. From 1947 until the late 1950s, some 60 per cent of all gas delivered for consumption in California came from the Permian and San Juan.[3] Since gas prior to that time came from California fields, the greatest part of all new field *purchases of reserves*

1. Based upon the reserve estimates for El Paso Transmission Company up to 1956, as estimated by Brobrow, Dixon, McKie, Oil and Gas Geologists. Those of the smaller lines are omitted for lack of evidence. Cf. Prospectus, "El Paso Natural Gas Company, 250,000 shares 5.50% cumulative Preferred Stock" (New York, White Weld and Co., 1956), pp. 20–25.

2. As estimated from reserve sumaries for El Paso and Pacific Northwest Pipeline Corporation, the only two large purchasers, up to January 1, 1957. The figure is inclusive of El Paso purchases up to 1956, additions in 1956, and Pacific Northwest purchases up to 1957. Cf. Prospectus 1956, and Prospectus, "El Paso Natural Gas Company, 100,000 shares Second Series 1957" (New York, White Weld and Co., 1957), pp. 16–19.

3. Cf. J. J. Parsons, "The Natural Gas Supply of California," 34 *Journal of Land Economics* 19 (February 1958).

for this western state must have been in these basins.[4] Washington, parts of Oregon, and Idaho have been receiving gas from reserves in the San Juan Basin as well. Local utilities along the entire West Coast have been seeking reserves of Southwest gas; at the same time the largest transporter to California has lateral lines into all parts of both basins, and the transporter to the upper Northwest has purchased 6.0 trillion cubic feet in the San Juan Basin. These basins have been the closest sources to the West Coast of large new volumes and continue to be the sources immediately accessible to the present transporters.

PREREQUISITES FOR POWER TO SET PRICE IN THE TWO BASINS

The owners of reserves in West Texas-New Mexico each operate in field markets where pipelines buy either for the West Coast or for local Texas utilities and industrial users. Each purchaser of new reserves has a supply area encompassing a number of producer's field markets. Competition in the sale of reserves depends upon power to control supply in the pipeline's supply market (and competition in the purchase of reserves depends upon ability to control demand in the producer's market area).

Relevant Markets for the Pipeline Buyers. In the 1950s, production and demand seem to have displayed a general pattern. The initial discovery of oil in the 1930s in the Permian Basin and gas in the 1940s in the San Juan led to intensive exploration of both regions. New "packages" of reserves became available at a fluctuating rate for contract sales in both basins. When one producer "spud-in" a successful gas exploratory well in a new sector of the basin, the other leaseholders soon drilled on adjoining holdings.[5] This meant that a new field

4. If *production* from these basins increased from 0 to 60 per cent of California deliveries, then the reserve base for production from these basins must have increased at a faster rate. For each year's *new* production source, twenty years of reserves have been added, while for each *retired* field, one year of reserves have been utilized.

5. Cf. the interesting paper of James McKie, "Market Structures and Uncertainty in Oil and Gas Exploration," *Quarterly Journal of Eco-*

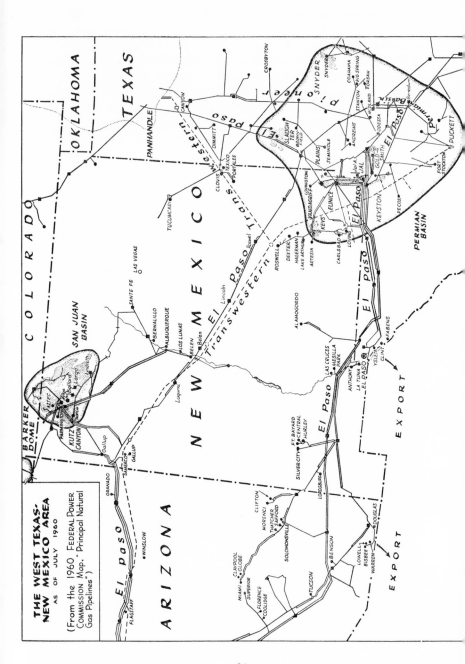

THE WEST TEXAS-
NEW MEXICO AREA
AS OF JULY 1960

(From the 1960 Federal Power
Commission Map. "Principal Natural
Gas Pipelines")

area became a source of supply one to three years after the first successful well. Then there may have been a period of unsuccessful exploration, succeeded by another rapid drilling program to determine the extent of a promising find elsewhere in the area. Once a wildcat well proved successful, exploration typically became concentrated at one location and a number of producers were prepared to supply reserves from the proved trap, or series of adjoining traps, in a short period of time.

The purchasers of reserves in this period were, as mentioned, either large interstate pipelines serving California and Washington or gas companies serving local consumers. The largest of the interstate transporters was El Paso Natural Gas Company, the only line to take gas to California from 1947 until the late 1950s. El Paso began as a gathering company for a number of Texas-New Mexico utilities and smelting industries. When California was seen to be a potential importing market for gas for home use, and the Permian Basin became a large source of reserves of dry gas, the company constructed a series of parallel 24"-26"-30" transmission lines to the West Coast. With the discovery of the large Barker Dome field in the San Juan Basin, the company constructed gathering lines there to supplement its transmission lines, and to carry gas directly to northern California.[6] During the 1950s, both the Permian and San Juan were included in El Paso's supply area and were traversed by more than 4,000 miles of gathering pipelines.[7]

---

nomics (November 1960), pp. 543–71, for a realistic explanation of the exploratory process in "old" producing regions. It is also suggested in Chapter 2 that minimizing the risk of drainage calls for quick exploration in jointly held fields.

6. For a short account of the company's physical growth, in its own language, cf. "The First Twenty-Five Years," 16 El Paso Pipeliner 4–19 (Winter 1953).

7. Cf. Prospectus 1957, p. 24, for "description of 1956 properties." It should be noted also that El Paso extended throughout the southwest section of the Panhandle field in North Texas, purchasing some reserves there, and operating a lateral line for gathering. During most of the 1950s, however, Panhandle Reserves were traded to Northern Natural Gas Company for some of Northern's Permian Basin reserves. The actual limits of the supply market for El Paso may not have included the Panhandle.

In the mid-1950s a second large transmission company, the Pacific Northwest Company, sought new reserves in the San Juan Basin for resale in the state of Washington. This transporter continued to purchase reserves in this basin (as a subsidiary of El Paso subsequent to 1954) but did not expand lateral and gathering facilities into the Permian Basin—although it may have purchased El Paso gas originating in West Texas.[8]

A third large interstate pipeline which purchased reserves in both the Permian and San Juan Basins, as well as in the Mid-Continent area, was the Transwestern Pipeline Company. It sought reserves in 1958–60 throughout West Texas and New Mexico and in the Oklahoma Panhandle for transmission to California.

These three transporters had supply areas that generally included all of West Texas-New Mexico. Smaller transporters operated by local utilities and industrial purchasers had more limited purchase areas. The Northern Natural Gas Company operated a gathering affiliate (the Permian Basin Pipeline Company) able to purchase new reserves throughout the Permian region in the 1950s.[9] Pioneer Natural Gas Company purchased reserves in the Permian Basin for home resale in Amarillo, Lubbock, Muleshoe, and other northwest Texas towns. Southern Union Gas Company operated a number of unconnected, short gathering lines from the San Juan Basin for home delivery in Santa Fe and from the Permian Basin for delivery in Roswell, New Mexico. (There was no connection between Southern Union gathering facilities in the two basins.) Both Pioneer and Southern Union also purchased 40 to 60 per cent of their new reserves from El Paso Natural Gas Company, an activity that helped to limit their supply areas.

Most of the other small pipelines were owned by oil companies and purchased gas for refinery fuel or for manufactur-

8. As an *independent source of demand,* Pacific Northwest was limited to the San Juan Basin and to the period 1953–55.
9. Northern relied on El Paso to carry gas from this lateral line in West Texas up to the Northern line in the Mid-Continent area, however. At the most, the Permian Basin Company could have bought reserves throughout the Permian Basin; at the least, it could have purchased reserves only at those locations agreeable to El Paso.

ing petrochemicals. Delhi-Taylor Oil Company, Sinclair Oil Company, and Phillips Petroleum Company recorded two or three contracts in three-year purchase periods. Their contract purchases were always in the same county (Phillips and Sinclair in West Texas, Delhi-Taylor in the San Juan Basin).[10]

While the geographical location and extent of the supply area were not the same for each pipeline in the 1950s, there seems to have been a region common to most of them. The largest lines had supply regions that included all of the Permian and San Juan Basins. The smaller lines each operated in one or the other of the basins, and were able to purchase throughout most of a basin if this did not interfere with purchases from El Paso (their principal source of supply). Moreover, when necessary the smaller line might have been able to increase the extent of its supply region over the whole two-basin area by purchasing through El Paso.

Product and time dimensions of relevant supply markets were similar for all buyers. The larger interstate lines and intrastate utilities sought reserves of standard quality that could be produced at a uniform rate over a twenty-year period. Contracts for dry-gas reserves were included in all pipeline markets. Gas from oil traps could be produced only at fluctuating rates of oil recovery so contracts for oil-well gas reserves involved a "low-grade" product. These contracts were included in supply markets only at substantial discounts in price. The length of the market period depended upon opportunities for transporters to postpone immediate purchase. Most of the lines seemed to have spent some years in accumulating reserves, so that emergency short-term purchases were not necessary. The large lines seemed willing to consider reserves that were likely to be available for delivery within five years. The smaller lines, with higher "inventory" costs, may have had somewhat shorter time periods. But at the least,

10. The recorded contracts include only those for gas to be transported across state lines. Of course, there were a number of intrastate purchases by local industries that remain unrecorded. These very well may have been larger than those of the recorded oil companies but this is doubtful, given the (estimated) limits on reserves in this area, and the large fraction of the (possible) maximum purchased by the large pipelines.

the period for considering alternative sources of new reserves must have been approximately four years in the 1950s.

The purchaser's market may not have been exactly the same for each pipeline. But in general, the relevant market included new reserves of dry gas to be found in West Texas or New Mexico, or both, during any three to five-year period in the 1950s.[11]

Relevant Markets for Producers. Producer's markets seem to have been considerably more limited than buyer's markets. Technological limitations on the location of gas production, here as elsewhere, confined producers to considering alternative sources of demand within the field area. It was not possible to sell reserves to a buyer that did not have established or proposed gathering facilities in the field. Most gas suppliers had to drill "step-out" exploratory wells, sell "proved" reserves, and begin production within five years of initial discovery in a field, in order not to lose the privileges of lessee.[12] The producer should have been limited in most cases, by both technology and "capture rights," to selling reserves in the field within two or three years of the completion of exploration.

THE STRUCTURE AND BEHAVIOR IN MARKETS DURING THE EARLY 1950s

Within the context of such buyer's and seller's markets, the price-setting power and behavior of firms determines the presence of competition or monopoly. Competition is present

11. This is not to suggest that oil-well gas or gas to be available further in the future would not be part of the "market supply" at *some price*. Rather, under the most likely legal constraints and pricing patterns, attention can be centered on a market for dry gas of at least three to five years duration. This is a simplifying condition that, if anything, would cause the *maximum* extent of any market for the pipeline to be underestimated.

12. It is difficult to document the conclusion that there are only five years from wildcat to production under a contract. Interviews with producers in the region, a confidential examination of a nonrandom sample of Permian Basin lease agreements, and discussions with lessees on interpretations of these agreements leave the impression that this is the prevailing limit.

when a large number of equal-sized firms operate as predicted by competitive price theory. Competition is lacking when few buyers or sellers set prices in relevant markets in accordance with monopsony or monopoly theory.

Power To Set Price in 1950–54 Markets. For there to have been monopoly of contract prices in West Texas-New Mexico in the early 1950s, some single producer should have controlled the supply of new reserves for one of the pipelines. A producer could have done this only by controlling uncommitted reserves in at least one of the two basins for approximately four years. A few producers also could have set prices if they had joint control of uncommitted reserves in this supply market.

Whether there was monopoly-type control of uncommitted gas reserves in the 1950s cannot be determined with any exactness, because ownership of uncommitted reserves is not a matter of public record. Some estimates can be made, however, by considering concentration in the sale of reserves, and "turnover" in the group of large sellers. If there was high concentration in the *sale* of reserves, there would be reason to suspect high concentration in the ownership of *uncommitted* reserves. When one producer can control reserves so as to restrict the amount of new contract sales, then this producer should have the greatest share of actual sales. Low concentration in sales is seldom a result of use of power to control supply.[13]

Concentration of actual sales in early 1950 *supply markets* was quite low, from all indications. The relevant supply markets extended, as has been suggested, throughout at least part of both basins over a period of close to four years. The first sample includes all new contracts for 1950 through 1953, for sales in West Texas-New Mexico to interstate pipelines that

13. Low (monopoly) sales concentration might follow from those with monopoly power not selling their majority share of total reserves but rather "shutting-in" for five to ten years. This is not profitable unless control extends to a substantial amount of *all* expected reserves over the longer period and the producer in question has a longer sales period than the assumed two to three years.

reported to the Federal Power Commission.[14] Concentration
of estimated newly committed reserves is shown in column 1

TABLE 5:1. *Concentration in the Sale of Reserves to Interstate
Transporters: The Early 1950s*

	West Texas-New Mexico 1950–53		West Texas-New Mexico 1951–54	
Estimated total new reserves (trillions of cu. ft.)		2.0027		2.4721
Total number of contracts		135		184
Total number of suppliers		69		96
Percentage of total new reserves dedicated by the four largest suppliers	Standard (Ind.) Oil and Gas	20.05	Gulf Oil Corporation	10.89
	Gulf Oil Corporation	12.07	Republic Natural Gas	10.49
	Humble Oil and Refining	6.34	Standard (Ind.) Oil and Gas	9.76
	Amerada Petroleum	5.14	Warren Petroleum	5.60
		44.00		36.74
Percentage of total new reserves dedicated by the ten largest suppliers		64.99		60.76

Source. All 1950–54 interstate contracts of sale of gas in West Texas-
New Mexico reported in F.P.C. form 301 as compiled in exhibit 2-LC of
Federal Power Commission Docket G-9277, *Champlin Oil and Refining
Co., et al.*

of Table 5:1. The total reserves from all contracts in this
sample were 2.0027 trillion cubic feet.[15] There were 69 sellers.

14. In accordance with Federal Power Commission requirements following after the *Phillips* decision, all producers had to file form 301 for
all pre-1955 contracts to obtain a "certificate of necessity." The contracts still in force were filed between 1955–57 and compiled in *Champlin Oil and Refinery,* Docket G-9277 (exhibit 2-LC). Contracts that
had lapsed before 1956 or that had not been reported due to negligence
were not included.

15. It has been assumed that 1955 deliveries in each contract were at
that contract's uniform rate of production, so that multiplying 1955 production by the number of years in the contract results in an indication
of the expected volume of recovered reserves. For a discussion of this
estimation method, cf. the Appendix at the end of the book.

The largest four sold 44.00 per cent of the total, and the largest ten sold 64.99 per cent.

During 1951–54, 96 producers signed 184 contracts. The largest supplier accounted for slightly more than 10 per cent of the estimated aggregate reserves, as did the second largest. The ten largest suppliers together signed contracts for approximately 60 per cent of 2.4721 trillion cubic feet as indicated in Table 5:1.

Structures of markets supplying new reserves in the two periods seem to have been similar. Each buyer's market was characterized by lack of any one dominant source of supply. In the first market Stanolind Oil and Gas Company sold some 20 per cent of reserves, but such a share hardly seems sufficient to earn Stanolind the title of "dominant firm." [16] Both markets had four producers who together controlled 40–45 per cent of market sales. It is doubtful that these four could have controlled price together, with less than half the sales.[17]

16. At this level of sales, it would require a 50 per cent decrease in Stanolind's sales to decrease *total sales* by 10 per cent. If the remaining producers are independent, diverse, and can increase their sales slightly, the 10 per cent decrease in *total sales* might not even take place. There would be little possibility of controlling market price with control of 20 per cent of the area supply of new reserves.

17. Professor George Stigler, in one of the many illuminating notes in *The Theory of Price*, shows that, if $Q + q = f(P)$ where Q is the output of r firms, q the output of the $(r+1)$ firm, $\dfrac{dq}{dp} = \left[f'(P) - \dfrac{dQ}{dP} \right]$ or $\dfrac{P(dq)}{q(dp)} = \left(\dfrac{Pf'(P)}{Q+q} \cdot \dfrac{Q+q}{q} \right) - \left(\dfrac{dQ}{dP} \cdot \dfrac{P}{Q} \cdot \dfrac{Q}{q} \right)$. Since elasticity is defined as the relative change of quantity, it follows that $\eta_{(r+1)} = \dfrac{Q + q(\eta_m)}{q} - \dfrac{Q}{q} \cdot \varepsilon_m$ where $\eta_{(r+1)}$ is the price elasticity of the $(r+1)$ firm, η_m is the market price elasticity, ε_m is the elasticity of supply of the r firms. Cf. George J. Stigler, *The Theory of Price* (New York, Macmillan, 1957), p. 301, n. 7. If the share of the largest firm is 10 per cent of sales and demand for reserves is elastic in the relevant range, then the largest seller's demand has an elasticity of at least 10.0. That is, $n_{r+1} = \left[\dfrac{1.00}{.10}(1.0) + 0 \right]$ (assuming zero supply elasticity of other sources of reserves). Differences between such demand and perfectly competitive demand can be ignored. The largest four would have had a *group demand* curve of elasticity 3.0 in the relevant range as a *minimum*. This,

These were not the same firms in the two markets, as well, so that they scarcely had sufficient group stability to even attempt control. The largest firm in the 1951–54 market replaced Stanolind by completing large new sales in 1954, the year Stanolind provided only a small new volume. The second largest firm in 1951–54 achieved its position by large relative sales during the last year also. The four largest in 1951–54 included two that were not among the four largest in the 1950–53 market period. The ten largest suppliers in 1951–54 included four that were not among the first ten in the 1950–53 market. Some producers must have had partially explored reserves, or reserves not yet to the limit of the two to three-year marketing period, that could have been sold in the 1950–53 market but were not. If these reserves had been sold in the earlier market they would have been sufficient to prevent any attempt by the four largest sellers to control new contract prices.

Some of the smaller pipelines may have had supply areas in only one basin for a shorter (two-year) time period. Concentration in actual sales in each basin for a two-year period may indicate possibilities of seller's control of prices to small transporters. Such figures for the 1953–54 market, for example, are shown in Table 5:2. Sales concentration in the San Juan Basin was as low as for larger markets, while that in the Permian Basin was somewhat higher. In the Permian area, for these two years, Republic Gas accounted for some 26 per cent of total sales with one contract for gas in the Pegasus Field. This one large sale, coupled with 9–11 per cent shares of three other sellers, resulted in the four largest sellers accounting for approximately 58 per cent of the aggregate amount sold in that basin.

---

again, would usually be judged as "highly elastic," if not of the order of similarity with competition shown by that for the largest firm. For the four largest firms to have acted on the basis of their collective demand, they would have had to control the collective supply of their group. Since the membership in the group experienced a 50 per cent change in the overlapping market period, group control would have been difficult. Since the two largest firms experienced a −50 per cent and −16 per cent change in market shares, control was not evident.

For similar markets, sales concentration was sometimes higher, and seldom lower, than shown in Table 5:2. The 1951–52 market was characterized by much higher concentration. The largest firm in the San Juan Basin committed some 40.80 per cent, and the largest four 67 per cent of the ap-

TABLE 5:2. *Concentration in the Sale of Reserves to Interstate Transporters in the More Narrowly Defined Supply Markets*

	Permian Basin 1953–54		San Juan 1953–54	
Estimated total new reserves (trillions of cu. ft.)	.9629		.3281	
Total number of contracts	62		57	
Total number of suppliers	44		44	
Percentage of total new reserves dedicated by the four largest suppliers	Republic Natural Gas	26.91	Skelly Oil Corporation	11.03
	Warren Petroleum	11.88	W. P. Carr Company	11.00
	Cities Service Products	9.86	Beaver L. Oil Corporation	9.80
	Sinclair Oil Company	9.13	East Development Company	8.39
		57.78		40.22
Percentage of total new reserves dedicated by the ten largest suppliers	77.84		69.94	

Source. As in Table 5:1.

proximately .310 trillion cubic feet sold. In the Permian Basin, approximately 58 per cent of all estimated sales of new reserves came from four producers, with the largest firm responsible for 24 per cent of the .870 trillion cubic feet sold.

If sales indicate relative holdings of reserves, any pipeline confined to purchasing in one basin for two years during the early 1950s would have been faced with few alternative sources of supply. However, perhaps reserves were more widely distributed than shown by sales data. There may have been many more alternative sources of gas, since there was considerable turnover in shares of large sales in a short period of time. The ten firms who dominated the highly concentrated 1951–52 sales were different from the ten who dominated the 1953–54 markets. For instance, the producer responsible for 42.80 per cent of 1951–52 sales in the San Juan Basin (Stanolind Oil and Gas), completed no new sales there in 1953–54. It would seem as if any attempt on the part of one producer to control sales volume in the small market would have been thwarted by more rapid sales on the part of others in a slightly later market period. There must have been a large number of producers with substantial volumes that could have been made available for sale.

Any pipeline able to purchase over part of two basins would have had at least thirty more sources of supply than the transporter in one basin. Additional suppliers would have included the larger sellers in the other basin (since no one of the large four in one basin was a member of "the four largest" in the other, at least for the period indicated in Table 5:2). Any pipeline able to consider supplies over a three or four-year time period, rather than a two-year period, would have had more alternatives because of the large turnover of ownership of the larger "packages of reserves."

In general, there was a continuum of supply markets. For the large pipelines transporting to the West, markets covered all of West Texas and New Mexico, over a period of at least four years. For the smaller lines, markets ranged down to the size of a single basin area for a two-year period. In the largest markets, there was no apparent opportunity for few producers to control total reserves; sales concentration and turnover indicate a lack of monopoly-type power during the early 1950s. In the smallest markets some producer's price control might have been possible, but extensive "turnover" indicates that control was unlikely. In markets neither the largest nor the smallest, monopoly power was unlikely because extensive additional sources of reserves were available in only slightly larger areas and slightly longer time periods. Since most pipelines operated in these last-mentioned markets, there would seem to have been no general monopoly or oligopoly power to control price.

Monopoly Buying Power in Producer's Markets. The lack of price-setting power for producers is not unexpected. Lease rights in West Texas and New Mexico have been widely sold and large traps of reserves have been jointly owned. There were no apparent barriers to entry of new producers, either in economies of large-scale development or in control of exploration by a few firms.[18] On the demand side of the market, however, economies of scale in transportation and regulation of entry of new transporters should have resulted in fewer pipelines than producers in West Texas-New Mexico. Indeed, there might have been *so few sources of demand* that pipelines could have controlled prices.

To have had power to determine new contract price, a pipeline would have had to control sources of demand in a producer's field area in a two to three-year selling period. There were hundreds of producer's field areas in the West Texas-New Mexico region for each two-year period in the early 1950s. In some, there might have been only one pipeline; in others, there could have been enough to have prevented control of demand. Each relevant market could be considered in terms of number of buyers, as an indicator of monopsony power. But this is a laborious analysis and since each transporter in his area had access to every field producer's market therein,[19] all fields in the same supply area can be considered together.

If all transporters traversed a supply area covering the

18. Control of exploration is dealt with more fully in the study by James McKie. He concludes that there might be some capital advantages of larger firms in wildcat exploration, and that the large firms as a group are more successful as indicated by per-well barrel recoveries. These are general conclusions that do not point to any oligopoly control, because the "large firms" would include most of the largest twenty-five sellers of reserves.

19. Assuming that the buyers had not agreed beforehand to allow each exclusive "demand rights" in separate fields in a common supply area. If this assumption can be made, then fields can be considered in groups because demand conditions in each in the supply area are the same.

Permian and San Juan Basins, the number of purchasers in the area would indicate the potential number of purchasers in each producer's field area. Also each buyer's share of actual purchases throughout the area should point to his relative capacity to purchase in each producer's market.[20] If all transporters did not extend throughout the two-basin region, then the number of buyers in the region would be an *overestimate* of potential sources of demand in those fields to which the smaller pipelines did not reach. The number of pipeline purchasers, and their relative shares, indicate the greatest possible extent of sources of demand in any field producer's market. Purchase concentration in producer's markets during 1950–54 is shown in Table 5:3. The figures indicate that El Paso, with some exceptions, was the primary source of demand in any collection of field markets. The 1950–51 producer's markets collectively were quite small, with 33 contracts for some .425 trillion cubic feet. Sales from the San Juan Basin were just beginning and sales of dry gas reserves from the Permian Basin were still minor.[21] El Paso purchased 100 per cent of all new contract reserves in 1950–51. Producers probably did not find more than one source of demand. El Paso must have had some power to set new contract prices.

Producing companies that could defer selling until the 1951–52 markets would have found few more buyers. El Paso continued to dominate the region, purchasing 52 per cent of total newly committed reserves. It purchased everything committed in the San Juan fields (27 contracts) and in the West Texas fields (4 contracts plus 12 oil-well gas contracts

20. Of course, it would be possible for a buyer with 10 per cent of area purchases to take 100 per cent of some fields, but it would not be likely to take 100 per cent in all fields (without "excess demand capacity"). A 10 per cent share would indicate capacity to purchase in the typical field.

21. The Federal Power Commission authorized construction of transmission from the San Juan in 1950. Cf. 9 *F.P.C.* 270 (1950) for discussion of certification of the El Paso transmission system that borders the San Juan Basin to California. The sales listed for the Permian Basin are dry-gas sales only, in accordance with the general definition of product "in the relevant markets," in order to make price comparisons possible.

not included in the sample). The Permian Basin Pipeline Company purchased 48 per cent of the entire Permian-San Juan Basin new reserves by signing contracts in fields confined to Lea County in southeast New Mexico. Considering Lea County fields alone, Permian Basin Pipeline purchased 73.3 per cent of new reserves sold there and El Paso purchased 27.7 per cent, giving producers in Lea County at most two effective alternative sources of demand.[22] But in the rest of the field producer's markets, concentration figures indicate only one effective buyer.

TABLE 5:3. *Concentration in the Purchase of Reserves, 1950–51*

	West Texas-New Mexico 1950–51		*West Texas-New Mexico 1951–52*	
Estimated volume of reserves (trillions of cu. ft.)	0.4246		1.1795	
Number of contracts	33		65	
Number of buyers	1		2	
Percentage of total new reserves purchased by the four largest buyers	El Paso Natural Gas	100.00	El Paso Natural Gas	51.90
			Permian Basin Pipeline	48.10
				100.00
Percentage purchased by the ten largest buyers	100		100	

Source. As in Table 5:1.

Demand conditions in 1952–53 producer's markets were similar to those in earlier years. El Paso increased its purchase share to 65 per cent of the aggregate new reserves in the two basins. Permian Basin pipeline accounted for 35 per cent, while three local buyers contracted for negligible percentages. El Paso's share increased and Permian Basin Pipeline's share decreased because El Paso took more than 90 per cent of what was sold in 1953. Permian Basin Pipeline made

22. Assuming that there had not been "an agreement" to share Lea County purchases on a ¾–¼ basis. There is no evidence that there was such an agreement, particularly since this ¾–¼ division of purchases took place only during one market period.

a few small purchases in 1953, and Southern Union Gas Company (one of the local retail utilities purchasing mostly from El Paso) signed one new contract. The industrial purchasers, C. V. Lyman and Delhi-Taylor Oil Company, purchased for limited refinery use. In effect, the producers in 1952–53 were faced with selling to the El Paso Natural Gas Company, or (in Lea County regions) to either El Paso or the Permian Basin Pipeline Company. El Paso must have had the power to set contract prices in most field markets.

In the 1953–54 field area markets, El Paso purchased more than 96 per cent of new contract reserves. Two smaller pipelines, Permian Basin Pipeline and Southern Union Gas Company, accounted for the 3–4 per cent of the new purchases not sold to El Paso. Such continued high concentration in purchases over the two-basin area might suggest that producers could rely only upon El Paso for consistent demand for any large amount of new reserves. From other sales information, however, it appears that this was true only up to the beginning of 1954. From January to November 1954, the newly organized Pacific Northwest Pipeline Company actively sought reserves in the San Juan Basin for a transmission line to the state of Washington. The new company provided pro-

TABLE 5:4. *Concentration in the Purchase of Reserves, 1952–54*

	West Texas-New Mexico 1952–53		West Texas-New Mexico 1953–54	
Estimated volume of reserves (trillions of cu. ft.)	1.5781		1.2926	
Number of contracts	102		119	
Number of buyers	5		5	
Percentage of total new reserves purchased by the four largest buyers	El Paso	64.52	El Paso	96.77
	Permian Basin	34.97	Permian Basin	2.64
	Southern Union	.33	Southern Union	.39
	C. V. Lyman	.16	C. V. Lyman	.19
		99.98		99.99
Percentage purchased by the ten largest buyers	100		100	

Source. As in Table 5:1.

ducers with an independent source of demand for "packages of reserves" in the San Juan Basin.

Pacific Northwest had the capacity to challenge El Paso's potential control of contract volumes and prices. The results were as stated in a Federal Power Commission staff brief:

> The competition in the San Juan Basin between El Paso and Pacific was acute. Early in 1954, Messrs. Fish, Wimbaly, Williams, Payne and McGee went to the San Juan Basin to interest producers in selling to Pacific. Mr. Fish claimed that, as to 90 to 95% of Pacific's (original) acreage in the San Juan Basin, the producers were backing Pacific. Competition for reserves occurs before contracts are signed. Aside from Pacific's original blocks of gas acquired, El Paso was successful in most instances in securing the gas.[23]

Pacific Northwest was able to obtain "producer's backing" and large blocks of reserves in the San Juan because of "discontent" with El Paso's terms in the past. Pacific apparently offered more favorable prices. This company certainly disrupted El Paso's control of volumes purchased in the San Juan Basin in 1954; informal contracting of reserves provided Pacific with more than 2.0 trillion cubic feet of new reserves.[24]

Producer's markets during 1950 to 1953 were characterized by El Paso Natural Gas Pipeline control of demand. Purchase shares of El Paso ranged from 50 to 100 per cent; there was little substantial change in purchase positions of the other lines. Purchase figures indicate there might have been one substantial alternative source of demand in 1952 in Lea County, New Mexico. Apart from this, and Pacific Northwest

23. Federal Power Commission Staff Brief, "In the Matter of El Paso Natural Gas Company, et al.," Dockets G-13018, G-13019 (April 1959), p. 19.

24. The contracts were "informal" because they were not certified until 1955–56. They provided 2.0 trillion of an estimated 7.0 trillion cubic feet this company obtained through 1956. Also, cf. Federal Power Commission Docket G-13019, pp. 13–17, for a discussion of methods El Paso used to gain "backing" in an earlier attempt to forestall entry. For example: "El Paso (in Utah) is offering two cents per thousand more than we" (p. 16).

competition in 1954, El Paso should have been able to control demand to an extent enabling control of price.

The "Power To Set Price" and Expected Price Behavior. If El Paso had, and used, the power to control demand, a rather distinctive pattern of price-output behavior should have followed. Rather than paying higher prices for larger volumes in "closer" locations, as the competitive buyer would have, El Paso should have paid similar prices for all volumes of reserves having the same marginal production costs.[25]

The expected monopsonistic pattern of price can be compared to actual prices on new contracts signed during 1950–54. It can be ascertained whether purchasers paid relatively higher prices for larger volumes of reserves, as expected from buyer's and seller's competition, or whether they paid similar prices for all-sized packages, as expected from monopsony. Similarly, it can be determined whether there was a competitive pattern of lower prices for gas in more distant reservoirs, or whether prices were the same regardless of trap distance, as expected from monopsony.

Differences in contract conditions should also have resulted in contrasting competitive and noncompetitive pricing patterns. Longer-term contracts should have had higher prices than shorter term [26] if there were buyer's competition in order to reflect increased offer prices and higher average production costs. If one buyer had power to set contract prices, then a premium also should have been paid on longer-term contracts

25. As outlined in the last chapter, the monopsony buyer cannot be expected to price according to higher maximum offer prices for closer reserves, or for larger volumes. Rather, this buyer should set a uniform price for all reserves having the same production costs at a level just sufficient to cover these (average) costs. Given that marginal production costs rise quite sharply for recovery of greater than 60–70 per cent of in-ground reserves, there should be little difference between monopsonistic volumes purchased under actual contracts and competitive volumes under the same contracts. Given that average production costs are roughly similar for traps in the same basin for 60–70 per cent recovery, monopsony prices should be similar on all contracts there.

26. The (competitive) maximum offer prices are higher for longer term because of buyer's advantages for resale and because of higher production costs. Monopsony prices may have to be greater for longer term, as well, to cover only the higher marginal production costs.

—but only to cover the greater marginal production costs of longer term.[27] Thus, higher prices on longer term should be observed in either case when there are large numbers of short and long-term contracts; but there can be distinctly higher prices (and fewer short-term contracts) under competitive demand conditions. Favored Nations and Renegotiation clauses in new contracts should have resulted in lower prices if there were competition: the presence of the clauses should reduce producer's unit costs of production and buyer's offer prices. If West Texas-New Mexico field markets were characterized by monopsony, prices should have been lower when these clauses were present, if the producer's marginal costs were lower. Again the price difference might have been greater under competition.[28]

"Competitive" price levels should be higher than those from "monopsony." It is exceedingly difficult to compare actual price levels with hypothetical "competitive" and "monopsony" price levels for particular markets unless actual demand and supply schedules are known. However, some indirect estimates of competitive-monopsony differences may follow from comparing price levels in fields where there was more than

27. Cf. discussion in the preceding chapter of the shift upward of marginal and average production costs from longer term-length of dedication. Crude calculations have suggested that the increase in average costs may be close to 2.0 cents per mcf for each five years of longer term. With competition among pipelines, the 2.0 cents per mcf differential should be equal to or less than the difference in *maximum demand prices* for fifteen and twenty-year contracts. But the monopsony buyer need pay no more than the *net addition* of longer term to *marginal production costs*. The increment to marginal production costs being less than that to average costs for longer term, in the relevant range of output, the monopsonist has to pay less for longer-term contracts. The monopsonist also pays less if the *competitive* premium in *maximum offer prices* is greater than the increased unit costs (i.e., if *all* contracts are long term) because he does not have to pay *maximum offer prices*.

28. That is, competitive buyers would be expected to offer the "maximum demand price" premium for a contract without these clauses. This premium may be greater than the increased costs of a clauseless contract, so that the producers sign contracts without clauses. The monopsonistic buyer should offer a premium equal only to the increased cost for the contract without clauses and this premium might well be lower than the competitive premium (and the number of clauseless contracts might be less).

one buyer, with price levels where El Paso Natural Gas was the only buyer. Competition between El Paso and other buyers at some locations should have forced El Paso to pay higher prices there than elsewhere.

In summary, if prices were competitive in West Texas-New Mexico during 1950–54, they should have been higher on larger volume sales, at closer locations, under longer-term contracts without contingency clauses. On the other hand, under monopsony, prices should not have differed with volume or distance, and they might not have differed with term-length or with the presence/absence of Favored Nations clauses.

Comparing Actual Prices with Expected Prices for 1950–54. The results of competition, in effect, imply a systematic relationship between price on a contract and the volume of reserves, distance to the trap, the particular aspects of the contract agreement. In contrast, the results of monopoly buying power should include the absence of the relationships resulting from competition. When there is buyers' and sellers' competition the relationship $P = f(V, D, T, C_1, C_2)$ should hold; when there is monopsony power being exerted, this relationship should not be apparent.[29] One method for determining the presence of this competitive relationship is to assume that it would be observable from testing for a linear relation between conditions of the contract and price for sales in any one market. Prices on contracts resulting from competition should be higher on large-volume contracts: that is, $(P = \alpha + \beta V + v)$ should be observed, where P is contract price, V is volume of reserves dedicated in that contract, and the coefficient β is positive.[30] When a large pipeline has power to set price, however, it can be assumed that this linear relationship would not hold—that β would be equal to, or close

29. Where P is initial price in the contract, V is volume of reserves dedicated, D is distance of the trap from the end of transmission, T is the term-length of the contract, Y is the year of contract signing, C_1 and C_2 are respectively the presence of Favored Nations and Renegotiation clauses.

30. And where v is a term indicating "disturbances" or "residuals" due to other unspecified factors affecting price.

to, zero. Prices on competitive contracts should vary with the other aspects of sales so that the equation ($P = \alpha + \beta_1 V + \beta_2 D + \beta_3 T + \beta_4 Y + \beta_5 C_1 + \beta_6 C_2 + v$) should be observable.[31] There should be positive values for the coefficients of volume and term (i.e., β_1, $\beta_3 > 0$) and negative coefficients for distance, and for the presence of the two contingency clauses (i.e., β_2, β_5, $\beta_6 < 0$). In contrast, the results of monopsony pricing should include values of all coefficients close to zero (i.e., the hypothesis that $\beta_1 = 0$, $\beta_2 = 0$, $\beta_3 \geqq 0$, $\beta_5 \leqq 0$, $\beta_6 \leqq 0$ cannot be disproved).[32]

This equation can be estimated with samples of contracts from actual markets during 1950–54. Estimation proceeds by fitting the equation: $P = a + b_1 V + b_2 D + b_3 T + b_4 Y + b_5 C_1 + b_6 C_2 + U$ (where the b's are estimates of β_1, β_2, etc.) such that the sum of the square of the deviations between computed prices and actual prices for each contract is minimized.[33] This method is utilized because it yields estimates b_1, b_2, b_3, etc., of β_1, β_2, β_3, etc., that allow testing of hypotheses concerning β_1, β_2, β_3, (i.e., the estimates are unbiased and efficient). For example, the competitive hypothesis $\beta_1 > 0$ (relative to the contrasting monopsony hypothesis $\beta_1 = 0$) can be tested with values of the distribution $t = \dfrac{b_1 - 0}{S_{b_1}}$.[34] This is accomplished by assuming, given the

31. Cf. footnote 29 above for definitions of the particular factors in the equation.

32. Zero values for the coefficients are equivalent to a finding that volume, distance, and so on have not affected price. This is a finding in accordance with monopsony predictions of no functional relationship between these factors and the contract price. Specific predictions for the coefficient of Y can be made from conditions of demand in particular supply areas as these supply regions are discussed. Specific predictions for β_3, β_5, β_6 under monopsony have to include values greater than or less than zero as well as values equal to zero, because the monopoly buyer may have to pay higher amounts for longer term or contracts without clauses as a result of increased development costs therefrom.

33. That is, $\displaystyle\sum_{i=1}^{n} [P_i - (a + b_1 V_i + b_2 D_i + b_3 T_i + b_4 Y_i + b_5 C_{1i} + b_6 C_{2i})]^2$ for n contracts, is a minimum.

34. Where S_{b_1} is the standard deviation of all values of computed b following from a series of sample contracts.

null-hypothesis $\beta_1 = 0$, that large values of $t = \dfrac{b_1 - 0}{S_{b_1}}$ could not follow by chance, but rather disprove the monopsony hypothesis in favor of the competitive.

The validity of the estimation procedure, and the tests for competition, depend upon characteristics of the sample of contracts. Prices on those contracts analyzed can be assumed to be influenced by very many factors in addition to those specified in the functional relationship, but the average price effect of the other factors must be zero. Also, the disturbance effect on prices of unspecified factors must be normally distributed about a mean value equal to zero, and the distribution must not be related to particular specified factors.[35] It is also assumed that statistical procedures for testing $\beta_i > 0$ as compared to $\beta_i = 0$ distinguish between competitive and monopsony price. There would seem to be little question that differences in maximum offer prices, for different volumes, distances to the trap, and so on, should have a distinctive effect upon *average* prices, given the inelasticity of individual producer supply.[36] The lack of differences between actual average prices should be indicative of the absence of maximum offer prices.[37]

35. Cf. Paul G. Hoel, *Introduction to Mathematical Statistics* (New York, John Wiley, 1954) chaps. 7 and 8; or more succinctly, R. Stone, *Consumers' Expenditure in the United Kingdom, 1920–38* (Cambridge, Cambridge University Press, 1954), *1*, pp. 280–84, on "Regression Analysis." Attempts are made to establish the validity of these assumptions in the appendix following Chapter 8.

36. That is, with *vertical* marginal cost curves and relatively higher prices "locational rents" should occur for the closer producers. The monopsonist should remove these rents and pay scarcely more than the marginal costs at the *low* point of the vertical curve.

37. It should be mentioned that actual relationships of prices and V, D, T, etc. may not be linear, but the linear equation is used since the test is limited to the *presence* or *absence* of any relationship. Most attention is centered upon whether contract price depends upon volume (that $\beta_1 > 0$), not on whether the actual relationship is positive and equal to .992, for example. It would seem sufficient to estimate only the sign of β_1 in the equation, and this can be done in a linear equation. In some cases, however, "non-linearity" in a variable may result in the insertion of a factor Δ in β_i and may result in unwarranted rejection or acceptance of the hypothesis $\beta_i > 0$. This does not seem likely but it can be considered in evaluation of the results.

The equation $(P = a + b_1V + b_2D + b_3T + b_4Y + b_5C_1 + b_6C_2 + U)$ can be calculated by "least squares" from samples of contracts signed between 1950–54. The samples consist of new contracts signed in two-year producer's market periods for gas-well gas, or for residue gas when stripped of liquids and deliverable at a uniform rate. All contracts in the samples contain complete information as to initial price, volume of 1955 production, term-length of production, the presence or absence of the contingency clauses, and the date on which the contract was signed. The contracts were for reserves committed "in interstate commerce" only, since these alone have been included in Federal Power Commission listings.[38] Initial price can be used to indicate revenue received per thousand cubic feet of gas reserves.[39] Volume of reserves committed by the contract can be estimated by multiplying 1955 production by the number of years of proposed production.[40] Distance of the trap can be estimated for each contract by measuring (on Federal Power Commission maps) miles along given transmission routes from fields and the location along the Arizona-New Mexico border designated the end of transmission.

The estimated equations shown in Table 5:5 are the results

38. The sample is from the exhibit 2-LC in the Federal Power Commission *Champlin Oil and Refining, et al.,* Docket G-9277 as microfilmed from F.P.C. form 301. The form contained the above information, as supplied by the producers.

39. Initial price does not provide a complete estimate since it is the per-unit revenue received for the *first year's production only* and is not subject to later scheduled increases et al. But initial price does provide an indication of the producer's estimate of the price he is receiving, while the future "base prices" in the contract data are too incomplete to provide any estimate.

40. This estimate is accurate if 1955 production was at the uniform rate assumed implicitly by the signers of the contract. For new contracts signed in the years immediately preceding 1955, the 1955 production may not differ from the per annum production estimated at the time of signing; but for contracts signed in 1950, five years of development may have resulted in a new, revised reserves estimate and new rates of production. For these early contracts, the initial reserve estimate of the producer may differ from 1955 volume multiplied by the term-length. Unfortunately, the paucity of information on reserves per contract make it impossible to determine the extent of the error from using what may not be an initial estimate.

TABLE 5:5. *Summary of Actual Price Behavior,*
West Texas-New Mexico, 1950–54

Given that: $P = \alpha + \beta_1 V + \beta_2 D + \beta_3 T + \beta_4 Y + \beta_5 C_1 + \beta_6 C_2 + v$

P = initial contract price, cents per mcf
V = volume of reserves, billions of cu. ft.
D = distance of trap, in hundreds of miles
T = term-length, in years
Y = either the first-year sample (zero) or the second year (one)
C_1 = presence of Favored Nations clause ($=$ one)
C_2 = presence of Renegotiation ($=$ one)
R^2 = coefficient of determination
S_u = standard error of estimate, cents per mcf
S_p = standard deviation of price, cents per mcf.

A. *1950–51*
   (*sample of 33 contracts*)

Regression equations

$P = \alpha + \beta_1 V + \beta_2 D + \beta_3 T + \beta_4 Y + \beta_5 C_1 + \beta_6 C_2 + v$
$P = 12.953 - .0010V - .4268D - .1064T + .1201Y - .4369C_1$
$(2.296)\ \ (.0042)\ \ \ (.0761)\ \ \ (.1314)\ \ (.3088)\ \ (.3950)$

$ -1.729C_2$
$\ \ (.5582)$
$R^2 = .611$
$S_u = .697$
$S_p = .978$

(*Competitive*) Predictions	(*Monopsony*) Predictions	*Tests of computed equations*
$\beta_1 > 0$	$\beta_1 = 0$	Given that $t_i = \left[\dfrac{b_i - \beta_i}{S_{b_i}}\right]$ for a value
$\beta_2 < 0$	$\beta_2 = 0$	of $t_i < |1.645|$ disproves the hypothesis
$\beta_3 > 0$	$\beta_3 \gtreqless 0$	that $\beta_i = 0$ in favor of $\beta_i \gtreqless 0$ (with a
$\beta_5 \lesseqgtr 0$	$\beta_5 \lesseqgtr 0$	95 per cent confidence interval)
$\beta_6 \lesseqgtr 0$	$\beta_6 \lesseqgtr 0$	$\beta_1 = 0$ since $t_1 = -\ .2442$

$\beta_2 < 0$ since $t_2 = -5.6053$
$\beta_3 = 0$ since $t_3 = -\ .8094$
$\beta_4 = 0$ since $t_4 = \ .3890$
$\beta_5 = 0$ since $t_5 = -1.1059$
$\beta_6 < 0$ since $t_6 = -3.0998$

B. *1951–52*
   (*sample of 65 contracts*)

Regression equations

$P = \alpha + \beta_1 V + \beta_2 D + \beta_3 T + \beta_4 Y + \beta_5 C_1 + \beta_6 C_2 + v$
$P = 7.906 + .0129V - .1887D - .0847T + 1.198Y + .9218C_1$
$(2.613)\ (.0047)\ \ (.0982)\ \ (.1161)\ \ (.381)\ \ \ \ (.9931)$

$ +.5023C_2$
$\ (1.0185)$
$R^2 = .307$
$S_u = 1.289$
$S_p = 1.474$

(*Competitive*) Predictions	(*Monopsony*) Predictions	Tests of computed equations
$\beta_1 > 0$	$\beta_1 = 0$	$\beta_1 > 0$ since $t_1 =$ 2.7109
$\beta_2 < 0$	$\beta_2 = 0$	$\beta_2 < 0$ since $t_2 = -1.911$
$\beta_3 > 0$	$\beta_3 \geqq 0$	$\beta_3 = 0$ since $t_3 = - .7294$
$\beta_5 \leqq 0$	$\beta_5 \leqq 0$	$\beta_4 > 0$ since $t_4 =$ 3.1430
$\beta_6 \leqq 0$	$\beta_6 \leqq 0$	$\beta_5 = 0$ since $t_5 =$ .9282
		$\beta_6 = 0$ since $t_6 =$ .4960

C. *1952–53*
(*sample of 102 contracts*)

Regression equations

$$P = \alpha + \beta_1 V + \beta_2 D + \beta_3 T + \beta_4 Y + \beta_5 C_1 + \beta_6 C_2 + v$$

$$P = 6.116 + .0158V + .0574D + .0306T + .8140Y + 1.315C_1 - .8379C_2$$
$$\quad (1.109)\ (.0050)\quad (.0832)\quad (.0475)\quad (.3227)\quad (.785)\quad (.7709)$$
$R^2 = .164$
$S_u = 1.465$
$S_p = 1.554$

(*Competitive*) Predictions	(*Monopsony*) Predictions	Tests of computed equations
$\beta_1 > 0$	$\beta_1 = 0$	$\beta_1 > 0$ since $t_1 =$ 3.0363
$\beta_2 < 0$	$\beta_2 = 0$	$\beta_2 = 0$ since $t_2 =$ .6906
$\beta_3 > 0$	$\beta_3 > 0$	$\beta_3 = 0$ since $t_3 =$ .6429
$\beta_5 \leqq 0$	$\beta_5 \leqq 0$	$\beta_4 > 0$ since $t_4 =$ 2.5224
$\beta_6 \leqq 0$	$\beta_6 \leqq 0$	$\beta_5 > 0$ since $t_5 =$ 1.6746
		$\beta_6 = 0$ since $t_6 = -1.0869$

D. *1953–54*
(*sample of 119 contracts*)

Regression equations

$$P = \alpha + \beta_1 V + \beta_2 D + \beta_3 T + \beta_4 Y + \beta_5 C_1 + \beta_6 C_2 + v$$

$$P = 7.923 + .0041V + .0230D + .0804T + 1.444Y + .8938C_1 - 2.225C_2$$
$$\quad (.663)\quad (.0034)\quad (.0558)\quad (.0329)\quad (.215)\quad (.5431)\quad (.598)$$
$R^2 = .426$
$S_u = 1.067$
$S_p = 1.385$

(*Competitive*) Predictions	(*Monopsony*) Predictions	Tests of computed equations
$\beta_1 > 0$	$\beta_1 = 0$	$\beta_1 = 0$ since $t_1 =$ 1.2007
$\beta_2 < 0$	$\beta_2 = 0$	$\beta_2 = 0$ since $t_2 =$ .4117
$\beta_3 > 0$	$\beta_3 \geqq 0$	$\beta_3 > 0$ since $t_3 =$ 2.5372
$\beta_5 \leqq 0$	$\beta_5 \leqq 0$	$\beta_4 > 0$ since $t_4 =$ 6.6995
$\beta_6 \leqq 0$	$\beta_6 \leqq 0$	$\beta_5 > 0$ since $t_5 =$ 1.6456
		$\beta_6 < 0$ since $t_6 = -3.7673$

from least squares calculations utilizing this data as to volume, location, etc.[41] They are indicative of average price differences for differences in contract volume, trap distance, term of production, etc. They can be compared with theoretical competitive or monopsony price behavior contrasting values for β_i in $[P = \alpha + \beta_1 V + \beta_2 D + \beta_3 T + \beta_4 Y + \beta_5 C_1 + \beta_6 C_2 + v]$.

Actual Price Behavior in 1950–54 Markets. The 1950–51 sample included 33 contracts covering an estimated .4246 trillion cubic feet. Given that El Paso purchased 100 per cent of these new reserves, the pattern of pricing should have been similar to the theoretical monopsony pattern. The one pipeline buyer should not have varied contract price with volume or distance, and might not have varied price according to length of contract term or with contingency clauses.[42] Production cost differences may have necessitated a slightly higher monopsony price in the Permian Basin, where reserves were at greater depth. There was no a priori reason for price levels to change between 1950–51. The computed pricing pattern was:

$$P = 12.953 - .0010V - .4268D - .1064T + .1201Y$$
$$(2.968)\ (.0042)\quad (.0761)\quad (.1314)\quad (.3088)$$
$$- .4369C_1 - 1.729C_2$$
$$(.3950)\quad (.5583)$$

(a measure of dispersion in each computed coefficient, the standard error of the coefficient, is shown in parenthesis below). Price in a new contract was insignificantly lower the greater the estimated volume of reserves committed in the

41. The method of "least squares" was utilized in the I.B.M. "one pass" regression program of Professor Harold Watts of Yale University. "Least squares" equations are discussed in Hoel, chap. 7.

42. That is, there should *not* have been differences in contract prices because of differences in *maximum* offer prices for longer term and for the absence of contingency clauses. But differences in prices might have been required to compensate for higher producers' marginal costs for longer term, or for not having Favored Nations clauses. These cost differences have been assumed to have been small in the preceding and in the theory of Chapter 3 as compared to differences following from *demand* prices, but they cannot be ignored.

contract.[43] Price was approximately .43 cents per mcf lower (for any given volume of reserves) 100 miles farther from the end of transmission. This was considerably less than the .70 to 1.10 cents per mcf expected to follow from maximum offer price differences in competitive supply areas.[44] The term of the contract had no significant effect upon price—probably because there is a lack of contracts with contrasting term in this sample.[45] Prices did not increase from 1950 to 1951 on contracts similar in all other respects (as indicated by β_4 not being different from zero). The presence of Favored Nations and Renegotiation clauses resulted in somewhat lower prices, but they were significantly lower only when there were Renegotiation clauses.[46]

Contract volume, term-length, the distance to the point of production, etc., explained some 61.11 per cent of the variation in price (since R^2, the coefficient of correlation, $= .6111$). The explained portion was 61 per cent of a remarkably small amount of total price variation, since most of the contracts had prices within one cent of the average (the standard deviation of all prices was .9784 cents per mcf).

The over-all impression is that prices followed the pattern expected from monopsony purchase of reserves. The "typical" 1951 contract in the San Juan Basin had average volume of 12.87 billion cubic feet, a twenty-year term, Favored Nations and Renegotiation clauses. This contract had an initial price of 8.28 cents per mcf (as calculated from inserting these

43. The customary test for *statistical significance* suggests that a hypothesis of no relationship between price and volume cannot be disproved. Assuming $\beta_1 = 0$, then $t = (b_1 - \beta_i)/S_{b_1} = b_1/S_{b_1}$ is distributed with *zero* mean and *unit* variance. A value of $t > 1.64$ should occur less than 5 per cent of the time because of chance; a value of t this large should lead to rejection of the hypothesis that $\beta_i = 0$ in favor of $\beta_i > 0$. Cf. Table 5:5 for computed values of t.

44. The observed value for the coefficient for distance is statistically significant, however, as shown in the last column of Table 5:5. It cannot be said that pricing was uniform at all locations, as expected from a strict interpretation of monopsony pricing.

45. There was only one contract of 15-year term while the remaining had 20 to 21-year term-lengths of production.

46. Statistical tests of significance for β_4, and β_5, β_6 are found in Table 5:5.

specifications in the regression equation: 12.87 billion for V, 20 for T, etc.). Estimated initial price for the contract covering the smallest volume of reserves, under the shortest-term contract without contingency clauses, was approximately 11.47 cents per mcf, more than for the large volume. A comparable "typical" contract in the Permian Basin had a price approximately 1.63 cents per mcf lower than this "typical" contract in the San Juan. The difference was approximately .43 cents per mcf per 100 miles of increased distance to the trap, which seems too little to be in accord with competitive demand differences. Nor did prices vary much with respect to contract conditions such as term-length and the presence of Favored Nations or Renegotiation clauses.[47] Over-all uniformity in prices and the absence, in particular, of systematic variation of prices with respect to volume and distance, suggest similarity between 1950–51 prices and monopsony price behavior.

Price behavior in larger samples of contracts for 1951–52, and for 1952–53, adds further to an impression of monopsony practice. The 65 contracts for 1951–52 list El Paso Natural Gas Company as the purchaser everywhere except in Lea County, New Mexico (where there were a number of contracts signed by Permian Basin Pipeline). El Paso was the buyer of 65 per cent of reserves in 1952–53 contracts (as shown in Table 5:3). The pricing pattern for 1951–52 was as indicated by the regression line (with the standard errors of the regression coefficients shown below):

$$P = 7.906 + .0129V - .1887D - .0847T + 1.198Y$$
$$\quad (2.613) \ (.0047) \quad (.0982) \quad (.1161) \quad (0.381)$$
$$+ .9218C_1 + .5023C_2.$$
$$\quad (.9931) \quad (1.0185)$$

47. The lack of variation with term-length provides no further indication of the type of behavior, since it follows from the lack of contracts of terms other than twenty years. The hypothetical "monopsonist" may have offered a premium for twenty-year reserve sales that induced all producers to sell according to this term-length on the 33 contracts, or hypothetical competitors may have offered a maximum price greater than increased production costs so that all contracts were dedicated for twenty years.

The pattern for 1952–53 was:

$$P = 6.116 + .0158V + .0574D + .0306T + .8140Y$$
$$(1.109)\ (.0050)\quad (.0832)\quad (.0475)\quad (.3227)$$
$$+ 1.315C_1 - .8379C_2.$$
$$(0.785)\quad (.7809)$$

The two samples of price behavior correspond with monopsony predictions or with some of the effects of *isolated* buyer's competition.

For both market periods there was little price variation with distance to the trap, or with the term-length of the contract. Contracts for reserves 100 miles farther from the western New Mexico border had prices .18 cents per mcf lower in the first market period, and .06 cents higher in the second market period. Of these two estimates (b_2) of the average effect of distance on price, only the first implies that prices were significantly different at different locations.[48] The term-length of contract had little perceptible effect upon prices. Again the reason is related to the calculation of the regression line: the sample contained only two contracts of term-length less than twenty years in 1951–52, and only five short-term contracts in 1952–53, so that the calculated effect of term on prices (the coefficient b_3) is based upon prices of twenty-year contracts and of only a few shorter-term contracts.

Contract prices varied with volume, and the level of price was higher in 1952 than in earlier years. Prices for large contracts (more than 24.0 billion cubic feet) were on the average .07 cents per mcf higher than prices on contracts of estimated average size (18.0 billion). Similar large contracts in 1952–53

---

48. The test for statistical significance of the null hypothesis that the difference between prices for different-sized dedications is zero (i.e., that $\beta_2 = 0$ where β_2 is the population coefficient for distance) assumes that $t = \dfrac{b_2 - \beta_2}{S_{b_2}}$ would have zero mean and unit variance so that a value of t greater than 1.645 would occur less than 5 per cent of the time. Values of greater than 1.645 lead to rejection of the hypothesis. Here the values of $t = \dfrac{b_2 - 0}{S_{b_2}} = -1.911, + .6906$ respectively, and the difference is statistically significant only in the first sample.

had prices .10 cents per mcf higher than that for the average volume.[49] There was an estimated difference of approximately 2.60 cents per mcf between the largest sale (200 billion cubic feet) and the smallest (.31 billion cubic feet). This premium for large volumes did not prevail on all sales, however; it was evident only in particular Permian Basin contracts. There were 14 contracts in 1951–52 for reserves greater than 24 billion cubic feet, seven having been signed by El Paso and seven by Permian Basin Pipeline. There were 19 contracts in 1952–53 for these larger volumes—El Paso signed twelve, and the other seven were the same Permian Basin 1952 contracts. El Paso purchased large "packages" at the same price as small, but Permian Basin Pipeline paid an average of 3.0 cents per mcf more than the El Paso price for its seven large-volume purchases. This had the effect of causing price (in the regression equation) to be higher for larger volumes. It also caused average price for 1952 to be greater than for 1951 by 1.198 cents per mcf.

Permian Basin Pipeline's prices do not necessarily mean the two-basin area had become more competitive. The pricing pattern observed in 1950–51 certainly had been disrupted. The uniformity of price imposed by one buyer was lacking [50] —but only in Lea County, New Mexico, where Permian Basin Pipeline purchased. The El Paso Company continued to offer the same prices as earlier.

The El Paso 1952 price for the "typical" contract in the San Juan Basin was 7.609 cents per mcf, somewhat lower than the 1951 price of 8.283 cents per mcf.[51] The 1953 price was 8.423 cents per mcf, slightly higher than during the two previous years. The San Juan Basin contracts had had relatively stable prices since 1950, while in the Permian Basin, prices

49. The price differences for "large" volumes were (statistically) significantly different from zero according to the test outlined in Table 5:5.

50. There was much more *general variation* in price as a result of these contracts as well: the standard deviation of initial prices was 1.457 cents per mcf for all contracts, compared with .9784 cents per mcf in 1950–51.

51. The characteristics of a "typical" contract are described below and in the note for Table 5:10.

increased for this "typical" contract from 5.655 cents per mcf in 1951, to 7.827 cents in 1952 and to 8.641 cents in 1953. The new purchase prices of Permian Basin Pipeline Company in Lea County caused these increases in the Permian Basin, since El Paso prices did not change. The purchase prices indicate only that one of two transporters in Lea County paid a higher than usual price for his new purchases of reserves there. Increased prices neither continued nor spread to other fields.[52]

In the 1953–54 market period, the El Paso Company again was the buyer in most of the contracts listed throughout both basins. Four lines other than El Paso purchased new reserves, but they accounted for no more than 3.3 per cent of the estimated aggregate volume sold. El Paso's overwhelming share of new contract reserves would seem to indicate general control of field demand; the only exception might have been in the San Juan Basin in 1954 where the entry of the new Pacific Northwest Pipeline Company was taking place. The capacity of this newer pipeline would have been sufficient to prevent any El Paso control of price in that basin, so that there should have been more competitive price behavior there than previously.

Actual price behavior for the 1953–54 sample of 119 contracts was as summarized by the linear regression equation: [53]

$$P = 7.923 + .0041V + .0230D + .0804T + 1.444Y$$
$$(.663)\ (.0034)\quad (.0558)\quad (.0329)\quad (.215)$$
$$+ .8938C_1 - 2.2255C_2.$$
$$(.5431)\qquad (.5984)$$

The (statistically) significant factors affecting average price were term T, year Y, and the presence of the Renegotiation clause C_2. The estimated volume of reserves in the contract did not affect price, nor did the distance of the point of production from final points of resale. El Paso did not pay higher prices for larger volumes of reserves, and actually

---

52. That is, the competitive "malaise" was quickly isolated. It was later cured, as will be seen below.

53. The figures in parenthesis indicate the standard errors of the coefficients.

offered somewhat lower prices in the San Juan Basin closer to California.[54] Longer-term contracts had higher prices on the average, but the number of contracts having terms less than 20 years was so small that this effect has to be disregarded. Prices in 1954 contracts were 1.44 cents per mcf higher than for 1953 comparable contracts in the sample. This increase in price levels represents one marked change from earlier markets. There was also a strongly negative relationship between the presence of Renegotiation clauses and average price while the presence of a Favored Nations clause resulted in slightly higher average price.[55]

Generally there seems to have been little difference between 1953–54 pricing patterns and those for earlier markets. The impression is that one buyer still had control of demand and price, with some exceptions. The uniformity of price with respect to volume and distance could only have followed from buyer's control of price. The price for the "typical" contract, however, rose from 8.42 cents per mcf in the San Juan in 1953 to 9.87 cents per mcf in 1954.[56] This increase was the first of more than 1.0 cents per mcf in the San Juan Basin in five years, and it coincided with the first attempts of Pacific Northwest to purchase reserves. Perhaps El Paso Natural Gas raised price to meet active bidding of Pacific Northwest in this market period, but it continued to have control sufficient to be able to set the uniform general price.[57]

Summary Evaluation of 1950–54 Markets. On the whole there were few deviations from a monopsony pattern of price

54. The test of "significance" is the same as above: testing to determine whether $b_i/S_{b_i} > 1.645$. If it is not, then the null hypothesis $\beta_i = 0$ cannot be disproved. Cf. "tests of computed equation" in Table 5:5.

55. The contrasting effects of C_1 and C_2 on price are not in accord with *either* competitive or monopsony predictions.

56. The "typical" contract still is for 12.87 billion cubic feet for twenty-year delivery, and contains Favored Nations and Renegotiation clauses.

57. Price on the "typical" contract increased between 1953 and 1954 in the Permian Basin from 8.641 cents per mcf to 9.951 cents, in the San Juan Basin from 8.423 cents to 9.874 cents. The increase was greatest in the San Juan Basin where Pacific Northwest provided an alternative source of demand.

formation. Throughout the years 1950–54, El Paso Natural Gas seems to have been the exclusive or dominant source of demand in producer's field markets. This company was responsible for most of the recorded purchases of reserves in any two-year period; and it shared markets only twice with another buyer. Where markets were not shared, the prices on new contracts closely followed the monopsony pattern (they did not vary with contract volume or the distance to the point of production).[58] The prices on new contracts were quite stable over time (there was no significant price rise between 1950 and 1951, 1952 and 1953). But where another pipeline purchased large amounts of new reserves, prices departed somewhat from this pattern. Prices were higher in Lea County, New Mexico, when Permian Basin Pipeline provided an extensive new source of demand there; prices rose throughout the San Juan Basin while Pacific Northwest began purchasing there. Prices varied more from contract to contract at these times, but not in the manner suggested by competitive price theory.[59] El Paso, in these particular instances, apparently merely altered a monopsony-type pricing policy somewhat. The general pattern of 1950–54 prices remained similar to the uniform monopsony pattern.

MARKET CONTROL AND MARKET BEHAVIOR IN THE
LATER 1950s

El Paso's control of price would have declined if Pacific Northwest Pipeline had continued as a large independent

58. Prices did not vary with the term-length of contract or the presence-absence of contingency clauses. The lack of variation with term may well have been due to characteristics of the particular sample of contracts, however.

59. The proportion of total variation in prices "explained" by the factors in the equation can be indicated by R^2, the coefficient of multiple determination. In 1950–51, $R^2 = .611$ when the standard deviation of prices $S_p = .978$ cents per mcf; in 1953–54 $R^2 = .426$ when $S_p = 1.385$ cents per mcf and Pacific Northwest was purchasing large amounts of reserves. It would seem that, in the earlier years, small variations in accordance with volume, distance, et al. were a significantly large proportion of exceedingly little price variation. In the later years, the uni-

source of demand over a considerable length of time. Pacific Northwest could have been expected to bid price to the level of "maximum demand price" and to have brought about an over-all pattern of variation with volume, distance, term, etc. But buyer's competition was thwarted as a result of agreements of the two pipelines to merge in the last months of 1954. By 1955, El Paso's share of demand in producer's markets was so extensive as to suggest that this company had re-established monopsony power.

Market structures did not remain entirely the same, however, either with respect to the supply, or to the purchase of reserves. Intensive exploration of the San Juan Basin and discoveries of a large proportion of dry gas volumes in the Permian Basin resulted in the offer for sale of a number of large "blocks of reserves" in the period 1955–60. The entry of another large new pipeline in 1957 significantly altered demand conditions in field markets. The new transporter, Transwestern Pipeline Company, sought contract reserves throughout West Texas and New Mexico for resale in competition with El Paso in California. It is possible that these new discoveries, and/or the new pipeline entry, changed the character of competition in the late 1950s markets.

The Power to Control Supply, 1955–60. The presence of a few producers with large holdings of reserves would have drastically changed the nature of price formation. Any one supplier, or a small group of suppliers, with a substantial share of total uncommitted reserves in the Permian or San Juan Basins, might have been able to increase price levels from the monopsony level and to have required premiums for large volumes in closer traps.[60] The extension of known reserves in the Mesa Verde and Pictured Cliffs Strata of the San Juan

form pricing pattern seems to have been disturbed by entry, but not to the extent that competitive demand factors play a large part in explaining total variation. This may result from most of the *recorded* contracts being those of the monopsonist adhering to his old pricing policy.

60. These price changes would only be part of a new "monopoly pattern of prices." Variation from buyer to buyer in the levels of prices charged would have been equally as important (as mentioned in the last chapter).

Basin to new discrete traps resulted in some large individual holdings of uncommitted reserves by 1955. The discovery and development of the Paradox Basin (particularly the Aneth Field) near the San Juan Basin took place in such a manner that a few producers were left with control of most of 2.0 trillion cubic feet of reserves there. The new traps of dry gas in the Permian Basin were discovered by some twelve producers. The question is whether these new volumes were actually so closely held as to allow the owners to set new contract prices.

Concentration of ownership of uncommitted reserves in the relevant supply markets was not high, according to all indications. The relevant markets were rather large, since most of the smaller transporters now purchased some reserves on resale from El Paso and thus had access to new gas volumes from both basins. The time-length of supply markets in the late 1950s might well have been greater than four years for all pipelines. The few largest producers of new reserves would have had to control most of the amount becoming available between 1955 and 1960 throughout West Texas-New Mexico to have had monopoly power in the relevant market. Ownership of uncommitted reserves between 1955 and 1957 and sales of reserves from 1956 to 1958 do not show that large owners controlled reserves sufficiently to control price.

Actual ownership of large volumes of reserves in the 1955–57 period has been estimated in Table 5:6. The largest holding, that of Warren Petroleum Company, consisted of reserves of 1.3 trillion cubic feet, mostly in the Puckett formation in the Permian Basin. This was a substantial amount in any supply area, but it was only about 15 per cent of known large volumes becoming available for production at that time, and only 12 per cent of all unsold reserves.[61] Warren scarcely could have set market prices on the basis of this small portion of total supply. Nor could Warren and the three next largest producers have set price together. The shares of Humble,

61. The total uncommitted reserves of 11.0 trillion cubic feet includes the large volumes listed and producers' or buyers' estimates of the aggregate amount available from smaller traps.

Sunray, and Phillips added to that of Warren accounted for no more than 37 per cent of total reserves.[62]

The producer with the largest amount of reserves newly

TABLE 5:6. *Ownership of Uncommitted Reserves of Natural Gas in West Texas-New Mexico, 1955–57*

	1	*2*	*3*
Producing company	*Estimated total reserves (trillions of cu. ft.)*	*Estimated uncommitted reserves throughout the country (trillions of cu. ft.)*	*Uncommitted reserves of dry gas available for sale to pipelines in West Texas-New Mexico (trillions of cu. ft.)*
Warren Petroleum and Gulf Oil Company (merged in 1956)	4.6	2.0	1.3
Humble Oil and Refining	16.0	5.3	1.1
Sunray Mid-Continent Oil Company	2.9	1.5	1.0
Phillips Petroleum Company	17.2	3.5	0.7
Texaco, Incorporated	11.5	4.8	0.5
Pan American (Standard Oil of Indiana)	9.9	4.8	0.4
El Paso Production (El Paso Natural Gas Pipeline Company)	4.4	3.5	3.5
Estimated total			11.0

Source. Column *1* has been obtained from company annual reports, unpublished compilations of particular producers, estimates of Merrill Lynch, Pierce, Fenner, and Smith and Herald's Reporting Service (Connecticut). Column *2* has been estimated by multiplying 1955 production by the average term-length of all outstanding contracts for that company in order to obtain an estimate of "committed reserves." "Uncommitted reserves" follow from subtracting this estimate from Column *1*. Column *3* is from estimates of personnel in the gas sales departments of most of the major producing companies, and particularly from estimates or recollections of personnel in gas purchasing departments of the major pipelines in West Texas and elsewhere. (Worksheets for preparation of the data can be made available upon request.)

62. To have increased prices 10 per cent would have required a decrease of *total* sales by at least 10 per cent and a decrease of sales by these four of at least 30 per cent (assuming "elastic" demand and no *increase* in sales of other firms at the higher price). This would appear to be less desirable than larger sales at a given (competitive) price.

available for production in 1955–57 was El Paso Production. This company, composed of the geological, geophysical, and reservoir engineering departments of the pipeline company, El Paso Natural Gas, had begun an enlarged program of exploration in the Permian and San Juan Basins and in Utah-Wyoming in the early 1950s, to provide reserves beyond the amounts coming from independent producers.[63] By 1955 the production departments had discovered and partially developed approximately 3.5 trillion cubic feet, to be delivered eventually into El Paso pipelines. Consequently, in the later 1950s, El Paso Production became the chief source of El Paso Pipeline's new reserves. The provisions for sale could not have been according to monopoly supply conditions, since El Paso was required to charge its pipeline a price equal only to exploration and production costs.[64]

Reserve holdings generally do not seem to have been highly concentrated in these three years. Holdings of uncommitted reserves in 1955–57, moreover, represented only shares in a *stock* of reserves that could be sold in that period. The buyer must have considered the *flow* of new reserve supplies over four or five years to have been more relevant. This flow of supply must have been derived from new contract offers to sell from the stock available in 1955–57, and also from volumes available in traps discovered after 1955. To estimate control of price, it seems necessary to indicate the extent of all new reserves available over the longer period, 1955–58.

One estimate of the flow of new reserves is the actual sale of new reserves. No producer would be expected to utilize

63. Cf. 17 *El Paso Pipeliner*, 2 (1954): "The company enters into a new phase of its development with the inauguration of a rigorous exploration program designed to find new reserves of gas."

64. At least there would not seem to have been *increased* opportunity to evade regulation by having the producing facilities "charge" pipeline facilities a monopoly price for new reserves that become legal costs of gas in the regulated "cost of service." Cf. *El Paso Natural Gas Company*, F.P.C. Docket G-4769 where El Paso argued for being allowed slightly more than 6 per cent on investment in "well mouth equipment." The Federal Power Commission allowed 8.61 per cent [but this finding was remanded by the fifth circuit court for "lack of evidence" in *El Paso v. F.P.C.* (281F2d 567)]. The important point is that utility rate principles were applied to El Paso's exploration expenses in the period considered.

control of price primarily to increase sales of other firms; rather, control of price would be expected when and where one firm has completed the majority of sales. Sales in 1956–58, as represented by a sample of new contracts, do not show one firm or few firms providing the majority of reserves.[65]

Sales over West Texas-New Mexico, as shown in Table 5:7, included 148 new contracts committing an estimated 2.36 trillion cubic feet.[66] There were 108 separate producers for the 148 contracts. The largest firm was responsible for approximately 13 per cent, and the four largest for approximately 34 per cent, of the total volume. Such levels of sales concentration probably do not indicate power to control price. It seems doubtful that the largest firm, or the four largest, could have controlled supply and price while accounting for less than 35 per cent of the relevant sales.[67]

Moreover, the four largest could not have controlled even 35 per cent of the reserves for the relevant length of time. None of them was a large seller in 1954 and two of them were not listed among the large reserve holders during 1955–57. This much turnover in membership of the dominant groups

65. The sample consists of all the contracts listed as pipeline purchases for resale interstate and signed during 1956–58.

66. The aggregate volume of reserves was obtained by adding together the estimates for new reserves in each 1956–58 contract. The contract estimate was obtained by multiplying estimated month's delivery by twelve times the number of years of contract term. On the assumption that the "estimated monthly production" listed in the contract data was at the uniform rate of production, the resulting volume is the buyer's and seller's estimated reserves. It is not the same as term times 1955 delivery in Table 5:1, and a priori may be a more accurate estimate of volume dedicated at contract signing because it is not subject to revision for errors in the original forecast (as is the 1955 production figure). That is, 1955 volume times term may not be an accurate estimate of dedicated reserves because the 1955 production may not be at the previously agreed uniform rate but at this rate revised for any changes in estimated volume (as more wells are drilled, etc). Much more can be learned in development; 1955 production may not be an indicator of each year's production *as estimated before development and signing the contract.*

67. It is probable that the "relevant market" was longer than three years and that concentration would be less in the longer period. Unfortunately data for sales over the entire 1955–58 period are not available.

in the relevant and adjoining years would have made it exceedingly difficult for a few firms to control supply and mar-

TABLE 5:7. *Concentration in the Sale of Reserves to Interstate Transporters in the Late 1950s*

West Texas-New Mexico
1956–58

Estimated total new reserves (trillions of cu. ft.)	2.3661	
Total number of contracts	148	
Total number of suppliers	108	
Percentage of total new reserves dedicated by the four largest suppliers	Pan American Petroleum Corporation	12.79
	Humble Oil and Refining Company	9.12
	Magnolia Petroleum Corporation	6.42
	Sun Oil Company	5.63
		33.96
Percentage of total new reserves dedicated by the ten largest suppliers	55.89	

Source. As in Table 5:1. Volume is estimated for each contract by multiplying "expected monthly rate of delivery," as shown in the contract, by number of months of term. "Total reserves" equals the sum of these estimates.

ket price; [68] there would always have been newly-large producers willing to increase their relative shares by violating any group output-price agreement. [69]

68. Large "turnover" in shares indicates that there might have been more sources of reserves than shown in sales concentration. Unsold, but available, reserves result in elastic supply so that the largest seller's demand curve with elasticity $\eta_{r+1} = \dfrac{Q + q(\eta_m)}{q} - \dfrac{Q}{q}\varepsilon_m$ is greater than first mentioned because ε_m (the supply elasticity) cannot be assumed to be zero.

69. Another indicator of lack of control is that "turnover" was complemented by the entry of 44 entirely new producers in 1956–58. These 44 firms, mostly small drillers or land-owners, were listed as new producers in interstate commerce after 1955 on the Federal Power Commission coding lists of sellers. Some were probably subsidiaries of old companies not cross-classified as such. But the majority of the 44 were new independent producers, and they supplied 15 per cent or more of new reserves. Each new firm was so small as to have no individual effect

Other sales of a less formal nature were made by a number of producers.[70] A new transporter, Transwestern Pipeline Company, began to buy reserves throughout the region in 1957, and managed to obtain commitments for more than 2.0 trillion cubic feet. The largest purchases were from Warren Petroleum and the Richardson and Bass Company. Warren committed 1.237 trillion cubic feet "in place"; approximately 70 to 90 per cent of this was recoverable and all of it was "inferior," since it contained 30 per cent carbon dioxide that had to be removed. Richardson and Bass committed .650 trillion cubic feet "in place" of sweet, dry gas in Winkler County, Texas, from a newly discovered field. There were a number of smaller sales in 1958–59 that represented Transwestern's original reserves as well as some informal commitments made to El Paso (to prevent sale to Transwestern). The total informal commitments probably exceeded 4.0 trillion cubic feet; they included most of the reserve holdings listed in Table 5:6 plus some additional findings, like those of Richardson and Bass. It is not likely that these sales resulted in sales concentration much different from that shown in Table 5:7.[71]

All indicators suggest a lack of producer's control of market supplies. In essence, market structures on the supply side in the late 1950s were quite similar to competitive supply conditions existing in 1950–54. There had been considerable change in demand conditions, however, by 1955. There were further changes in the extent of monopsony control of demand in 1957–58.

By 1955 the El Paso Company removed the one other major independent purchaser by means of a merger. Negotiations for the merger between El Paso and Pacific Northwest began in December 1954 with an informal agreement for coopera-

on supply (only one was in the largest ten). Each would dedicate the maximum possible, given marginal production costs. All together could supply an aggregate volume that could offset any attempt at supply control by established firms.

70. These sales have to be considered "less formal" because they had not been certified in the Federal Power Commission by 1959.

71. This can only be inferred from Table 5:6, since records of these sales were not available before Transwestern certification was complete (or before 1960–61 new contract sales data had been listed).

tion. The message of the chairman of Pacific Northwest Pipeline included mention of merger for the reason that "El Paso's California market will be protected from future competition and further it results in all parties now working together for a common end rather than fighting each other." [72] In particular, "The agreements with El Paso provide for complete cooperation in the development of the San Juan Basin field, and for the joint support of each company's (expansion) applications." [73] Cooperation in the San Juan Basin effectively meant that future purchases of new reserves were made by one company rather than two.[74] El Paso Natural Gas, with Pacific Northwest as a subsidiary, retained the control over field purchases from West Texas-New Mexico that was endangered by Pacific's entry in 1953–54.

Purchases in 1956–57, and in 1957–58, indicate the extent to which El Paso's domination of demand allowed it to control actual markets. As shown in Table 5:4, El Paso-Pacific took 78 per cent of the estimated 1.80 trillion cubic feet in 1956–57, and approximately 82 per cent of a similar amount in 1957–58. The second largest buyer in both market periods, the Permian Basin Pipeline Company, purchased only 13 per cent of reserves. The remaining pipeline buyers, either local utilities (Pioneer Natural Gas and Southern Union) or local industrial users, purchased no more than 8 per cent of total reserves as a group. There would seem to have been no more than three sources of demand in most fields in the two-year seller's market period.

At times there may have been fewer than three buyers.

72. Letter of R. C. Fish, Pacific Northwest Pipeline Corporation, Dec. 24, 1954, as reproduced in full in Federal Power Commission Staff Brief, "In the matter of El Paso Natural Gas Company, et al.," Dockets G-13018, G-13019 (April 1959), pp. 27–29.

73. Ibid., p. 28.

74. Negotiations to complete the merger took place over an extended period. El Paso officially proposed merger to Pacific Northwest in April 1955. Negotiations continued without success until the middle of 1956, while Pacific continued to stand by the "end of year" message and also continued to make independent sales of Canadian gas. Finally, letter agreement was reached on Oct. 24, 1956, to exchange Pacific Northwest for El Paso stock, and the exchange was completed Jan. 31, 1957. Cf. Federal Power Commission Staff Brief, p. 9.

During 1956–58 El Paso completed an agreement with Permian Basin Pipeline "to avoid the costly duplication of facilities" [75] and for the purpose of extensive cooperation in transporting reserves. It seems reasonable to suspect that the agreement was completed successfully only if there was a minimum of independent bidding for reserves between the two lines.[76]

TABLE 5:8. *Concentration in the Purchase of Reserves, 1956–58*

	West Texas-New Mexico 1956–57		West Texas-New Mexico 1957–58	
Estimated volume of reserves (trillions of cu. ft.)	1.8073		1.7535	
Number of contracts	119		69	
Number of buyers	5		6	
Percentage of total reserves purchased by the four largest buyers	El Paso-Pacific	77.70	El Paso-Pacific	81.99
	Permian Basin Pipeline	13.32	Permian Basin Pipeline	12.97
	Pioneer Natural Gas	6.59	Pioneer Natural Gas	4.07
	Phillips Petroleum	1.15	Southern Union Gas	0.51
		98.76		99.54
Percentage of total reserves purchased by the ten largest buyers	100		100	

Source. As in Table 5:1.

Records show Permian Basin Pipeline purchased almost all of its new reserves in one field in Yoakum County, Texas, in 1956–58. El Paso did not purchase reserves there in those years. Pioneer and Southern Union also cannot have purchased independently because they have received a major part of their reserves from El Paso. This may have left, in reality, only one source of demand for new reserves, at least during most of the first market period.

75. Prospectus 1956, p. 17, as mentioned above.
76. If Permian Basin Pipeline were to carry El Paso's Gas, then surely the El Paso reserves should not have been obtained by outbidding Permian Basin Pipeline.

However, a second large source of demand entered the area in 1957. Transwestern Pipeline sought reserves sufficient for certification of a transmission line to California. This transporter provided new demand in both the Permian and San Juan Basins and a number of informal sales were made of reserves that were sought by El Paso.[77] Such purchases prevented El Paso's control of demand in at least some fields. For example, this transporter encountered new difficulties in purchasing the reserves in the Aneth field: after making a customary offer of 14 cents per mcf for the package of more than 2 trillion cubic feet, El Paso was informed that Transwestern was willing to pay 17 cents per mcf.[78] El Paso raised its price to 20 cents per mcf; so did Transwestern, and El Paso obtained the gas "by reason of the proximity of the existing (El Paso) lines (allowing it) to take the gas sooner than Transwestern." [79] The Federal Power Commission noted that "El Paso is concerned over the fact that Transwestern is bidding for gas in the Permian Basin, because it will not be able to purchase gas at less than the price named by Transwestern.

77. The first few of these informal dedications were listed in certification proceedings in *Transwestern Pipeline, et al.,* F.P.C. Docket G-14871 (Opinion no. 328). They have been mentioned below in connection with sales concentration. It has been pointed out that the reserve estimates on known sales are probably too large (because of the amount of inferior gas) while the number of contracts is too small. As given, they increase dedications in the 1957–58 markets to 3.6815 trillion cubic feet with the following purchase shares: Transwestern, 53.390 per cent; El Paso, 39.049; Permian Basin Pipe, 6.177; Pioneer, 1.939; with the total equal to 99.555 per cent. Transwestern's share includes only contracts signed in 1957; the 1958 contracts would increase its buying market share even more (while decreasing the selling share of Warren, Richardson and Bass, most likely). Transwestern's large purchases are dominated by the Warren contract (for 1.2367 trillion cubic feet) which is actually a sale of "inferior" gas. If this is to be included "in the market," then perhaps El Paso's purchases of oil-well gas of approximately the same amount should also be included. Questions of the amount and quality of further reserve sales for the new line and for El Paso make it impossible to precisely determine relative shares. It can only be concluded that Transwestern was a significantly large new source of reserve demand.

78. Testimony of Mr. Stern of El Paso in Docket G-13018, *El Paso Natural Gas, et al.,* and F.P.C. Staff Brief (of April 1959), pp. 19–20.

79. Staff Brief, p. 21.

It will have to meet that price." [80] In other words, El Paso was not able to maintain its own price policies after the entry of this independent buyer.

It would appear that El Paso had been able to re-establish its earlier monopsony power by 1956, through the merger with Pacific Northwest, and the working agreements with the smaller pipelines. But by 1958, while El Paso may have continued to purchase more than 80 per cent of *reported* new contract reserves, the producers had the alternative of selling to Transwestern Pipeline Company. Transwestern's capacity to purchase new reserves throughout the area, and its policy of independent purchasing, should have interfered with El Paso's control of demand and price. The erosion of monopsony power resulting from the entry of Pacific Northwest may have been repaired, but another, more extensive erosion had started.

Price Behavior in 1956–58 Markets. With monopsony power in 1955–56, El Paso should have set prices to minimize its purchase costs. Prices should have been uniform and at a level equal to average production costs. There would have been no need to offer significantly higher prices for large-volume contracts than small-volume ones, given that the large volume was forthcoming at the same price. And price offers should have been the same, regardless of the location of the trap so long as buyer competition was not present to bid up prices for volumes in closer reservoirs. There might have been need for higher offer prices only on longer-term contracts, or on those without contingency clauses (in both cases because of higher producer's costs).

By the 1957–58 market period, with decreased monopsony power, El Paso might have had to offer prices higher than those that would barely cover production costs. In competition with Transwestern, higher prices might have been offered for larger volumes in closer reservoirs, at least in some cases.

To test the presence or absence of the monopsony pattern, the equation

$$P = \alpha + \beta_1 V + \beta_2 D + \beta_3 T + \beta_4 Y + \beta_5 C_1 + \beta_6 C_2 + v$$

80. Ibid., p. 21.

can again be estimated. If price formation was according to the monopsony pattern outlined, β_1, β_2, $\beta_4 = 0$; $\beta_3 \gtreqqless 0$; β_5, $\beta_6 \leqq 0$; if prices were competitive, then $\beta_1 > 0$, $\beta_2 < 0$, $\beta_3 > 0$, $\beta_4 \gtreqqless 0$, $\beta_5 \leqq 0$, $\beta_6 \leqq 0$ because of the mentioned variations in maximum offer prices. The equation for 1956–57 for a sample of 119 contracts proves to be:

$$P = 5.463 + .0225V - .2059D + .2683T + 2.3409Y$$
$$(3.192) \ (.0579) \quad (.1463) \quad (.1600) \quad (.4522)$$

$$- .1419C_1 - 0.5932C_2.$$
$$(.4539) \quad (.5724)$$

The regression equation for 1957–58, based on a sample of 69 contracts, can be compared to that of the earlier market:

$$P = 6.830 + .0234V + .0682D + .1937T - .4891Y$$
$$(3.926) \ (.0066) \quad (.1523) \quad (.1974) \quad (.5722)$$

$$+ 2.6397C_1 - 1.0922C_2.$$
$$(.9980) \quad (.9957)$$

Prices in the two market periods were largely uniform. Both distance D of the trap from the end of transmission and the term of contract T had no significant impact upon contract price.[81] The coefficient of D was negative in the first equation and positive in the second, but not statistically different from zero in either. Term-length of contract, T, was not significant in either of the two market periods (but again because there were few contracts having a term other than twenty years).[82] There was also little observed effect of Favored Nations and Renegotiation clauses on prices in these market years, since

81. Tests for significance, i.e., $\beta_i = 0$ as compared to $\beta_i \gtreqqless 0$, are shown in Table 5:9.

82. There were a number of contracts having a term of 19 years but only one of shorter term; it seems likely that the coefficients are not satisfactory estimates of the effect of term on price for other than 19–20 year contracts. The paucity of shorter-term contracts *may indicate* that El Paso was able to induce all sellers to dedicate long term by offering long-term prices higher by the increased cost of longer term. Or the lack of short-term contracts *may indicate* that producers were offered the entire (competitive) difference between *maximum* short and long-term demand prices (an amount greater than the cost increase of longer 'erm).

the coefficients of C_1 and C_2 were not different from zero in all instances but one.[83]

The contrast between the two equations is found in the behavior of price with volume and with the year of the contract. The volume of reserves, V, had some influence upon average initial price in 1957–58, and the level of prices on all

TABLE 5:9. *Summary of West Texas-New Mexico Price Behavior, 1956–58*

Given that: $P = \alpha + \beta_1 V + \beta_2 D + \beta_3 T + \beta_4 Y + \beta_5 C_1 + \beta_6 C_2 + v$
P = initial contract price, cents per mcf.
V = volume of reserves, billions of cu. ft.
D = distance of trap, in hundreds of miles
T = term-length, in years
Y = either the first-year sample (zero) or the second year (one)
C_1 = presence of Favored Nations clause (=one)
C_2 = presence of Renegotiation (=one)
R^2 = coefficient of determination
S_u = standard error of estimate, cents per mcf.
S_p = standard deviation of price, cents per mcf.

A. *1956–57*
  (*sample of 119 contracts*)

Regression equations

$P = \alpha + \beta_1 V + \beta_2 D + \beta_3 T + \beta_4 Y + \beta_5 C_1 + \beta_6 C_2 + v$

$P = 5.463 + .0225V - .2059D + .2683T + 2.3409Y - .1419C_1$
    (3.192) (.0579)   (.1463)   (.1600)   (.4522)   (.4539)

    $+ 0.5932C_2$
     (.5724)

$R^2 = .435$
$S_u = 1.82$
$S_p = 2.35$

(Competitive) Predictions	(Monopsony) Predictions	Tests of computed equations
$\beta_1 > 0$	$\beta_1 = 0$	If $b_i/S_{b_i} \gtrless 1.645$, the hypothesis $H_0 : \beta_i = 0$
$\beta_2 < 0$	$\beta_2 = 0$	can be rejected.
$\beta_3 > 0$	$\beta_3 \geqq 0$	$\beta_1 = 0$ since $t_1 =$ .3886
$\beta_5 \leqq 0$	$\beta_5 \leqq 0$	$\beta_2 = 0$ since $t_2 = -1.4081$
$\beta_6 \leqq 0$	$\beta_6 \leqq 0$	$\beta_3 > 0$ since $t_3 =$ 1.6769
		$\beta_4 > 0$ since $t_4 =$ 5.1761
		$\beta_5 = 0$ since $t_5 =$ .3126
		$\beta_6 = 0$ since $t_6 =$ 1.0363

83. The exception, the coefficient for Favored Nations in 1957–58, was positive so that the presence of a Favored Nations clause in the contract resulted in a higher average price. (This should not have followed from either competitive or monopsony behavior.)

TABLE 5:9 (cont.)

B. 1957–58
(sample of 69 contracts)

Regression equations

$$P = \alpha + \beta_1 V + \beta_2 D + \beta_3 T + \beta_4 Y + \beta_5 C_1 + \beta_6 C_2 + v$$

$$P = 6.830 + .0234V + .0682D + .1937T - .4891Y + 2.6397C_1$$
$$\quad (3.926) \quad (.0066) \quad (.1523) \quad (.1974) \quad (.5722) \quad (.9980)$$

$$\quad - 1.0922C_2$$
$$\quad (0.9957)$$

$R^2 = .411$
$S_u = 2.14$
$S_p = 2.64$

(Competitive) Predictions	(Monopsony) Predictions	Tests of computed equations
$\beta_1 > 0$	$\beta_1 = 0$	$\beta_1 > 0$ since $t_1 = \quad 3.5255$
$\beta_2 < 0$	$\beta_2 = 0$	$\beta_2 = 0$ since $t_2 = \quad .4483$
$\beta_3 > 0$	$\beta_3 \geqq 0$	$\beta_3 = 0$ since $t_3 = \quad .9807$
$\beta_5 \leqq 0$	$\beta_5 \leqq 0$	$\beta_4 = 0$ since $t_4 = - \quad .8508$
$\beta_6 \leqq 0$	$\beta_6 \leqq 0$	$\beta_5 > 0$ since $t_5 = \quad 2.6449$
		$\beta_6 = 0$ since $t_6 = -1.0969$

Source. As in Table 5:1.

contracts rose appreciably in 1957. Coefficients for volume were much higher in both markets than they had been previously, and significantly higher prices were paid for larger volumes of new reserves in the second market sample. Prices on larger dedications (at least 25 billion cubic feet) were .50 to 2.50 cents per mcf greater than on smaller contract sales. The level of prices rose by more than 2.0 cents per mcf in 1957, the largest increase in any year since 1950.

The continued uniformity of prices for gas from spatially-separated traps was in the tradition of El Paso's earlier pricing policy, and must have followed from the use of monopsony power. The presence of competitive bidders for reserves would have raised prices in the closer San Juan Basin to a significantly higher level than those in the Permian Basin some 500 miles farther away.[84] But the much higher prices

84. The saving in transmission costs from purchasing gas 100 miles closer to points of resale must have been between .50 and 1.50 cents per mcf. Prices under competition should have been that much higher in the closer field. Any such difference of .50 to 1.50 cents per mcf would have been statistically significant under the tests outlined in the discussion above.

for larger volumes and the observed increase in the price level may point to a partial change in monopsony pricing policy to meet new buyer's competition. The largest number of raised prices occurred in November and December 1957 and throughout 1958, for El Paso purchases of approximately 420 billion cubic feet under 16 uniform-sized contracts in Winkler County, Texas. The prices El Paso offered for these larger volumes were in the range of 16 cents per mcf,[85] and were offered at the time that Transwestern Pipeline sought reserves in this county.[86] These Winkler County prices had the effect of raising the average price for all larger volumes sold in the area, and of raising the level of price for the "typical" contract in the Permian Basin from 10.827 cents per mcf in 1956 to 13.051 cents per mcf in 1957.[87] At the same time, El Paso's purchases of approximately 2,000 billion cubic feet in the Aneth Field for 20 cents per mcf, indicated a breakdown of the old pricing pattern in that region. Federal Power Commission hearings included testimony to the effect that "Transwestern needed the (Aneth Field) gas as a part of its supply and had entered into a contract with one of the producers at 20 cents before El Paso bid away (this) volume of reserves."[88]

THE UTILIZATION OF MONOPSONY POWER

The 1957–58 informal price offers of Transwestern and the concurrent changes in the established pattern of El Paso

85. The "typical" contract in 1956 in the Permian Basin had a price of 10.827 cents per mcf, cf. Table 5:10 below.

86. The higher prices for the larger volumes were the first indication of a disruption in El Paso's pattern. Transwestern itself seems to have been paying consistently higher prices for all volumes. The Warren Oil dedication of 1.237 trillion cubic feet of inferior-quality gas was for 12 cents per mcf. After refining, this volume cost Transwestern 17–20 cents per mcf (cf. F.P.C. Docket G-1487, p. 8). The Richardson and Bass reserves of .6500 trillion cubic feet in Winkler County cost 21.8 cents per mcf, and a smaller Warren dedication of .0413 trillion in Lea County was for 18.0 cents per mcf.

87. The "typical" contract continued to have the specifications of volume et al., mentioned at the end of Table 5:10.

88. Cf. "El Paso Natural Gas Co." F.P.C. Dockets G-13018, G-13019, Commission Staff Brief, p. 20. The Aneth Field Contracts are not part of the 1957–58 sample because they were not submitted or "certified" at the time compilations of the data were made.

prices point to a disruption in the historical pricing pattern for new reserves. In the early 1950s, the number and relative size of buyers were such that El Paso evidently had control of price in all but a few instances. Pricing patterns in the 1950–54 markets departed from a monopsony-type pattern only twice. Those instances occurred when there were changes in the number of independent buyers: In the Permian Basin during 1952, when the Permian Basin Pipeline Company purchased a large block of reserves in Lea County; in the San Juan Basin during 1954, the year the Pacific Northwest Company completed its first and last independent campaign to purchase reserves. Otherwise, there was a monopsony-type stable price level over time and a monopsonistically uniform pattern of prices regardless of contract volume or distance to the field. In 1957–58, after El Paso's control of demand had been re-established by merger, another new buyer began to seek reserves, and bidding between two large pipelines followed. El Paso's market share of purchases decreased. Price on the "typical" contract rose by more than 2.0 cents per mcf (as shown in Table 5:10) and prices for large volumes rose even further. Increasing price variation testifies to the breakdown of the old pattern: As shown in Table 5.11, prices in the "smallest" contract conformed closely to that in the "typical" contract in the early years of sale but

TABLE 5:10. *Computed Prices for a "Typical" Contract*

	San Juan Basin		Permian Basin	
	Price, cents per mcf	Standard error of estimate	Price, cents per mcf	Standard error of estimate
1950	8.163	.676	5.835	.676
1951	8.283	.676	5.655	.676
1952	7.609	1.464	7.827	1.464
1953	8.423	1.464	8.641	1.464
1954	9.874	1.067	9.951	1.067
1956	11.509	1.819	10.827	1.819
1957	13.850	2.143	13.051	2.143
1958	12.303	2.143	12.562	2.143

Source. Price is obtained by computing P in the regression equations given that contract volume V is 112.87 billion cubic feet, that D is 3.5 hundred miles for the San Juan Basin and 7.3 hundred miles for the Permian Basin, that term T is 20 years and that clauses C_1, C_2 are present. These values for V, D, T were average values in 1951–52.

TABLE 5:11. *Computed Prices for "Typical" and "Smallest" Contracts*

| | Permian Basin | | | San Juan Basin | | |
	1	2	3	4	5	6
	Price on the "typical" contract,* cents per mcf	Price on the "smallest" contract,** cents per mcf	Price ratio of "typical" to "smallest" (R = 1/2)	Price on a "typical" contract	Price on the "smallest" contract	Price ratio of "typical" to "smallest"
1950	8.163	11.352	.730	5.835	9.730	.581
1951	8.283	11.472	.712	5.655	9.850	.592
1952	7.609	6.363	1.196	7.827	6.581	1.189
1953	8.423	7.177	1.174	8.641	7.395	1.168
1954	9.874	9.532	1.036	9.951	9.618	1.034
1956	11.509	5.033	2.287	10.827	4.251	2.547
1957	13.850	7.374	1.878	13.051	6.592	1.980
1958	12.303	6.797	1.810	12.562	7.056	1.780

* The "typical" contract is defined in Table 5:10.
** The "smallest" contract is for 1.0 billion cubic feet to be delivered in one year. There are Favored Nations and Renegotiation clauses in the contract and the reserves are found at 3.5 hundred miles in the Permian Basin, and 7.3 hundred miles in the San Juan Basin.

were relatively lower in the later years. The ratio of the "typical" price to the "smallest" price clearly indicates a substantial change in the pattern of prices at the time of new buyer entry.

Market structure and field price behavior in the 1950s indicate that there was, in general, buyer's monopoly. The El Paso Company must have had power to determine price on most contracts, and must have been responsible for the monopsony type pattern of actual prices. This transporter experienced some difficulty in the middle 1950s in maintaining its control, and faced serious bidding for reserves by Transwestern Pipeline at the end of the 1950s. Nevertheless, the El Paso Natural Gas Company generally determined price formation for sales of new reserves.

This was in contrast to the nature of markets and actual prices in the Gulf region of Texas and Louisiana.

6. *The Sale of Reserves in the Gulf Coast Region*

The greatest source of new reserves during the 1950s was the "Gulf Coast Salt Basin" located along the Gulf of Mexico in Texas and Louisiana. The fields here have been more of a collection of small traps in the same general area than traps in closely related geological formations as in the San Juan Basin. Gas has been found at almost every depth from 2,000 to 12,000 feet, but most larger volumes have been discovered at the greater depths under high pressure. Hundreds of traps have been found along the Gulf of Mexico, within 120 miles of the shoreline, and in similar formations throughout North Louisiana and Mississippi.

DEVELOPMENT OF THE GULF COAST AS A SOURCE OF RESERVES

A few large sources of dry gas reserves had been found in the Gulf region by the early 1940s. There were a series of separate supply areas for local utility gathering lines and industrial users in the Carthage and Panola fields of East Texas, in the vast East Texas field, and in the Monroe and Cotton Valley fields of Louisiana.[1] Further reserves of dry gas were being discovered in the search for oil. Some part of the new volumes were being "shut-in" because unit development costs were greater than price, and with this "worthless" hydrocarbon being accumulated in sealed-in traps, amounts became

1. Each of these fields had reserves of more than 500 billion cubic feet by 1948 for local industrial and utility sale. The Monroe field had

available sufficient to fill long-distance transmission lines to capacity for ten or more years.

The development of technology permitting large pipelines to extend over longer distances made it possible, at this time, for transporters to buy gas in the Gulf for resale in Pennsylvania and New York. By the middle 1940s a few interstate transporters had constructed supply lines into the Gulf Coast Salt Basin.

Continued exploration resulted in large new packages of "salable" reserves in the early 1950s. The established transporters expanded gathering and lateral transmission facilities into new fields to purchase these reserves. Because the reserves were found in unordered sequence, the expanding pipelines began to overlap gathering facilities. At the same time, new transporters were demanding reserves sufficient to justify their construction of pipeline facilities.

By the late 1950s the Gulf Coast Basin was the largest gas producing (and buying) region. There had been exploration for gas fields out into the Gulf of Mexico. Large "packages" of reserves became available on-shore from the development of gas in oil fields after the oil had been depleted, and from intensive drilling of step-out wells that encountered new traps.

---

been estimated to contain 6,000 billion cubic feet shortly after discovery in 1916. In the other large fields there were the following estimated dry gas reserves (by 1946):

Bethany (East Texas)—2,000 billion cu. ft.
Carthage (Louisiana)—3,000 billion cu. ft.
Cotton Valley (Louisiana)—500 billion cu. ft.
Katy (Texas Coast)—5,000 billion cu. ft.
Lake Arthur (Louisiana)—700 billion cu. ft.
Lirette (Louisiana)—550 billion cu. ft.
McAllen (Texas Coast)—600 billion cu. ft.
McFadden (Texas Coast)—900 billion cu. ft.
North Houston (Texas Coast)—600 billion cu. ft.
Rodessa (Louisiana)—2,000 billion cu. ft.
San Salvador (Texas Coast)—800 billion cu. ft.
Ville Platte (Louisiana)—550 billion cu. ft.
Willow Springs (East Texas)—900 billion cu. ft.

There were numerous smaller fields producing gas from oil wells (for undetermined uses). Cf. the American Institute of Mining and Metallurgical Engineers, *Statistics of Oil and Gas Development* (New York, 1948), and the 59 *Oil and Gas Journal* 106–08 (April 1961).

There were at least eight pipelines willing to purchase reserves in most field areas in the region after 1955. The five largest transporters had gathering lines throughout the area, and the rest had pipelines in North Louisiana leading into either South Louisiana or into the Texas Gulf area. Some could purchase elsewhere through pipelines that served as gathering lines for both local and interstate buyers.

With the growth of Gulf Coast gas fields and of the number of buyers, there was a distinct growth in competition for reserves. In the 1940s, a paucity of purchasers had resulted in buyers having had the power to control prices for reserves. The levels of concentration in sales and purchases and the patterns of actual price behavior point to there having been monopsony similar to that in West Texas-New Mexico. By the early 1950s the entry of new transporters and the extensive overlapping of older buyers had led to a partial breakdown of monopsony power. The new price behavior reflected the establishment of competition in at least part of the Gulf region. During the late 1950s there was an apparent lack of buyer's power to set price throughout the region. There were a number of buyers in each field and a large number of sellers in the region. Actual market prices were distinctly similar to those expected from pervasive competition in both buying and selling. The power to set price had withered away in the space of ten years.

This decline in price control was not continuous. The 1945–47 period was one of general monopsony in market structure and performance. The 1950–54 period was one of partially established buyer's competition, while the 1956–58 period was one of generally competitive structure and performance.

GULF COAST MARKETS, 1945–47

"A market" for natural gas reserves in the eastern Texas-Louisiana region became established with the consolidation of a number of gathering lines into the United Gas Pipeline Company. A series of small-diameter lines had transported gas from a few fields to utility companies in Texas-Louisiana cities since the 1930s. By the end of World War II these lines had been merged into United Gas and stretched along the Gulf shore from central Louisiana to Refugio County, Texas. This company was able to purchase new reserves throughout the Gulf Coast Salt Basin for intrastate users in the later 1940s, and was the purchaser in the first long-term contracts signed for large volumes in that region.

During this period two additional buyers—the Tennessee Gas Transmission Company and Transcontinental Gas Pipeline—constructed lateral lines over most of the region. Tennessee began purchasing throughout the Gulf Coast in Texas in 1945 for resale in Tennessee, Kentucky, Ohio, and New York. In 1948–49 it contracted for reserves in the larger fields in Refugio and Matagorda counties, in the counties farther south that bordered on Mexico,[2] and in the Panola field of East Texas-Northwest Louisiana. By the end of 1949 it operated more than 3,000 miles of pipeline and was constructing or seeking certification for an additional 2,600 miles of equipment. The Transcontinental Gas Pipeline Company traversed an equally broad area along the Gulf by 1949–50. "Transco" sought reserves throughout South Louisiana and the Texas Gulf for transmission to locations east of Tennessee's resale customers. Before certification, it sought more than two trillion cubic feet within 50 miles of Tennessee's coast lines.

These three large pipelines were the leading sources of demand for the accumulated Gulf reserves. There were other purchasers, but they did not seek reserves over any extensive supply area. Among them the Texas Eastern Transmission Corporation was the largest after having leased the government-constructed "Big Inch" and "Little Inch" crude oil transmission lines in 1947. Texas Eastern demanded as large reserves as Tennessee or Transcontinental, but only in that part of the Gulf Coast region northwest of Houston where the "Inch" lines were located.[3] In addition, there were a dozen smaller local lines purchasing gas in the 1940s for oil-refinery boiler fuel or buying reserves on longer term for local dis-

2. The fields farthest south were in the Rio Grande Basin that adjoins the Gulf Coast Salt Basin.

3. From the period beginning with the leasing of the "inch" lines in 1947 to the expansion of these lines in 1951, Texas Eastern remained confined to the lines' old crude oil supply area.

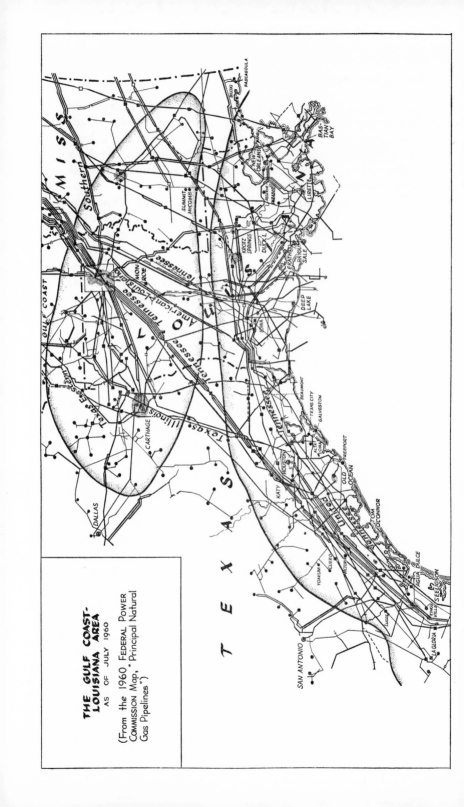

THE GULF COAST-
LOUISIANA AREA
AS OF JULY 1960

(From the 1960 Federal Power
Commission Map, "Principal Natural
Gas Pipelines")

tribution in the smaller cities. These transporters were only small sources of demand for new reserves (since such home and boiler fuel use was quite limited), and they operated only over narrow supply regions.

The three large transmission companies purchased the greatest part of new reserves in the 1940s. Of the long-term contracts for dry gas reserves signed in the Texas Gulf between 1940 and 1949, some 242 were still in force in 1955.[4] The Tennessee Gas Transmission Company, United Gas Pipeline, and Transcontinental together signed 88 of the 91 contracts in the area within 150 miles of Houston. These same three transporters were responsible for 78 of the 100 contracts for gas located between Houston and the Mexican border (with United Gas Pipeline signing only one of the 78, however). Tennessee and Transcontinental were the purchasers in 37 of 51 contracts for reserves in fields between the Houston area and the Louisiana border. United Gas Pipeline reputedly accounted for 20 per cent and Tennessee and Texas Eastern together for 70 per cent of the contracts in the East Texas-North Louisiana Panola field.[5]

Power to Control Price, 1945–47. Tennessee, United, and Transcontinental not only signed most of the contracts but they seem to have had a collective share of *total demand* sufficient to allow control of new contract prices. In order to have had effective control, the three lines together would have had to provide the only extensive source of demand in undeveloped fields during any two to three-year (seller's market) period. Their share of the actual purchases indicate they were capable of such control.

In field markets during 1945–46 and 1946–47 these three transporters purchased shares as shown in Table 6:1. The United Gas Pipeline Company purchased 75 per cent of estimated reserves in all contracts listed for the Gulf region

4. These are the contracts listed for gas well gas in exhibit 2-LC of F.P.C. Docket G-9277 from Federal Power Commission form 301, for January 1940–December 1949.

5. According to the estimates of these and other buyers in the field (in private interviews) in 1958.

TABLE 6:1. *Concentration in the Purchase of Reserves, Texas-Louisiana Gulf Coast, 1945–47*

	1945–46 market period		*1946–47 market period*	
Estimated volume of reserves (trillions of cu. ft.)	1.8588		2.4251	
Number of contracts	75		130	
Number of buyers	6		9	
Percentage of reserves purchased by the four largest buyers	United Gas Pipeline	75.22	United Gas Pipeline	35.09
	Tennessee Gas Transmission	11.94	Transcontinental Gas Pipeline	23.19
	Texas Gas Transmission	5.23	Tennessee Gas Transmission	18.88
	La Gloria Corporation	4.54	Texas Eastern Transmission	16.16
		96.93		93.32
Percentage purchased by the ten largest buyers	100		100	

Source. All 1945–47 contracts submitted to the Federal Power Commission in 1954 as purchases for resale in interstate commerce. Cf. exhibit 2-LC, *Champlin Oil and Refining et al.*, F.P.C. Docket G-9277.

152

during 1945–46, with the remainder divided between Tennessee Gas, Texas Gas Transmission,[6] and three local industrial purchasers. United Gas Pipeline, Transcontinental Gas Pipeline, and Tennessee Gas Transmission together purchased 75 per cent of the reserves in 1946–47. Each took roughly comparable amounts and Texas Eastern Transmission, in its restricted area, was the only other large buyer. In *most* Gulf fields, producers had no customers alternative to the three big pipelines.

Nor did producers in these fields seem to have had any *monopoly* power by which to control supply and set new contract prices. There were a large number of independent sources of newly discovered or shut-in reserves in the Gulf Coast and North Louisiana basins over three-year periods: the four largest sellers contributed only 40.4 per cent of all new contract sales of reserves in the region for 1945–47, and the ten largest firms accounted for only 61.3 per cent of the estimated total volume. There were at least 100 active suppliers and an unknown number of potential suppliers with shut-in reserves.[7] To have had control of contract prices, the largest producer should have had a larger portion of sales than 12 per cent.[8] The four largest producers would have encountered conditions unsuitable for controlling price through

6. Texas Gas Transmission purchased only two large volumes of reserves in the Monroe Field in North Louisiana and had no gathering lines elsewhere at that time.

7. The "potential" suppliers had volumes that were "shut-in" for the lack of any previous market or else owned reserves in one trap and shut them in in expectation of higher future prices. The first would have had to sell within two years of that time at which price was greater than average cost. The second could sell over any longer time period. Both groups would sell reserves in the event of a ("monopoly") increase in price levels, perhaps to an extent sufficient to prevent price-setting.

8. The elasticity of demand η_r for reserves of the largest seller =
$$\frac{Q+q}{q}\,\eta_m - \frac{Q}{q}\,\varepsilon_{r-1} = \frac{1.00}{.12}\,(1.0) + 0 = 8.33 \text{ at the minimum, where } Q$$
indicates reserves of other than the large producer, q is reserves of the large producer, ε_{r-1} is elasticity of supply of reserves from other firms. This is assuming that market share $q = 12$ per cent, market demand elasticity (η_m) is 1.0, and supply elasticity of the other sources is zero. Such firm price elasticity makes for conditions of demand little different from those under perfect competition.

collusion. They were located in four separate field areas so that concerted effort to control collective sales from partially proved traps would have been difficult.[9] Their share of new reserves (as indicated by shares of sales) was not extensive; to have restricted total sales by an appreciable amount would have required severe group restriction.[10]

TABLE 6:2. *Concentration in the Sale of Reserves throughout the Gulf Coast-Louisiana Region, 1945–47*

		1945–47 market supply period
Estimated total new reserves (trillion of cu. ft.)		3.5027
Total number of contracts		163
Total number of suppliers		100
Percentage of total new reserves dedicated by the four largest suppliers	Stanolind Oil and Gas	12.01
	Arkansas Fuel Oil	10.84
	Skelly Oil Company	9.51
	Sun Oil Company	8.03
		40.39
Percentage of total new reserves dedicated by the ten largest suppliers		61.29

Source. As in Table 5:1

With low concentration in sales but high concentration in purchases, the three largest transporters must have had *collective* opportunity to set price. There is only the question whether they did cooperate to the extent necessary for effective control of demand in each field in the region. If they did not, but rather sought reserves by independent bidding, field prices should have reached the competitive level. No one of the lines could have controlled price alone, because the capacity for increased purchases of the other two would have been sufficient to absorb market supply. If the three lines did cooperate, however, by following a common purchase pattern, they could have controlled total demand and set the general level of prices in the monopsony manner.

It is not possible to state that the three lines cooperated in this manner in the 1945–47 period. At a later time they did

9. None of the large four had reserves in the same field, except in the Carthage field of East Texas.

10. Their collective demand curve would have had *minimum* elasticity of $\{1.00/.40\ (1.0) + 0\} = 2.50$.

enter into agreements for resale and transfer of gas (United became one of Tennessee's major sources of reserves, and Transcontinental transported 26 billion cubic feet per day for Tennessee). They might have had "cordial relations" earlier but this would not prove that they had agreed earlier to a common Gulf purchasing policy. There is no direct proof of collusion; it can only be hypothesized.[11]

Price Behavior, 1945–47. If the three buyers acted to purchase new reserves in concert, prices should have followed the monopsony pattern. There should have been little variation of prices between traps because producers' rents would thus be avoided, and because uniform prices for different traps of reserves would have been a simple pattern for the three to adopt. But if the group did not act together to set price, then market behavior should have been quite different. There should have been "more intense" bidding and higher prices for reserves in traps closer to points of resale. There should have been a competitive pattern of higher prices on larger volume contracts, on contracts with longer production periods, and on contracts without Favored Nations and/or Renegotiation clauses.

Prices, to have been competitive in the markets during 1945–46 and 1946–47, should have followed the pattern $P = \alpha + \beta_1 V + \beta_2 D + \beta_3 T + \beta_4 Y + \beta_5 C_1 + \beta_6 C_2 + v$. Price in any one contract should have been higher for longer production periods and for larger volumes of reserves (for larger values of T and V). Contract price should have been lower for reserves in more distant fields (with larger values of D) and lower for agreements with Favored Nations and Renegotiation clauses (with C_1, $C_2 = 1$). That is, a competitive pricing pattern should provide evidence that $\beta_1 > 0$, $\beta_2 < 0$, $\beta_3 > 0$, $\beta_5 < 0$, $\beta_6 < 0$. In contrast, a monopsony pricing pattern would not have been dependent upon variations in "max-

11. It should be remembered that *two* pipelines were enough to cause a breakdown of the monopsony pattern in West Texas-New Mexico. It should also be remembered that monopsony was established by agreement (and, finally, merger) between the two lines in 1954–55. Competition, in West Texas, between two buyers occurred upon *entry* of one of them; it may well have been that competition did not prevail between three *established* buyers in the Gulf Coast.

imum offer prices." If prices were being set by one buyer, they should not have varied significantly with volume V or distance D (β_1, $\beta_2 = 0$). Generally, no rents of location nor rents from advantageous reserve size should have been paid to the producer.[12] Monopsony prices might have been somewhat higher on contracts with longer term-length and on contracts without contingency clauses, because of higher production costs ($\beta_3 \geqq 0$, β_5, $\beta_6 \leqq 0$). Such cost differences should have been the only source of monopsony price variation.[13]

Calculations of the equation $\{P = a + b_1V + b_2D + b_3T + b_4Y + b_5C_1 + b_6C_2 + U\}$ for two samples of contracts (1945–46 and 1946–47) are shown in Table 6:3. For 1945–46, new contract initial prices did not vary in accordance with either contract volume, trap distance, or term-length of production. The coefficients for Volume V, distance D, and term T (b_1, b_2, and b_3) were not different from zero (i.e., the hypotheses $\beta_1 = 0$, $\beta_2 = 0$, $\beta_3 = 0$ could not be disproved). The regression equation indicates the difference between the price of the average volume consigned (24.78 billion cubic feet) and the largest volume (375.93 billion cubic feet) to have been only .702 cents per mcf. Prices in various traps throughout the supply area were generally the same, and longer-term contracts had prices comparable to those with term-lengths of 1–15 years.[14]

12. The difference in the amount of gas recovered from the trap because of price differences would not have been large, given that the marginal production costs have been considered to be close to zero for 50 per cent recovery, but infinite for some amount in the range of 80–90 per cent recovery. The discussion in Chapter 2 of the marginal cost curve is pertinent to outlining hypothesized monopsony pricing: sharply increasing marginal costs at 80–90 per cent recovery result in dedication of *this portion,* at *either* the low monopsony price *or* the higher competitive price.

13. Prices under monopsony should not have increased over time but they *might* have been expected to do so under competition (because of demand increases). Under monopsony, $\beta_4 = 0$, as compared to $\beta_4 \geqq 0$ under competition.

14. The sample contained at least 25 short-term contracts, mostly of 10–15 years duration, so that coefficient b_3 may be more indicative of price changes with shorter term than in the West Texas samples.

There was very little variation in the general pattern of prices. The level of average price increased in 1946 by only .11 cents per mcf. The presence of both contingency clauses in a contract had a net (positive) effect of more than one cent on contract price.[15] The proportion of the variation in prices explained by all the mentioned factors was only 12.1 per cent (given that the coefficient of determination $R^2 = .121$). This was a small proportion of a small total price variation: the standard deviation of price was .916 cents per mcf.

The pattern of price in the regression equation is quite similar to that expected from the utilization of monopsony power. The lack of variation of price with volume V, distance D of the trap, and the term T of the contract conform to the uniform price that the monopoly buyer would offer in order to avoid paying rents to producers. The uniformity of price over time is consistent with the use of monopsony power. The remarkable uniformity of all prices suggests the presence of "market discipline" for price-setting by one or few firms on the buying side of the contracts.

The observed pricing pattern for 1946–47 differed somewhat from that of 1945–46. Price in the 1946–47 regression equation did not vary with the term-length of production, or with the presence of Favored Nations, and/or Renegotiation clauses. Price did vary with contract volume and trap distance, however. Changes in "contract price" according to values of V and D were small (in terms of cents per mcf) but were significantly different from zero. The estimated difference between the price for the largest volume of reserves in the 1946–47 market (310.86 billion cubic feet) and the average volume (18.66 billion cubic feet) was 1.87 cents per mcf, an amount much smaller than the difference in transportation costs for the two.[16] Price for a volume of new reserves "at the end of transmission" [17] was .22 cents per mcf higher than

15. The difference was not negative, as expected from competition, but *was* close to zero, as expected from monopsony.

16. Cf. the tables in Chapter 3.

17. The "end of transmission" was arbitrarily chosen to be the area in Kentucky where the great majority of lines to the East intersect. From here distances are the same for the majority of the lines, so that

price for that volume in a field 100 miles farther away. This difference was approximately one-third the additional transportation costs from the more distant location. Also, prices on 1947 contracts were on the average .99 cents per mcf greater than on 1946 contracts—a statistically significant increase.

TABLE 6:3. *Summary of Gulf Coast-Louisiana Price Behavior, 1945–47*

Given that: $P = \alpha + \beta_1 V + \beta_2 D + \beta_3 T + \beta_4 Y + \beta_5 C_1 + \beta_6 C_2 + v$

P = initial contract price, cents per mcf.
V = volume of reserves, billions cu. ft.
D = distance of trap, in hundreds of miles
T = term-length, in years
Y = either the first-year sample (zero) or the second year (one)
C_1 = presence of Favored Nations clause (= one)
C_2 = presence of Renegotiation (= one)
R^2 = coefficient of determination
S_u = standard error of estimate, cents per mcf.
S_p = standard deviation of price, cents per mcf.

A. *1945–46*
   (*sample of 75 contracts*)

Regression equations

$P = \alpha + \beta_1 V + \beta_2 D + \beta_3 T + B_4 Y + B_5 C_1 + B_6 C_2 + v$

$P = 4.861 + .0020V - .1465D - .0030T - .1127Y + 1.9569C_1$
$\quad\;\;(.593)\;\;(.0018)\;\;(.0908)\;\;(.0091)\;\;(.2155)\;\;(1.0609)$

$\quad - .9417C_2$
$\quad\;\;\,(.9176)$

$R^2 = .121$
$S_u = .896$
$S_p = .916$

(Competitive) Predictions	(Monopsony) Predictions	Tests of computed equations
$\beta_1 > 0$	$\beta_1 = 0$	If $t = b_i/S_{b_i} > \lvert 1.645 \rvert$, the hypothesis
$\beta_2 < 0$	$\beta_2 = 0$	$H_o : \beta_i = 0$ is rejected and the alternative
$\beta_3 > 0$	$\beta_3 \gtrless 0$	hypothesis $\beta_i \gtrless 0$ is accepted.
$\beta_5 \leqq 0$	$\beta_5 \leqq 0$	$\beta_1 = 0$ since $t_1 = \quad 1.0839$
$\beta_6 \leqq 0$	$\beta_6 \leqq 0$	$\beta_2 = 0$ since $t_2 = -1.6131$
		$\beta_3 = 0$ since $t_3 = - \;.3263$
		$\beta_4 = 0$ since $t_4 = - \;.5163$
		$\beta_5 > 0$ since $t_5 = \quad 1.8446$
		$\beta_6 = 0$ since $t_6 = -1.0263$

variations in (competitive) offer prices for any marginal purchaser would likely be in accord with mileage from this location.

TABLE 6:3 (cont.)

B. 1946–47
  (Sample of 130 contracts)

Regression equations

$$P = \alpha + \beta_1 V + \beta_2 D + \beta_3 T + \beta_4 Y + \beta_5 C_1 + \beta_6 C_2 + v$$

$$P = 5.321 + .0064V - .2187D - .0051T + .9946Y + .2951C_1 + .1089C_2$$
$$\quad\;\; (.392)\;\; (.0019)\;\; (.0405)\;\; (.0074)\;\; (.1573)\;\; (.3865)\;\; (.4133)$$

$R^2 = .368$
$S_u = .804$
$S_p = .988$

(Competitive) Predictions	(Monopsony) Predictions	Tests of computed equations
$\beta_1 > 0$	$\beta_1 = 0$	$\beta_1 > 0$ since $t_1 = \;\;\;3.3221$
$\beta_2 < 0$	$\beta_2 = 0$	$\beta_2 < 0$ since $t_2 = -5.3952$
$\beta_3 > 0$	$\beta_3 \geqq 0$	$\beta_3 = 0$ since $t_3 = -\;\;.6753$
$\beta_5 \leqq 0$	$\beta_5 \leqq 0$	$\beta_4 > 0$ since $t_4 = \;\;\;6.3216$
$\beta_6 \leqq 0$	$\beta_6 \leqq 0$	$\beta_5 = 0$ since $t_5 = \;\;\;.7634$
		$\beta_6 = 0$ since $t_6 = \;\;\;.2634$

C. 1946–47

(sample of 121 contracts, excluding Texas Eastern Transmission)

Regression equations

$$P = \alpha + \beta_1 V + \beta_2 D + \beta_3 T + \beta_4 Y + \beta_5 C_1 + \beta_6 C_2 + v$$

$$P = 4.204 + .0035V - .0855D + .0022T + .6353Y + .3734C_1$$
$$\quad\;\; (0.356)\;\; (.0018)\;\; (.0378)\;\; (.0063)\;\; (.1385)\;\; (.3239)$$

$$- .3076C_2$$
$$\;\;(.3499)$$

$R^2 = .201$
$S_u = .669$
$S_p = .729$

(Competitive) Predictions	(Monopsony) Predictions	Tests of computed equations
$\beta_1 > 0$	$\beta_1 = 0$	$\beta_1 > 0$ since $t_1 = \;\;\;2.0282$
$\beta_2 < 0$	$\beta_2 = 0$	$\beta_2 < 0$ since $t_1 = -2.2647$
$\beta_3 > 0$	$\beta_3 \geqq 0$	$\beta_3 = 0$ since $t_3 = \;\;\;.3519$
$\beta_5 \leqq 0$	$\beta_5 \leqq 0$	$\beta_4 > 0$ since $t_4 = \;\;\;4.5869$
$\beta_6 \leqq 0$	$\beta_6 \leqq 0$	$\beta_5 = 0$ since $t_5 = \;\;\;1.1520$
		$\beta_6 = 0$ since $t_6 = \;\;\;0.0879$

Source. As in Table 5:1: all contracts submitted to the Federal Power Commission as being sales to interstate pipelines and included in exhibit 2-LC *Champlin Oil and Refining et al.*, Docket G-9277.

This variation of price with volume and distance, together with the increase in the price level in 1947, was a departure from earlier price uniformity.[18] Most of it can be attributed to the purchase of reserves in 1947 by the Texas Eastern Transmission Company in its narrow supply area. Texas Eastern signed nine contracts for the nine highest prices in the Gulf Coast. Compared to 1946 prices of 4.097 cents per mcf (as computed from the earlier regression equation for contracts with comparable volume, distance, term, etc.) the new Texas Eastern contracts had prices of 6.58 cents per mcf and 7.14 cents per mcf. These contracts were for larger volumes, at smaller distances, and could have been the cause of the rising average price for larger-volume, shorter-distance contracts. The extent of this effect can be indicated by the regression equation for all *other* purchases. This "residual" sample of 121 contracts exhibits a pricing pattern of greater uniformity (cf., the last rows of Table 6:3). Other contracts than Texas Eastern's had slightly higher prices for larger volumes and for volumes sold from closer traps. The size of the differences was, however, similar to that observed in the 1945–46 market sample.[19] Nor did prices vary with term-length of the contract. The regression equation explained only 20.1 per cent of all price variation (while the standard deviation of prices was limited to .729 cents per mcf).

Texas Eastern's offers were the first purchases of a new company. They were made in a supply area limited to a few counties in the upper Texas Gulf region, and prices offered did not "spread" to other companies. The pricing pattern of all contracts other than Texas Eastern's was similar to the 1945–46 pattern, with only slightly higher average price and slightly higher prices for larger volumes. The impression is that there was continued similarity between calculated regression patterns and the monopsony predictions. The lack of a systematic correspondence between price differences and differences in theoretical "maximum offer" prices point to price having been set by the buyers.[20]

18. It was extensive enough for the regression equation "to explain" approximately 36.8 per cent of the variation in price (with $R^2 = .368$).

19. Variation in all prices was so slight, however, that the coefficients b_1, b_2 for volume and distance were both statistically different from zero.

20. That is, the pattern in 1946–47 contracts can *best* be described by the monopsony model for pricing outlined in Chapter 4.

GULF COAST MARKETS, 1950–54

During 1950–54 there were striking changes in the character of markets. The most important change was in the number of sources of demand in producer's field markets: a number of new transporters entered the Gulf region and the more independent established transporters expanded their supply areas. The coastal portion of the Gulf Salt Basin became the source of reserves for a number of buyers large enough to cause intensive (competitive) bidding there for new volumes of gas. Elsewhere in the region, particularly in North Louisiana, established buyers maintained collective control of demand. As a result, the pricing pattern on new contracts in the coastal region was different from that on new contracts in the inland fringes.

Conditions of Demand in the Texas Gulf Region. The coastal region of Texas was the primary supply area for Tennessee Gas Transmission and for Transcontinental Gas Pipeline Companies. The two continued expansion of reserve holdings and replacement of produced reserves by signing new contracts for gas within 100 miles of the Gulf of Mexico. The third established transporter, the United Gas Pipeline, continued to purchase quite large volumes in the same area to be transported through a major new transmission line from Corpus Christi to Port Arthur. United provided a large and immediate source of demand.

These three transporters were overlapped by three further sources of demand. The largest of the other sources, the Texas Eastern Transmission Company, was prepared in 1950–51 to purchase more new reserves than previously. Texas Eastern extended its supply area to fields southwest of Houston through the subsidiary "Wilcox Trend Gathering Company." Another, and newer, purchaser was the Trunkline Gas Company. During 1949–50 Trunkline sought reserves for a proposed new pipeline along the Texas Gulf Coast from the Mexican border through Louisiana (that was to connect to the main lines of Panhandle Eastern Pipeline Company from

Oklahoma). In 1950 Trunkline completed construction of the line after contracting for 3.2 trillion cubic feet of reserves, and it continued to expand until some 4.3 trillion cubic feet had been purchased. A third new transporter, the Texas-Illinois Natural Gas Pipeline Company, concentrated purchases of approximately 2.2 trillion cubic feet in the Old Ocean and La Gloria fields on the Texas Gulf and sought reserves in the regions of the Clayton, Hagist Ranch, and Chocolate Bayou fields spaced along the length of the Gulf Coast in Texas.[21]

Where there had previously been three buyers in close contact with all Texas Gulf sellers and with each other, there now were six. Such an increase in the number of buyers should have changed demand in the field markets sufficiently to prevent collective (monopsony) control of price. These new, large buyers should be sufficient to destroy the previously observed "cooperation" between three established pipelines.

Entry of Pipelines into South Louisiana. Buyers in South Louisiana in 1950–55 were also operating in changed markets. In the years preceding 1950, the United Gas Pipeline Company was sole purchaser in the Mississippi delta region where reserves for sale were sparse. United obtained some volumes for resale to local Louisiana utilities and refineries, but it was not until the late 1940s that substantial volumes were found in Cameron and Plaquemines Parishes. Further large gas discoveries followed,[22] and a number of transporters already in Texas built lateral transmission lines into South Louisiana. Transcontinental Gas Pipeline and Tennessee Gas Transmission expanded down into the Louisiana Gulf. Transcontinental followed the policy of purchasing a greater part of its new reserves in South Louisiana while

21. Texas-Illinois' supply area was limited to the Texas Coast since the main transmission line was constructed through central Arkansas rather than through Louisiana.

22. The Houma field (1945), the Lake Sand and Mud Lake (1949) along with Turtle Bayou (1949) provided more than 2.0 trillion cubic feet of uncommitted reserves by the early 1950s. The off-shore exploration began at that time, as well, and promised even greater additions.

purchasing minor additions in the Texas Gulf region.[23] Tennessee sought reserves in this region for new lateral transmission facilities close to the Louisiana-Texas border. Both of these buyers completely overlapped United's former region of purchases.

During 1950–54, four more transporters entered the Louisiana delta—Southern Natural Gas Company, Texas Eastern Transmission Company, United Fuel Gas Company, and the American Natural Gas Company. The Southern Natural Gas Company built new lateral lines into South Louisiana from North Louisiana and Mississippi. This company had operated transmission lines from the North Louisiana Monroe field to Georgia since the early 1940s but did not begin a program of constructing new laterals into the southern sector until 1952. In order to obtain sufficient volumes for the new line, Southern Natural accumulated reserves from the end of the Mississippi River delta ("Breton Island Field") to field areas bordering on Texas ("Duck Lake Field"). This company had previously purchased reserves from United Gas Pipeline and Tennessee Gas Transmission and continued to receive delivery of some 15 per cent of its yearly "throughput" from United.

Texas Eastern and United Fuel Gas built lines into South Louisiana as an alternative to purchasing more reserves from gathering pipelines already there. In 1948–49, Texas Eastern had constructed a new main line from Kosciusko, Mississippi, to western Pennsylvania to transport reserves purchased in Mississippi from United Gas Pipeline. It subsequently proposed reconverting the "inch" lines to petroleum carriers and expanding the Kosciusko line to carry the gas. To make this possible, the company built a link from Kosciusko to its older gas gathering lines in the Texas Gulf region. This linking transmission lateral passed directly through South Louisiana fields, "making accessible to the company large reserves pre-

23. This policy derived from the large costs of "triggering" Favored Nations clauses on old Gulf Coast contracts while paying comparable prices. Cf. T. P. Wallser, "Buying Gas for Pipelines," *Gas Age* (Dec. 15, 1954), p. 394, for discussion of such by a Transcontinental official.

viously outside the range of its gas purchasing activities," [24] and resulting in Texas Eastern signing contracts for reserves there during and after 1953. At the same time, the United Fuel Gas Company was in the process of bidding for reserves in South Louisiana, as an alternative to buying more from Tennessee Gas Transmission and the other large gatherers. (United Fuel, a subsidiary of the Columbia Gas System serving western Pennsylvania, West Virginia, and Ohio, had followed a policy of purchasing at wholesale from the large interstate transporters.) The company purchased more than three trillion cubic feet to be delivered by a new pipeline (Gulf Interstate Pipeline Company) and thus provided a wholly new source of demand in South Louisiana.[25]

The American Natural Gas Company built an entirely new line into the Gulf Coast Basin. It had long served the Great Lakes area with gas delivered from the Texas Panhandle region by the subsidiary Michigan-Wisconsin Pipeline Company. To supplement these deliveries, American started to purchase reserves in South-central Louisiana in 1951 and built a new transmission pipeline (the "American Louisiana Pipeline Company") in 1953. This company signed contracts for more than two trillion cubic feet in field areas in Cameron-Acadia Parishes to the west of Baton Rouge.

As a result of all this entry, each South Louisiana field contained a number of potential buyers. Where there had been one interstate pipeline in the late 1940s, there were seven transporters with overlapping supply areas by 1955. This entry of new buyers, and the presence of so many buyers, could not help but have disrupted any control over demand that previously existed.

Entry of Pipelines into North Louisiana. The number of new pipeline buyers was far larger in the Texas Gulf and South Louisiana areas than in North Louisiana and adjoining East Texas. North Louisiana fields were spaced so widely that established pipeline supply areas did not overlap very much, and available new reserves were not copious enough to induce

24. As noted in a recapitulation, Texas Eastern Transmission Company, *Annual Report* (1956), p. 9.
25. Eventually, United Fuel absorbed Gulf Interstate.

new buyers. Without the entry observed elsewhere, and with only a small number of established buyers, there was more opportunity for monopsony control of demand and price in these fields.

The North Louisiana area had become a source for large volumes of gas reserves in the 1940s with the development of the Carthage, Monroe, and Panola fields. Because of these reserves, both United Gas Pipeline and Southern Natural Gas installed gathering systems in some portion of the northern section of the state. Southern's main line was constructed only to the eastern end of the Monroe field for purchases there and for repurchases from United Gas of gas gathered elsewhere. United purchased reserves throughout the entire North Louisiana region.

One further line, the Arkansas-Louisiana Gas Company, operated an extensive network of small gathering lines into every field for gas for limited home resale in Arkansas. Arkansas-Louisiana could bid for small volumes of reserves throughout North Louisiana, but probably could not purchase a large share of total reserves. Two transporters "passing through" the region, Texas Eastern and Texas Gas Transmission, confined themselves to purchasing on the western fringes of the area.[26]

The impression is that United Gas Pipeline was the only important source of demand in most fields. The Arkansas-Louisiana company purchased in the same fields as United, but with limited demand. Southern Natural Gas, Texas Eastern, and Texas Gas all overlapped only on the edges of United's supply area. The region was more or less the exclusive domain of United Gas in the beginning 1950s, and this company probably had the power to set price and sales volumes.[27]

In summary, there was obviously some dissimilarity in three

26. These two lines operated in close cooperation: Texas Gas received 86 per cent of its transported volumes of gas from Texas Eastern.

27. Whether this power was retained is open to investigation. The closeness of American Louisiana's new line in 1953–54 and large expansion programs of Tennessee Gas Transmission in these same years provided new sources of demand for reserves. Perhaps these new lines could have been sources of (competitive) offer prices for new gas.

parts of the Gulf region with respect to demand conditions in the early 1950s. A number of interstate buyers were clustered in one common supply area the length of the Texas Gulf Coast. A number of transporters had entered the South Louisiana delta region as well. But in North Louisiana fields there were few, and separated, sources of demand for new reserves. There were also separated supply areas containing no more than one or two buyers on the inland edges of the Gulf Coast Basin in Texas. These conditions point to a lack of buyer's power to control price in the Gulf Coast and in South Louisiana. But large buyers elsewhere probably possessed continuing monopsony power, by virtue of their small numbers.

Concentration in Purchases in the Relevant Producer's Markets. Whether the inland buyers actually proved able to exercise their potential control over prices depended upon further considerations—the relative capacity of each to have purchased large volumes of reserves at various locations and the ability of all buyers to have agreed to a common purchase policy. If there were a half dozen pipelines in each field but only one had the transmission capacity for most of the new reserves, then that one would have had some power to set price. If there were a number of lines that agreed on a common price, there should have been agreement on shares of new reserves (in order to prevent "cheating" at the monopsony price). There should have been an observable pattern of stable purchase shares, in either case, during 1950–54.[28]

28. The producing fields in the Gulf Coast Salt Basin by (geological) happenstance were concentrated within 50 miles of the Gulf of Mexico but were scattered in the inland areas. Buyers in the Texas portion of this region had gathering lines that overlapped along the coast. The coastal "overlap" appears to have been complete enough in the 1950–54 period to have resulted in the same number of sources of demand in each of the coast fields. Each had such similar demand conditions that buyer's shares of purchases in the whole Texas Gulf should have been the same as in each field. (That is, if the buyer were in the region he would have to be considered a source of demand in *each* field. Any field market for any producer would have had demand conditions the same as for *all* Gulf fields.) In fields located inland, concentration in purchases in each trap should have been greater than indicated by area figures because not all buyers were effective sources of demand in all the (wide-spaced) fields there.

TABLE 6:4. *Concentration in the Purchase of Reserves in the Texas Gulf Coast, 1950–54*

	1950–51	1951–52	1952–53	1953–54
Estimated volume of reserves (trillions of cu. ft.)	6.806	4.912	5.859	2.848
Number of contracts	101	151	285	261
Number of buyers	10	12	16	16
Percentage of total reserves purchased by the four largest buyers	Tennessee Gas Transmission Company 38.86 Texas-Illinois Natural Gas Pipeline 33.03 United Gas Pipeline Company 20.81 Transcontinental Gas Pipeline Company 4.39 97.09	Tennessee Gas Transmission Company 53.99 Texas-Illinois Natural Gas Pipeline 18.54 United Gas Pipeline Company 13.71 Texas Eastern Transmission Company 10.52 96.76	Tennessee Gas Transmission Company 52.53 Texas Eastern Transmission Company 17.88 Texas Illinois Natural Gas Pipeline 12.81 United Gas Pipeline Company 6.09 99.22	Tennessee Gas Transmission Company 43.29 Texas Eastern Transmission 20.72 United Gas Pipeline Company 9.78 Texas-Illinois Natural Gas Pipeline 8.96 82.75
Percentage of reserves purchased by the ten largest buyers	100	99.09	99.22	99.23

Source. As in Table 5:1.

167

Concentration in actual purchases was extensive in 1950–54 markets throughout the Texas Gulf. As indicated in Table 6:4, there were seldom more than ten buyers and the four largest buyers purchased all except a very minor share of the total reserves. Producers in each of the various fields probably could not have sold to more than four buyers in 1950–54; even then, it does not seem likely that the largest purchasers could have set prices. They may have had sufficient *collective* control of demand to lower price below the competitive level (similar to P_1 in Figure 4:9) but they do not seem to have purchased according to the prearranged pattern of stable share to be associated with collective control.

The largest purchaser, Tennessee Gas Transmission Company, was responsible for from 38 to 54 per cent of the contracted volumes of reserves in the various market periods. Two of the other large lines, Texas-Illinois Natural Gas Pipeline and the Texas Eastern Transmission Company, show significant changes in market purchase shares. Texas-Illinois' share of total purchases declined systematically from a high of 20 per cent (achieved upon entry) while Texas Eastern's share doubled between 1951–52 and 1952–54 in the process of accumulating reserves for its new pipeline. Other lines were expanding their purchases and, consequently, decreasing the share of the largest four: the new Trunkline Gas Company, for one, increased its share from zero in 1950–52 to 5.17 per cent in 1953–54. This "turnover" in purchase concentration would seem to point to a lack of a common (monopsony) purchase policy. Rather, fluctuating purchase shares must have followed from independent bidding for reserves.[29]

The pattern of purchases in South Louisiana was similar to that in the Texas Gulf. Louisiana fields were concentrated in the region bounding the coast, as in Texas, and pipelines along this coastal boundary overlapped so that demand conditions in one field were the same as demand conditions in

29. The lack of control may have been confined to "pipeline alley" along the coast, however. In fields farther inland there may still have been one buyer (such as United Gas Pipeline) and "turnover" in purchase shares for the entire area would not indicate competitive demand for reserves there.

all. Shares of purchases over the whole South Louisiana area in two-year market periods were as concentrated as in Texas, but there was entry of a larger number of buyers and even more "turnover" (as indicated in Table 6:5).

Purchases the first two years were dominated by the incumbent United Gas Pipeline Company, with only Southern Natural Gas providing a second source of demand for reserves of any size.[30] Purchases in 1951–52 and 1952–53 were dominated by newly entering lines. The United Fuel Gas Company bought the major share of new reserves, between 46 and 48 per cent, while providing a new source of demand. Transcontinental Gas Pipeline increased its share from less than 1 per cent in 1951–52 to approximately 11.6 per cent in 1952–53. Meanwhile, United Gas Pipeline's share declined from 68.9 per cent in 1950–51 to 19.05 per cent in 1952–53. This change in United's share, when there was entry of independent buyers, might well have resulted in loss of control over aggregate field purchases.

Shares of purchases in 1953–54 indicate the establishment of the new transporters as continuous demanders of new reserves. United Gas Pipeline was the largest buyer, but its share was only 5 per cent greater than that of United Fuel Gas and only 10 per cent greater than that of Transco. All these pipeline companies purchased in fields in which there were other new pipelines. Texas Eastern began to bid for reserves in central and South Louisiana, and American Louisiana Pipeline was also in the first stages of acquiring initial reserves (although their contracts were not listed until 1955 when the Federal Power Commission certified the projects). In general, in the early 1950s, the United Gas Pipeline Company probably was the only important source of demand. In 1952–54, apparent control of purchases decreased as new buyers entered South Louisiana.

30. Southern Natural as was still closely allied to United through repurchase agreements in North Louisiana, and Southern purchased only 16 per cent of estimated total reserves while United purchased 69 per cent of the total. Perhaps the producers could *not* have considered Southern an effective alternative source of demand to United in any field market.

TABLE 6:5. *Concentration in the Purchase of Reserves in the South Louisiana Gulf Coast, 1950–54*

	1950–51		1951–52		1952–53		1953–54	
Estimated volume of reserves (trillions of cu. ft.)	2.895		3.479		4.639		1.785	
Number of contracts	33		43		52		50	
Number of buyers	9		7		11		11	
Percentage of total reserves purchased by the four largest buyers	United Gas	68.89	United Fuel	48.19	United Fuel	46.54	United Gas	31.97
	Southern Gas	16.02	United Gas	27.78	Southern Gas	19.05	United Fuel	26.70
	Tenn. Gas	8.46	Southern Gas	20.84	United Gas	14.65	Transco	21.56
	La. Natural	2.64	La. Natural	1.50	Transco	11.59	Niagara Gas	11.15
		96.01		97.31		91.83		91.38
Percentage of total reserves purchased by the ten largest buyers	100		100		99.75		99.19	

Source. As in Table 5:1.

In North Louisiana, concentration in purchases was as high as elsewhere. Throughout the northern portion of this state and adjoining areas of Texas, there were nine buyers in 1950–51, taking an estimated 3.149 trillion cubic feet. The following four transporters signed contracts for 93.51 per cent of this volume: Arkansas Louisiana Gas Company (57.27 per cent) Mississippi River Fuel Company (20.27 per cent), United Gas Pipeline (11.13 per cent), and Southern Natural Gas Company (4.84 per cent). During 1952–54, Mississippi River Fuel was replaced by Texas Eastern Transmission Company and Texas Gas Transmission Company (both making new purchases on the northwest fringe of the region). But concentration figures indicate that Arkansas-Louisiana, United, and Southern retained their positions as largest purchasers.

These three established lines continued to each purchase in a different part of North Louisiana. Listed purchases of Arkansas-Louisiana and United were for gas in northwest Louisiana (in Caddo, Webster, Bossier, and Claiborn Parishes). Southern Natural Gas purchased in the older fields in northeast Louisiana, or in new fields in central-North Louisiana (in DeSoto Parish or Panola County, Texas). As a result, there was seldom more than one buyer in any one field and there were never as many as indicated by shares of purchases over the entire area.

In those wide-spaced North Louisiana fields there must have been opportunities for each transporter to have set some prices. In fields where there was one buyer, he could have determined prices if other lines did not enter (and generally they did not). In fields having more than one buyer, prices could have been controlled if there was prior agreement on the purchase shares of each buyer (stable shares for the established pipelines suggest that this was not impossible).

Concentration in Sales in Supply Markets. Buyers could *not* have set prices, in inland fields, if a few producers controlled supply in the Gulf region. It remains to be seen whether there was counterbalancing control of supply of new reserves.

The degree of predominance in sales varied according "to the relevant supply market." For some of the smaller pipelines, the relevant area in which to purchase reserves consisted of part of North Louisiana and bordering areas of Texas. Concentration of sales in North Louisiana-East Texas may be indicative of producer's control of the supply to these pipelines during the early 1950s. For other pipelines, sales concentration in South Louisiana is indicative of producer's control of the supply of reserves (if these pipelines could have purchased only in that restricted region). For transporters such as Texas-Illinois Natural Gas Pipeline, the relevant area was limited to the Texas Gulf region; concentration of sales there would indicate control of supply to this (and any similar) pipeline.

The new contracts signed during the 1950–53 period for reserves in the northern half of Louisiana (to the border of Beauregard-Allen-Evangeline-St. Landry Parishes) included some 275 "sales for resale in interstate commerce." [31] Contracts were signed by 129 producers, with the four largest accounting for approximately 48.2 per cent of the estimated total sample reserves and the ten largest supplying 68.5 per cent of the total. Those buyers confined to North Louisiana would have found ten producers capable of providing at least 150 billion cubic feet of new reserves. Similarly in the 1951–54 buyer's market period, the share of the largest four sellers was 42.4 per cent of the total. It is doubtful that the largest four in collusion in either market could have effectively controlled total sales and set price for North Louisiana.[32]

31. Where such was the criteria for inclusion in the sample reported to the Federal Power Commission. Cf. exhibit 2-LC, 3-LC, 4-LC, *Champlin Oil and Refining, et al.* Federal Power Commission Docket G-9277. Because of the proximity to Texas fields and to Texas resale purchasers, the transporters from North Louisiana fields all had some interstate transactions, so that most new contracts should be in the sample.

32. Demand elasticity for the four firms together would have been greater than 2.08 given that $\eta = \left\{ \dfrac{Q+q}{q} \cdot \eta_m \right\} = \dfrac{1.00}{.48}$ (1.00). But *individual* elasticity would have been from 5.0 to greater than 13.0 for each of the four. Unless there were collusion, profit maximizing sales policies would not have differed to any extent from the perfectly com-

Of course, transporters with larger supply areas had available further alternatives not suggested by the concentration figures in Table 6:6. Any pipeline able to purchase *both* in North Louisiana and in the Texas Gulf region would have been in a supply market where 17.272 trillion cubic feet were sold. The four largest producers in this extended supply area were: Union Oil of Louisiana with 10.14 per cent of total estimated reserves; Skelly Oil Company with 8.37 per cent; Chicago Corporation with 5.40 per cent; and Southwest Gas Production Company with 5.26 per cent. Together they accounted for 29.17 per cent of 1951–54 sales. The transporter within this larger gathering area would have found more than 200 sources of supply, at least 20 of which each could have provided more than 500 billion cubic feet of gas. Any attempt of the largest *four* producers to control sales and prices would have resulted in new purchasers transferring to other producers possessing uncommitted large volumes.

Concentration in the sale of reserves in both South Louisiana and the Texas Gulf Coast was similar to that in North Louisiana. South Louisiana sales involved larger reserve dedications, primarily because reservoirs in the delta region contained larger volumes for any given surface area. It was possible for one producer to offer 300 billion cubic feet of reserves from under a five-well tract. But there were enough of these highly productive traps to preclude any one seller from providing a significant part of total reserves. Forty-nine producers supplied more than 7.8 trillion cubic feet in 1950–53, with the largest four producers supplying 46.4 per cent of this amount. There continued to be a large number of sellers of large volumes of reserves in 1951–54, with the largest four supplying only 45.9 per cent of total reserves. Moreover there was considerable "turnover" in shares: one of the four largest and three others in the first ten in the 1951–54 period were not in the first ten in 1950–53. Transporters must have been able to purchase large-sized volumes of reserves from

petitive given such elasticities. If there were collusion, these four still would have had difficulty controlling supply with such small market shares.

at least a dozen sources in South Louisiana. This is a number usually considered sufficient to result in competitive supply conditions.

The Texas Gulf region was part of the supply area for most

TABLE 6:6. *Concentration in the Sale of Reserves in the Smallest Supply Areas of the Gulf Coast Basin, 1950–54*

A. *North Louisiana*

	1950–53		1951–54	
Estimated total new reserves dedicated (trillions of cu. ft)	7.161		7.356	
Number of contracts	275		279	
Number of sellers	129		133	
Percentage of reserves dedicated by the four largest companies	Skelly Oil Company	20.28	Mayfair Minerals	16.71
	Union Oil Company	11.80	Union Oil Company	11.48
	Southwest Gas	8.92	Skelly Oil	7.23
	Carter Foundation	7.18	Carter Foundation	6.99
		48.18		42.41
Percentage of reserves dedicated by the ten largest companies	68.48		64.24	

B. *South Louisiana*

	1950–53		1951–54	
Estimated total new reserves dedicated (trillions of cu. ft.)	7.836		6.383	
Number of contracts	83		93	
Number of sellers	49		54	
Percentage of reserves dedicated by the four largest companies	Pure Oil	17.24	Pan American	14.52
	Pan American	11.83	Texaco	11.11
	Southern Gas	9.00	Southern Gas	10.83
	Texaco	8.33	Tidewater	9.39
		46.40		45.85
Percentage of reserves dedicated by the ten largest companies	79.24		78.84	

TABLE 6:6 (cont.)

C. Texas Gulf

	1950–53	1951–54
Estimated total new reserves dedicated (trillions of cu. ft.)	10.114	7.760
Number of contracts	376	412
Number of sellers	201	115

Percentage of reserves dedicated by the four largest companies	Chicago Corporation	9.20	Chicago Corporation	12.44
	Union Oil Company	8.97	Humble Oil	9.15
	Skelly Oil	8.96	Shell Oil	6.35
	Seaboard Oil	7.25	Sunray Oil	5.75
		34.38		33.69

Percentage of reserves dedicated by the ten largest companies	56.88	52.76

Source. As in Table 5:1.

of the interstate transporters during 1950–54, and the sole supply area for some of the smaller Texas state transporters. Transporters purchasing there exclusively in 1950–53 had access to at least 10.11 trillion cubic feet from some 201 producers. The largest four producers sold approximately 34.4 per cent of this amount; consequently it is unlikely that they had any control over the selling price (since such would have required control of more than 60–80 per cent of the available reserves [33] and of more than 60–80 per cent of actual sales).

The same applies to producers supplying the larger transporters. A number of the interstate lines had supply areas that included all of the fields along the Gulf of Mexico from New Orleans to the Mexican border; they had access to more than 17.8 trillion cubic feet of new reserves during 1950–53 and

[33]. If less than 60–80 per cent of reserves were owned by the largest four producers, other producers would have been able to increase total sales substantially if the large firms were to raise price. That is, if $\eta_r = \dfrac{Q+q}{q} (\eta_m) - Q/q \; \varepsilon_{r-1}$, the elasticity of demand η_r for the group r would be quite high as a result of small shares of sales.

more than 14.0 trillion cubic feet during 1951–54. For these lines, there were more than twenty producers each having at least 500 billion cubic feet of reserves. The largest four producers actually sold the following shares:

1950–53

Pure Oil Company:	9.71 %
Pan American Producing:	6.67 %
Texaco Company:	6.65 %
Southwest Gas Production:	5.07 %
	28.10 % of total
	reserves

1951–54

Texaco Company:	8.00 %
Chicago Corporation:	6.83 %
Pan American Producing:	6.56 %
Humble Oil Company:	5.02 %
	26.41 % of total
	reserves

There was an obviously large number of producers able to supply reserves comparable to the greatest-volumed sales. With four producers supplying little more than 25 per cent of total reserves, there is no indication of effective producer's control of reserves and price in those supply markets. Similar conditions are found in other example markets extending into more than one part of the basin.

Pricing Patterns in 1950–54 Markets. As has been noted, fields in North Louisiana probably did not have pipelines bidding competitively for reserves, while fields in both South Louisiana and the Texas Gulf Coast seem to have experienced a thorough revision of demand conditions toward more competition between 1950 and 1954. At the same time, *supply* conditions were competitive throughout the Gulf Coast and Louisiana. Therefore actual prices, at least in the Gulf region, should have conformed to the theoretical competitive pattern. Prices should have been higher than under monopsony. Prices should have also been relatively higher on contracts involving larger volumes of new reserves, on contracts for gas closer to points of resale, and with longer term-length. But where there was power to set monopsony prices (as in North Louisiana and scattered fields on other fringes of the region), actual prices should not have varied with contract volume, the location of the trap, or term-length.[34]

Actual price behavior along the Gulf Coast should have been similar to the competitive pattern $\{P = \alpha + \beta_1 V + \beta_2 D + \beta_3 T + \beta_4 Y + \beta_5 C_1 + \beta_6 C_2 + v\}$ with β_1, $\beta_3 > 0$ (larger volume and longer term resulting in significantly higher contract price), $\beta_2 < 0$ (greater distance to the trap resulting in lower contract price), and β_5, $\beta_6 < 0$ (contracts with contingency clauses having a lower price). This would be in contrast to the monopsony pattern in which β_1, β_2, β_3, β_5, $\beta_6 = 0$ (or possibly $\beta_3 \gtrless 0$; β_5, $\beta_6 \leq 0$ because of differences in production costs from these contract options). Price formation data from contracts signed during 1950–54 are organized in Tables 6:7–6:10 to test these expected pricing patterns. The contracts for the Texas Gulf Coast region (from sixty miles west of the Louisiana border to Brownsville on the Mexican border) are analyzed first, since this region was the first to experience entry of larger numbers of buyers. Contracts for reserves from North and South Louisiana are analyzed together to bring to light any contrast between pricing patterns in the two parts of this state.[35]

In the computed regression for the Texas Gulf 1950–51 market, there was distinct variation of average contract price P with volume V, distance D, and term T. Price increased .0035 cents per mcf, on the average, for each billion cubic foot increase in reserves (an amount significantly greater than zero). Average contract price for reserves at the "end of transmission," [36] was .756 cents per mcf greater than for reserves

34. The lack of variation minimizes rents paid to producers from "windfall" advantages of location or of discovery of large volumes et al.

35. Also, North and South Louisiana have been combined because the range of values for distance and term for the sample of contracts in one half of Louisiana was too small to calculate reliable estimates of co-efficients b_2, b_3.

36. This "end of transmission" was arbitrarily defined as the central Kentucky area through which almost all transporters pass. The common axis results in field distances from 5.0 to 11.0 hundred miles.

in traps one hundred miles distant.[37] Price was on the average
1.61 cents per mcf greater in a contract with twenty-year term-
length than on a ten-year contract. Average contract price
was not higher in 1951 than in 1950, nor did prices vary between contracts with contingency clauses and contracts without.[38] The over-all pattern of prices in the Texas regression

TABLE 6:7. *Summary of Texas Gulf Coast-Louisiana Prices, 1950–51*

Given that: $P = \alpha + \beta_1 V + \beta_2 D + \beta_3 T + \beta_4 Y + \beta_5 C_1 + \beta_6 C_2 + v$
P = initial contract price, cents per mcf.
V = volume of reserves, billions of cu. ft.
D = distance of trap, in hundreds of miles
T = term-length, in years
Y = either the first-year sample (zero) or the second year (one)
C_1 = presence of Favored Nations clause (= one)
C_2 = presence of Renegotiation clause (= one)
R^2 = coefficient of determination
S_u = standard error of estimate, cents per mcf.
S_p = standard deviation of price, cents per mcf.

A. *Texas Gulf Coast*
   (*sample of 91 contracts*)

Regression Equations

$P = \alpha + \beta_1 V + \beta_2 D + \beta_3 T + \beta_4 Y + \beta_5 C_1 + \beta_6 C_2 + v$
$P = 11.374 + .0035V - .7560D + .1614T - .5234Y - .3041C_1$
$\quad\;\;(2.014)\quad(.0021)\quad(.2064)\quad(.0581)\quad(.4270)\quad(.4381)$

$\quad - .4076C_2$
$\quad\;\;(.4759)$

$R^2 = .223$
$S_u = 1.80$
$S_p = 1.98$

(*Competitive*) Predictions	(*Monopsony*) Predictions	*Tests of computed equations*
$\beta_1 > 0$	$\beta_1 = 0$	If $t = b_i/S_{b_i} > \|1.645\|$ hypothesis
$\beta_2 < 0$	$\beta_2 = 0$	$H_0: \beta_i = 0$ is rejected.
$\beta_3 > 0$	$\beta_3 \geqq 0$	$\beta_1 > 0$ since $t_1 =$ 1.6713
$\beta_5 \leqq 0$	$\beta_5 \leqq 0$	$\beta_2 < 0$ since $t_2 =$ −3.6616
$\beta_6 \leqq 0$	$\beta_6 \leqq 0$	$\beta_3 > 0$ since $t_3 =$ 2.7767
		$\beta_4 = 0$ since $t_4 =$ −1.2256
		$\beta_5 = 0$ since $t_5 =$ .6942
		$\beta_6 = 0$ since $t_6 =$ .8564

37. This is within the range of .50–1.25 cents per mcf per hundred
miles from competitive price variations equaling differences in transportation costs.

38. This lack of variation with C_1, C_2 could have followed from competitive *or* monopsonistic price formation. If the addition of the clauses

TABLE 6:7 (*cont.*)

B. *Louisiana*
   (*sample of 164 contracts*)

Regression equations

$$P = \alpha + \beta_1 V + \beta_2 D + \beta_3 T + \beta_4 Y + \beta_5 C_1 + \beta_6 C_2 + v$$

$$P = 6.227 - .00012V - .2628D + .0191T + .2459Y + .5052C_1$$
$$\quad (1.532) \ (.00095) \quad (.2027) \quad (.0346) \quad (.2802) \quad (.3113)$$

$$\quad - .2692C_2$$
$$\quad (.3653)$$

$R^2 = .247$
$S_u = 1.75$
$S_p = 1.97$

(Competitive) Predictions	(Monopsony) Predictions	Tests of computed equations
$\beta_1 > 0$	$\beta_1 = 0$	$\beta_1 = 0$ since $t_1 = -.1242$
$\beta_2 < 0$	$\beta_2 = 0$	$\beta_2 = 0$ since $t_2 = -1.2966$
$\beta_3 > 0$	$\beta_3 \geqq 0$	$\beta_3 = 0$ since $t_3 = .5521$
$\beta_5 \leqq 0$	$\beta_5 \leqq 0$	$\beta_4 = 0$ since $t_4 = .8775$
$\beta_6 \leqq 0$	$\beta_6 \leqq 0$	$\beta_5 = 0$ since $t_5 = 1.6231$
		$\beta_6 = 0$ since $t_6 = -.7369$

equation explains only some 22.3 per cent of the total variation in prices (given that $R^2 = .223$). Remaining price variation was undoubtedly due to further factors—such as sales of reserves in inland fields at prices comparable to those during 1945–47.

The Louisiana price pattern during 1950–51 can be contrasted to that in Texas. Prices did not vary with volume, distance, or term-length of the contract in Louisiana. Rather, there seems to have been general price uniformity. A uniform pattern of price is not surprising, since North Louisiana contained a series of separated monopsony buying areas and South Louisiana was the exclusive domain of United Gas Pipeline. With the exercise of buying power by different pipelines in traps with similar production conditions, "one price" should have been set at a level that covered uniform average production costs. Louisiana new contract prices were so similar that "one monopsony price" seems to have actually resulted.

---

did *not decrease pipeline demand* and producer's costs, then competitive price should not differ from that without the clause (as argued in Chapter 4). Monopsony price might not vary for the same reason.

The levels of contract price in the Texas Gulf on the one hand and in Louisiana on the other were even more in contrast than were the patterns of price. Prices for "typical" contracts can be estimated from each sample by inserting average volume, distance, and term in the two regression equations. In Louisiana during 1950, the typical contract involved 67.386 billion cubic feet in a trap 6.35 hundred miles from the end of transmission for a twenty-year term, and the contract included both Favored Nations and Renegotiation clauses. The "regression price" for this sale would have been 5.185 cents per mcf.[39] A typical contract in the Texas Gulf during 1950 (for the same volume and the same conditions of term, Favored Nations, etc., but at a distance of 9.75 hundred miles) would have had a price computed from the Texas regression equation of 6.767 cents per mcf—an amount greater than in the closer Louisiana field. Moreover, the price from the Texas regression equation for a distance comparable to that in Louisiana would have been 9.326 cents per mcf. There is a significant difference between the typical Louisiana price of 5.185 cents per mcf and the comparable Texas price of 9.326 cents per mcf, that points to there having been different types of market behavior in the two states.[40] Louisiana fields generally were characterized by single buyers with considerable monopsony power, while Texas fields each had a number of pipeline buyers bidding for reserves. Monopsony power seems to have been utilized in the closer Louisiana field, to depress prices below competitive prices in the more distant Texas field.

Later market periods indicate a continuation of price formation similar to monopsony, but to a lesser extent. The 1951–52 contracts in the Texas Gulf followed the same pattern

39. If assumptions concerning normal distribution of residuals v are correct and the standard error of residuals $S_u = 1.745$ cents, then 95 per cent of all comparable contracts should have prices within $\{\pm 1.96 \cdot (1.745)\}$ cents of 5.185 cents per mcf.

40. It might be possible to consider the Texas regression price a "forecast" of typical Louisiana price, and the Louisiana regression price can be considered a "realized" price. The difference of 3.528 cents per mcf is greater than $1.96 \cdot S_f$ (where S_f is the "standard error of forecast" equal to 1.834 cents per mcf). The difference then is "significant."

TABLE 6:8. *Summary of Texas Gulf Coast-Louisiana Prices, 1951–52*

A. *Texas Gulf Coast*
   (*sample of 151 contracts*)

Regression equations

$$P = \alpha + \beta_1 V + \beta_2 D + \beta_3 T + \beta_4 Y + \beta_5 C_1 + \beta_6 C_2 + v$$

$$P = 10.280 + .00367V - .6048D + .1270T + 1.636Y - .3531C_1$$
$$\quad\ (1.898)\ \ (.00248)\ \ \ (.1810)\ \ \ (.0558)\ \ (0.539)\ \ \ (.5546)$$
$$\quad - .4184C_2$$
$$\quad\ \ (.5736)$$

$R^2 = .195$
$S_u = 2.47$
$S_p = 2.70$

(*Competitive*) Predictions	(*Monopsony*) Predictions	Tests of computed equations
$\beta_1 > 0$	$\beta_1 = 0$	$\beta_1 = 0$ since $t_1 =\ \ \ 1.4825$
$\beta_2 < 0$	$\beta_2 = 0$	$\beta_2 < 0$ since $t_2 = -3.3410$
$\beta_3 > 0$	$\beta_3 \gtrless 0$	$\beta_3 > 0$ since $t_3 =\ \ \ 2.2802$
$\beta_5 \lessgtr 0$	$\beta_5 \lessgtr 0$	$\beta_4 > 0$ since $t_4 =\ \ \ 3.0346$
$\beta_6 \lessgtr 0$	$\beta_6 \lessgtr 0$	$\beta_5 = 0$ since $t_5 = -\ .6369$
		$\beta_6 = 0$ since $t_6 = -\ .7295$

B. *Louisiana*
   (*sample of 168 contracts*)

Regression equations

$$P = \alpha + \beta_1 V + \beta_2 D + \beta_3 T + \beta_4 Y + \beta_5 C_1 + \beta_6 C_2 + v$$

$$P = 1.0808 + .00211V + .6744D + .1141T + .8157Y + .8181C_1$$
$$\quad\ (2.2757)\ (.00176)\ \ (.3026)\ \ (.0474)\ \ (.4123)\ \ (.4650)$$
$$\quad + 1.004C_2$$
$$\quad\ \ \ (.5341)$$

$R^2 = .234$
$S_u = 2.63$
$S_p = 2.95$

(*Competitive*) Predictions	(*Monopsony*) Predictions	Tests of computed equations
$\beta_1 > 0$	$\beta_1 = 0$	$\beta_1 = 0$ since $t_1 = 1.1974$
$\beta_2 < 0$	$\beta_2 = 0$	$\beta_2 > 0$ since $t_2 = 2.2287$
$\beta_3 > 0$	$\beta_3 \gtrless 0$	$\beta_3 > 0$ since $t_3 = 2.4985$
$\beta_5 \lessgtr 0$	$\beta_5 \lessgtr 0$	$\beta_4 > 0$ since $t_4 = 1.9783$
$\beta_6 \lessgtr 0$	$\beta_6 \lessgtr 0$	$\beta_5 > 0$ since $t_5 = 1.7894$
		$\beta_6 > 0$ since $t_6 = 1.8790$

as the 1950–51 contracts. Volume of reserves contracted had a positive (but this time insignificant) effect upon contract price. The distance of the trap had a significant negative effect upon price, while the term of the contract had a significant positive effect. The 1952 contracts had an "average price" that was more than 1.60 cents per mcf greater than in the 1951 contracts. The variation of price with volume, distance, and term duplicated the pattern following from competition, while the level of prices rose with a large expansion in demand. (Both Texas-Illinois Natural Gas Pipeline and Texas Eastern Transmission Company purchased reserves for new lateral lines in 1952.)

The 1951–52 contracts in the Louisiana area included the first signed by newly entering pipelines. Contracts to entering transporters were in South Louisiana and had a marked effect upon the regression pattern of prices. Prices were higher in South than in North Louisiana, even though the northern fields were approximately 150–200 miles closer to points of resale (average price was .674 cents per mcf *greater* for each additional 100 miles of transmission). For the first time in Louisiana, average contract price was higher for larger than for smaller contracts and was increasing. (The 1952 price was .816 cents per mcf greater than the 1951 price.) [41]

The price level in Louisiana also changed relative to that in Texas. South Louisiana had a higher "typical" contract price than Texas during 1952: The South Louisiana price was 10.790 cents per mcf as computed from the regression equation (for a volume of 48.238 billion cubic feet, distance of 7.0 hundred miles, and 20-year term), while the corresponding Texas price was 9.664 cents per mcf (at 800 miles). The difference corresponds approximately to transportation cost differences, and is consistent with competition in purchasing reserves along both the Texas and Louisiana coasts. The North Louisiana price for a comparable contract was 9.440 cents per mcf,

41. Prices were higher on contracts with contingency clauses as well. This price difference and the increase in price over time seem attributable to the South Louisiana contracts with generally higher prices signed in 1954. (Most of the "south contracts" contained contingency clauses while the "north contracts" did not.)

which was lower than in either South Louisiana or Texas. Lower prices in North Louisiana could have followed only from separated, monopsonistic field markets.

Market pricing patterns for 1952–53 and for 1953–54 continued to reflect gradual attrition of monopsony. The Texas Gulf prices followed the competitive regression pattern more systematically than previously. The Gulf Coast-Louisiana prices continued to be higher than North Louisiana prices, and the level of all prices rose during 1953.

Texas Gulf prices in the three years 1952–54 varied with the size of volumes dedicated, the term of the contracts, and distances to the new reserves. The estimated price in a 1953–54 contract was .02 cents per mcf higher for each additional billion cubic feet of reserves (a price difference roughly of the magnitude of the decreased costs of transporting the larger reserves).[42] Price was .47 cents per mcf lower for each additional 100 miles between the reserve and the points of resale (an amount slightly below the range of price differences expected to follow from transportation cost differences).[43] Estimated average price in 1953–54 contracts was .630 cents per mcf greater for each additional five years of term-length of production. The price level increased in 1953 by approximately 1.10 cents per mcf, but did not change significantly in 1954. The addition of a contingency clause to the contract had no effect upon average price. But the overall variation in accordance with factors in the regression

42. Assuming the buyer to have costs as in Tables 3:2 and 3:3, the unit costs for transporting an *additional* 100 billion cubic feet in 12″–20″ lines would be approximately 2.0 cents less for the larger volume. The larger volume lowers transportation costs for all reserves so that the *marginal* transmission costs *savings* may be greater than 2.0 cents for the larger volume. The increased "maximum offer price" should reflect the 2.0 cents per mcf transmission cost saving.

43. The price difference reflecting transportation cost differences mentioned in Chapters 3 and 4 is in the range of +.50 to +1.25 cents per mcf for each 100 miles of greater distance. For a *number* of samples of 261 contracts 95 per cent of the *differences* in contract prices for each 100 miles of distance would be .4694 + {1.96 (.0932)} cents per mcf according to Table 6:7. Only a few contracts for reserves 100 miles apart would have had price differences, due to distance, outside the predicted range.

TABLE 6:9. *Summary of Texas Gulf Coast-Louisiana Prices, 1952–53*

A. *Texas Gulf Coast*
   (sample of 285 contracts)

Regression equations

$$P = \alpha + \beta_1 V + \beta_2 D + \beta_3 T + \beta_4 Y + \beta_5 C_1 + \beta_6 C_2 + v$$

$$P = 10.235 + .0037V - .4905D + .0780T + 1.7642Y + .3262C_1$$
$$\quad\;(1.175)\;\;(.00213)\;\;(.1115)\;\;(.0395)\;\;(0.2549)\;\;(.3717)$$
$$\quad + .8953C_2$$
$$\quad\;\;(.4257)$$

$R^2 = .245$
$S_u = 2.05$
$S_p = 2.34$

(*Competitive*) Predictions	(*Monopsony*) Predictions	*Tests of computed equations*
$\beta_1 > 0$	$\beta_1 = 0$	$\beta_1 > 0$ since $t_1 = \quad 1.7574$
$\beta_2 < 0$	$\beta_2 = 0$	$\beta_2 < 0$ since $t_2 = \; -4.4001$
$\beta_3 > 0$	$\beta_3 \geqq 0$	$\beta_3 > 0$ since $t_3 = \quad 1.9744$
$\beta_5 \leqq 0$	$\beta_5 \leqq 0$	$\beta_4 > 0$ since $t_4 = \quad 6.9212$
$\beta_6 \leqq 0$	$\beta_6 \leqq 0$	$\beta_5 = 0$ since $t_5 = \quad\;\;.8777$
		$\beta_6 > 0$ since $t_6 = \quad 2.1028$

B. *Louisiana*
   (sample of 196 contracts)

Regression equations

$$P = \alpha + \beta_1 V + \beta_2 D + \beta_3 T + \beta_4 Y + \beta_5 C_1 + \beta_6 C_2 + v$$

$$P = 0.2566 + .00349V + .9631D + .0585T + 1.0982Y + 1.2460C_1$$
$$\quad\;(1.8912)\;\;(.00199)\;\;(.2670)\;\;(.0397)\;\;(0.3849)\;\;(0.4290)$$
$$\quad + 2.0804C_2$$
$$\quad\;\;(0.4641)$$

$R^2 = .379$
$S_u = 2.61$
$S_p = 3.27$

(*Competitive*) Predictions	(*Monopsony*) Predictions	*Tests of computed equations*
$\beta_1 > 0$	$\beta_1 = 0$	$\beta_1 > 0$ since $t_1 = 1.7530$
$\beta_2 < 0$	$\beta_2 = 0$	$\beta_2 > 0$ since $t_2 = 3.6074$
$\beta_3 > 0$	$\beta_3 \geqq 0$	$\beta_3 = 0$ since $t_3 = 1.4744$
$\beta_5 \leqq 0$	$\beta_5 \leqq 0$	$\beta_4 > 0$ since $t_4 = 2.8525$
$\beta_6 \leqq 0$	$\beta_6 \leqq 0$	$\beta_5 > 0$ since $t_5 = 2.9045$
		$\beta_6 > 0$ since $t_6 = 4.4829$

equation: ($R^2 = .245$ in 1952–53, and $R^2 = .274$ in 1953–54).
Louisiana price behavior was affected by the entry of buy-

TABLE 6:10. *Summary of Texas Gulf Coast-Louisiana Prices, 1953–54*

A. *Texas Gulf Coast*
  (*sample of 261 contracts*)

Regression equations

$P = \alpha + \beta_1 V + \beta_2 D + \beta_3 T + \beta_4 Y + \beta_5 C_1 + \beta_6 C_2 + v$

$P = 11.3269 + .0227V - .4694D + .1261T + .3608Y + .5483C_1$
$\quad\;\; (0.9639)\;\; (.0050)\;\; (.0932)\;\; (.0308)\;\; (.2137)\;\; (.3022)$

$\quad\;\; - .1172C_2$
$\quad\;\;\;\;\; (.3606)$

$R^2 = .274$
$S_u = 1.63$
$S_p = 1.88$

(*Competitive*) Predictions	(*Monopsony*) Predictions	*Tests of computed equations*
$\beta_1 > 0$	$\beta_1 = 0$	$\beta_1 > 0$ since $t_1 = \quad 4.5043$
$\beta_2 < 0$	$\beta_2 = 0$	$\beta_2 < 0$ since $t_2 = -5.0399$
$\beta_3 > 0$	$\beta_3 \geqq 0$	$\beta_3 > 0$ since $t_3 = \quad 4.0967$
$\beta_5 \leqq 0$	$\beta_5 \leqq 0$	$\beta_4 > 0$ since $t_4 = \quad 1.6883$
$\beta_6 \leqq 0$	$\beta_6 \leqq 0$	$\beta_5 > 0$ since $t_5 = \quad 1.8144$
		$\beta_6 = 0$ since $t_6 = \quad\;\; .3251$

B. *Louisiana*
  (*sample of 201 contracts*)

Regression equations

$P = \alpha + \beta_1 V + \beta_2 D + \beta_3 T + \beta_4 Y + \beta_5 C_1 + \beta_6 C_2 + v$

$P = 4.534 - .00238V + .5782D + .0594T + .0764Y + .7016C_1 +$
$\quad\; (1.8151)\; (.00283)\;\; (.2540)\;\; (.0352)\;\; (.4004)\;\; (.4418)$

$\quad\; + 1.7631C_2$
$\quad\;\;\;\; (.4566)$

$R^2 = .173$
$S_u = 2.80$
$S_p = 3.03$

(*Competitive*) Predictions	(*Monopsony*) Predictions	*Tests of computed equations*
$\beta_1 > 0$	$\beta_1 = 0$	$\beta_1 = 0$ since $t_1 = -\;\; .8396$
$\beta_2 < 0$	$\beta_2 = 0$	$\beta_2 > 0$ since $t_2 = \quad 2.2763$
$\beta_3 > 0$	$\beta_3 \geqq 0$	$\beta_3 > 0$ since $t_3 = \quad 1.6874$
$\beta_5 \leqq 0$	$\beta_5 \leqq 0$	$\beta_4 = 0$ since $t_4 = \quad\;\; .1909$
$\beta_6 \leqq 0$	$\beta_6 \leqq 0$	$\beta_5 = 0$ since $t_5 = \quad 1.5884$
		$\beta_6 > 0$ since $t_6 = \quad 3.8614$

ers during 1953–54, much as it was in 1952. Where entry took place in South Louisiana, there were higher prices than on comparable contracts in North Louisiana (contracts 100 miles farther south had prices .963 cents per mcf greater). The level of all prices in Louisiana increased, because the South Louisiana transporters (Texas-Illinois, United Fuel Gas, and Trans-Continental Gas) offered higher initial prices. At the same time, prices were not consistently higher for larger-volume contracts or for longer-term contracts. Prices were not lower on contracts with Favored Nations and/or Renegotiation clauses.[44]

In general, there was considerable lack of over-all conformity with the competitive pattern of price,[45] and prices were markedly lower in North Louisiana. Both the diversity of pricing and the lower level of North Louisiana prices indicates a lack of competition among buyers *throughout* the state. Prices must have been set according to a monopsony pattern in North Louisiana, while those in South Louisiana resulted from competitive bidding.

A Summary of Gulf Coast-Louisiana Markets' Structure and Behavior, 1950–54.   Characteristics of buyers and the results of price formation point to emerging competition in the 1950–54 markets for reserves. A number of new buyers entered the supply areas of established pipelines along the Gulf Coast during the early 1950s. Fluctuating shares of purchases along with continued low concentration in sales indicate that established pipeline buyers in the Texas Gulf and in South Louisiana had lost their power to set price in

44. But in 1952–53 prices were significantly *higher* when these clauses were in the contracts. This is the opposite of either a competitive or monopsonistic pricing pattern for the area, while it is consistent with higher price offers in South Louisiana (where most contracts had clauses) and with contracts from competitive purchase fields having clauses, while those elsewhere did not.

45. The "diversity of price" is indicated by the coefficient of determination. The value of the coefficient (R^2) was .374 for 1952–53 (chiefly because of the large *positive* effect of distance and the *positive* effect of the Contingency clauses—both of which would not have followed from a pattern of competition). $R^2 = .173$ in 1953–54 so that the (competitive) regression pattern "explained" only 17.3 per cent of price variation.

favor of competition. At the same time, extensive concentration in purchases in separate supply regions of North Louisiana continued; the buyers there should have been able to control new contract prices. Prices on new contracts should have conformed to a competitive pattern along the Gulf of Texas-Louisiana and followed a monopsony pattern elsewhere. Actual prices in the regression analyses became more similar to the competitive pattern in Texas, and South Louisiana, as time passed (particularly after 1950–51). North Louisiana prices were lower than comparable South Louisiana prices. There must have been emerging competition for Gulf Coast reserves in 1950–54, and some lack of buyer's competition in North Louisiana.[46]

THE MARKETS FOR NEW RESERVES IN THE LATER 1950s

During 1956–58, most transporters completed their coverage of the larger fields in the Gulf Coast and Louisiana, so that the extent of buyer's competition became the same in all fields. The expansion of individual supply areas resulted in each transporter becoming a potential buyer of new reserves in each field. With more than a dozen purchasers in each field, it was no longer possible for one or a few buyers to control new contract prices anywhere. Since there continued to be a large number of sources of supply for each buyer, there were competitive conditions for both demand and production. Competitive price formation was consequently most likely, and actual prices conformed quite closely to the competitive theoretical pattern.

Entry and Expansion of Buyers. The first condition for competition was further "overlapping" of pipeline supply areas. The extent of common purchasing increased after 1955 with the entry of the Coastal Transmission Company. This company sought gas along the entire Gulf Coast for resale in Florida. The established pipelines themselves generally extended gathering facilities throughout the Gulf Coast. The

46. There were obviously "fringe fields" along the coast in which there was monopsony as well, given the lack of close approximation of the pricing pattern to the competitive pattern over the area.

Texas Eastern Transmission Company completed coverage of the Texas Gulf fields by building transmission laterals parallel to its old lines all the way to the Mexican border. Transcontinental Gas Pipeline Company purchased reserves on the western fringes of the Texas producing region (where it did not already have contracts with Favored Nations clauses). Trunkline Gas Company expanded its purchase capacity into the northeastern portion of the Gulf Coast of Texas. Given that Tennessee Gas Transmission, United Gas Pipeline, and Texas-Illinois Natural Gas Pipeline continued gathering throughout the area, at least six transporters covered both the eastern and western fringes of the Gulf Coast by 1955.

The older transporters were responsible for the development of a common supply area in Louisiana. The original lines, such as Transcontinental, Texas Eastern, and Tennessee Gas Transmission, began to buy gas in new fields in both North and South Louisiana in order to obtain reserves at rising prices without "triggering" Favored Nations clauses in contracts in older supply regions. Transcontinental's new purchases were in the newly discovered areas in the Gulf of Mexico off the Louisiana coast.[47] Texas Eastern Transmission Company constructed new lateral lines in east Texas-northwest Louisiana that completed its coverage of North Louisiana fields. Tennessee increased the extent of its North Louisiana supply area while building new lines in the Monroe field area.

Other established transporters also expanded their supply areas. Texas Gas Transmission purchased reserves for a new transmission lateral south of its established system and in the Monroe field region. Southern Natural Gas purchased in most of the northwest Louisiana fields for the first time. As a result there were at least six sources of demand in all fields in Louisiana (including the United Gas Pipeline, which had been established throughout the state much earlier).

By 1955 most transporters could purchase reserves throughout a greater part of the whole Gulf Coast–Louisiana, not only

47. United Gas, Tennessee Gas, and Trunkline Gas Company all purchased new volumes off the coast as well.

in one part or the other. The four largest pipelines had the entire basin as a common supply area (United Gas Pipeline, Tennessee Gas Transmission, Texas Eastern Transmission, and Transcontinental). There were other buyers that covered all of Louisiana (Southern Natural and Texas Gas Transmission) or the Texas-Louisiana Gulf (Trunkline Gas, Coastal Transmission Company, and Texas-Illinois Natural Gas Pipeline).[48] The producer in any one field area was guaranteed at least six potential buyers and in most fields there were more (because of the demands of United Fuel Gas, Houston Gas, Arkansas-Louisiana, American Louisiana, and of local industrial purchasers of long-term reserves).

Concentration in Demand and Supply of Reserves. It would have been difficult for any one or a few buyers to have controlled prices in new contracts, given this extensive overlapping of supply areas. With the buyers purchasing throughout the area, potential price-setters would have had to control demand over the region to have had control in any one field, and they would have had to purchase the greatest share of reserves.

Indications from a sample of actual 1956–58 sales are that no small groups of firms did purchase a significantly large share of reserves. Shares of purchases in 922 interstate contracts are shown in Table 6:11. The largest four purchased approximately 60 per cent of the reserves. Shares for each were so evenly distributed that there would seem to have been four transporters in any field able to buy most of the reserves there. Also, the four transporters apparently were bidding independently for the reserves in any seller's market period—or so it would seem from "turnover" in purchase shares. United Gas Pipeline was able to increase its share from 12.2 per cent in the first market period to 22.2 per cent in the second. Texas Eastern managed to decrease its share

48. With the qualification, of course, of limited offers to suppliers in the *original buying areas* where Favored Nations clauses in large number would be "triggered." These suppliers could obtain offers from the established line of prices close to the 1940–49 level only, and these prices may not have been reasonable alternatives.

from 19.1 per cent to an amount (7.4 per cent) that no longer merited a place in the largest four by 1957–58. Both Southern Natural and Hope Natural Gas increased purchases in the last two years by enough to replace Texas Eastern and Texas Gas Transmission as two of the largest four buyers. These fluctua-

TABLE 6:11. *Concentration in the Purchase of Reserves throughout Gulf Texas and Louisiana, 1956–58*

	1956–57		1957–58	
Estimated volume of reserves (trillions of cu. ft.)	10.3014		9.7076	
Number of contracts	648		659	
Number of buyers	40		38	
Percentage of total new reserves purchased by the four largest buyers	Texas Eastern	19.07	United Gas Pipeline	22.23
	Transcontinental	18.66	Transcontinental	20.25
	United Gas Pipeline	12.23	Southern Natural	10.67
	Tennessee Gas	9.52	Hope Natural Gas	7.48
		59.48		60.63
Percentage of reserves purchased by the ten largest buyers	87.53		85.12	

Source. The contracts include all new sales in 1956–58 submitted to the Federal Power Commission and certified as "necessary and convenient" for resale in interstate commerce. The sample for 1958 was not complete because some producers had not submitted the required information by 1959, and because some of the contracts had not been certified. Information in the contracts did not include an estimate of reserves contracted, but the producer's estimate of "the uniform monthly rate of production" was included. The uniform monthly rate multiplied by the term-length provided an estimate of contract reserves, and the estimates for all contracts were summed to provide a figure for aggregate reserves. The reliability of the resulting estimates is discussed in the Appendix.

tions in shares of demand follow most likely from competitive bidding for reserves in adjoining market periods.

Most transporters were able to obtain reserves in the late 1950s from a "large" number of producers. Discovery of numerous reservoirs of dry gas continued throughout the Gulf Coast. With continued dispersed ownership of discovered traps, the larger transporters had access to at least 250 different sources during 1957–60 throughout the Gulf and Louisiana.[49] The smaller transporters with supply areas in only one state could have purchased from at least 150 sources of new reserves.[50] There was dispersed ownership of relative amounts of uncommitted reserves as well. Ownership of actual reserves from 1954 to 1956 was not highly concentrated, nor were sales of reserves during 1956–58. Buyers had access to a large number of sources of new volumes of gas during any three to five-year period.

Known "stocks" of uncommitted reserves in 1954–56 are shown in Table 6:12. Humble Oil and Refining, with large volumes of gas in unit-operated traps on the King and Hopper Ranches of southeast Texas, accounted for 15.2 per cent of estimated total uncommitted reserves. The three next largest owners together accounted for another 33.7 per cent. The ten producers with the largest uncommitted volumes together owned 79.3 per cent of the total. These shares of aggregate reserves, and the size of individual reserve holdings, would not seem to have been sufficient for group control of total supply. A new transporter seeking more than one trillion cubic feet in the Gulf Coast Basin could have obtained this amount from any one of ten producers. Any established or entering pipeline seeking more than this amount could have secured it from those smaller producers that together owned 5.0 trillion cubic feet.

No pipeline in the 1954–58 market was confined to purchasing from the 1954–56 stock of reserves but rather possessed opportunities to take reserves both from known uncommitted volumes in 1956 and from volumes newly discovered in 1957–58. Producer's shares of actual contract volumes over 1956–58

49. The sample of sales for 1956–58 included 361 producers or suppliers of new reserves for a three-year period only, so that a number of alternatives were not listed. For the relevant period of three to five years, the largest four buyers had additional sources of reserves.

50. For 1956–58 alone, there were at least 236 independent Texas suppliers of new reserves. There were 157 independent producers in Louisiana in the same period (as indicated from the sample of 922 Gulf-Louisiana contracts in interstate commerce 1956–58).

indicate concentration in supply over this pertinent buyer's market period. The largest four suppliers in the sample of new interstate contracts for 1956–58 were responsible for only 17.28 per cent of aggregate reserves sold.[51]

TABLE 6:12. *Ownership of Uncommitted Reserves in the Gulf Coast and Louisiana during 1954–56*

Company	Estimated Total reserves (trillions of cu. ft.)	Estimated uncommitted reserves (trillions of cu. ft.)	Uncommitted reserves for sale to pipelines in the Gulf Coast–Louisiana Region (trillions of cu. ft.)
Humble Oil and Refining	16.0	5.3	3.2
Texaco, Incorporated	11.5	4.8	2.5
Standard Oil of Indiana (Pan American Production Company)	9.9	4.8	2.4
C.A.T.C. Company	2.0	2.0	2.0
Standard Oil (New York) (Magnolia Production Co.)	8.0	3.1	1.6
Phillips Petroleum	17.2	3.5	1.5
Union Oil (California)	2.2	1.6	1.0
Superior Oil Company	2.7	1.3	1.0
Pure Oil Company	3.2	1.8	0.9
Republic Oil Company	2.5	0.7	0.9

Estimated total uncommitted reserves of all Gulf Coast-Louisiana producers = 21.0

Source. "Total reserves" have been obtained from company annual reports, stock prospectuses, and estimates from the production departments of a number of the above companies. "Uncommitted reserves" follow from subtracting estimates of "reserves committed to production" from "total reserves." ("Reserves committed to production" have been derived from multiplying the average term-length of a company's outstanding contracts by that company's 1955 production.) "Gulf Coast-Louisiana uncommitted reserves" are partly from private records of the mentioned companies and from estimates of pipeline buyers. Worksheets for most company estimates will be provided upon request.

51. These four producers had almost equal shares of this percentage,

Actual sales of the largest ten were of such small relative size as to account for only 33.82 per cent of all sales. Sales of the ten next largest firms accounted for approximately 17.44 per cent of total newly committed reserves. The large interstate transporter must have had the opportunity to purchase more than twenty separate volumes of reserves of 100 billion cubic feet each. Ownership of reserves and sales of reserves both point to there having been at least a dozen large sources of reserves—a number sufficient to establish competition among sellers.

Not all pipelines were able to purchase throughout the entire basin, although the majority of large ones did so. But the smaller transporters must not have found different conditions of supply, even in *much* smaller purchase areas. Discovery of reserves had resulted not only in dispersed ownership, but also in dispersed geographical holdings for each producer. In Louisiana alone, the largest four sellers accounted for only 25.67 per cent of the total 7.344 trillion cubic feet, with almost equal shares for each: Humble Oil with 6.938 per cent, Pan American with 6.905, Superior Oil with 6.827, and Union Oil of California with 5.003. The ten largest sellers were responsible for 43.00 per cent of the total.[52] Ownership of uncommitted reserves, as well as sales, in smaller supply markets was not highly concentrated. Holdings of reserves in 1955 in South Louisiana alone are summarized in Table 6:13. The addition of the C.A.T.C. off-shore reserves of 2.0 trillion cubic feet, and of 1.5 trillion cubic feet in various fields in the northwest corner of Louisiana, to these

---

as follows: Columbian Carbon Co., 4.573 per cent; Pan American Prod. Co., 4.528 per cent; Humble Oil and Refining, 4.197 per cent; Superior Oil Co., 3.986 per cent; total, 17.284 per cent of 13.784 trillion cu. ft.

52. Transporters confined to Texas could have purchased from as many producers as were in Louisiana. The largest four suppliers accounted for 13.43 per cent of 4.889 trillion cubic feet, while the largest ten were responsible for 40.72 per cent of the total in 1956–58. Concentration in sales of this minor extent belies suggestions that reserves were held by few firms over any three to five-year period. Concentration in sales were high, however, in one smaller supply submarket: Columbian Carbon Co. accounted for 52.0 per cent of the 1.13 trillion sold in West Virginia. But no buyers were confined to that region alone.

South Louisiana holdings of Standard, Sun Oil, and Humble, indicates concentration of reserves of slightly over 50 per cent for the largest four owners.

The firms controlling one-half the uncommitted reserves (in one year) could not have controlled sales over the relevant three to five-year period, since they failed to provide the majority of new reserves during 1956–58.

In still smaller markets, there might have been high concentration in the ownership of newly available reserves. Without doubt, the discovery process resulted in one or few sellers having most of the new reserves in some very narrowly defined supply area at some time. A buyer confined to a particularly small region might have been in a producer-controlled market for a period.[53]

One exceedingly narrow market limited to "large purchases" —purchases of volumes greater than 24 billion cubic feet— has been reputed to have had so few producers that there was control of price.[54] There is no indication of noncompetitive structure in this market, however. The 1956–58 sales of "larger volumes" were completed by 85 different producers in the Gulf-Louisiana area. The larger pipelines with a desire to bid for these sales could not have found any small group of producers with a significantly large portion of the total

53. Monopoly control of price in *small geographical* supply markets would have been severely limited, however, by the buyer's opportunity to purchase from United Gas Pipeline Company (at regulated resale rates) gas gathered from other supply areas.

54. Cf. testimony of Professor A. E. Kahn in the Omnibus hearings. The large volumes were supposed to have been sold in a market "distinct" from that for the smaller volumes. They were of sufficient uniqueness for transportation and "resale value" that there was no tendency for offers to reflect transmission costs as compared to transmission for smaller volumes. Rather the interstate buyers sought *only* the large volumes given all alternative prices. There seems to be no apparent reason for this division of all sales into "two products." To be specific, that the pipeline did so suggests the above description of its regulatory, resale, and cost conditions of field demand is irrelevant for price determination. They are irrelevant reputedly because large blocks of reserves have been important "for strategy"—which they certainly have if they became *part of a reserve* sufficient to allow certification. (But the volumes of small contracts have been "strategic" in this sense as well.) This argument can be tolerated for the length of time necessary to discuss its implications, however.

9.069 trillion cubic feet. The four producers that sold the largest shares were able to account for only 22.340 per cent of total newly committed reserves, while the ten largest sold only 44.864 per cent. The four largest were the following: Columbian Carbon with 6.412 per cent, Pan American Petroleum with 5.543, Superior Oil Co. with 5.423, and Standard

TABLE 6:13. *Copy of a Producer Memorandum Entitled: Gas Fields in South Louisiana Not Dedicated to Contract, Houston, Texas (October 27, 1955)*

Field	Parish	Owner	Estimated reserves (mmcf)
Thibodaux	LaFourche	Stanolind	400
Rousseau	LaFourche	H. L. Hunt	50
Raceland	LaFourche	Stanolind	150
Bully Camp	LaFourche	Robstock	100
Napoleonville	Iberville	Cities Service	50
Sullivans Lake	Iberville	Shell	75
Bayou De Glaises	Iberville	Texas Co. and Humble	
Section 28	Iberville	Texas Co. and Humble	400
Plumb Bob	Iberville	Texas Co. and Humble	
Bayou Boullion	Iberville	Texas Co. and Humble	
Lake Mongoulois	Iberville	Amerada	50
Darrow	Ascension	Temple Hargrove	30
Grand Chenier	Cameron	Fifteen Oil	60
Bayou Sorrel	Iberville	Shell	75
Chichoula	Assumption	Sun	500
Des Allemands	John the Baptist	W. T. Burton	50
Lucy	John the Baptist	California	30
Hahnville	John the Baptist	Callery	30
Jeanerette	St. Martin	Atlantic	20
Atchafalya and Happy Town	St. Martin	Shell	40
Bayou Des Allemands	St. Charles	Amerada	40
Bayou Jean De Croix	Terrebonne	Humble	60
Bayou Penchant	Terrebonne	Superior	20
Crab Lake	Cameron	Forrest	225
Deer Island	Terrebonne	Humble	150
Four Isle Dome	Terrebonne	Superior	145
Halter Island	Terrebonne	Shell	95
East Lake Pallourde	Assumption	Humble	170
			3,015

Source. Reproduced in full from an interoffice memorandum of one of the above-mentioned companies. The table is preceded by the sentence: "Based on information we have been able to obtain from conversations with other companies, the gas production from the following listed fields in southern Louisiana is uncommitted so far as we can determine."

Oil (Texas) with 4.910. If sales concentration can be presumed to reflect potential supply, the four largest producers would have had to decrease their sales by 50 per cent in order to reduce aggregate sales by 10 per cent.[55] This would not have been possible without collusion, nor as profitable as selling maximum volumes at competitive prices.

In effect, in almost all sizes of supply markets, sources of new reserves were sufficiently numerous to have prevented any producer from setting price. In producer's selling markets, the presence of more buyers and extensive changes in buyer's shares of newly committed reserves point to far less opportunity for monopsony control. Most likely, there was competition among both buyers and sellers.

Pricing Patterns in Relevant Markets. Competition should have required each successful buyer to offer maximum prices for new reserves. Contract prices should have varied with the distance of the trap from resale areas, with the volume committed, with the term-length of production, and with the presence of contingency clauses in the contract. Additional transmission costs should have resulted in lower maximum offer prices for more distant reserves. The presence of Favored Nations and/or Renegotiation clauses in the contract should have increased the cost equivalent of *buyer's* risk, so that competitive maximum prices for Favored Nations contracts should have been lower then for clauseless contracts. The costs of transporting larger volumes from one trap were less, so that the maximum offer prices for larger amounts of reserves should have been greater. A longer term-length of production increased "certifiable" reserves for the transporter; there should have been higher offer prices for reserves under longer-term contracts because certification increased resale opportunities.

55. The "large four" in the (more realistic) market for all Gulf Coast reserves apparently attained their position by selling a few blocks of larger reserves—except for Humble Oil Company. Humble is one of the largest four in this market in the listing on page 192 but is not one of the large four in the "large sales" group. The elasticity of *group* demand would be greater than 5.0, given that

$$\eta_g = \frac{(Q+q)}{q}\,\eta_m + \frac{Q}{q}\,(\varepsilon_{r-1}) = \left[\frac{1.00}{.20}\right](1.0) = (5.0).$$

Prices in an extensive sample of contracts should have conformed to the pattern $[P = \alpha + \beta_1 V + \beta_2 D + \beta_3 T + \beta_4 Y + \beta_5 C_1 + \beta_6 C_2 + v]$ with β_1, β_3 positive, β_2 negative and β_5, β_6 negative for the results to be termed "competitive." If prices did not follow this pattern, they can be compared with the monopoly and/or monopsony patterns. The results from actual price formation can be examined for "monopoly seller" discrimination between pipeline buyers.[56] If there were discrimination, the regression pattern should exhibit *different price levels* for each buyer. The pattern of prices on all contracts can be compared with the monopsony pattern of β_1, β_2, $\beta_3 \geqq 0$, $\beta_5 \leqq 0$, $\beta_6 \leqq 0$, as well.

Data from a sample of 922 contracts include information on the "pattern of prices" comparable to these theoretical patterns. Price on each contract was "initial price" (the price for reserves delivered in the first years of term).[57] Volume for each contract was estimated by multiplying the designated "expected monthly rate of delivery" by the number of months of term in the contract. Distance of the trap was the same as for 1950–54 sales in the same county, while the pertinent data on term-length and contingency clauses were in the contract listings.

56. A pattern involving interbuyer discrimination as well as price variation with term, volume, and distance would strongly suggest the presence of monopoly. As noted in Chapter 4 the variation with volume, et al., may or may not be canceled by strong elements of discrimination. Then too, the pattern may be canceled arbitrarily by decree of a group of "oligopoly producers" seeking to set a workable collusive (high) level of price. This last price policy should be easily recognizable.

57. It should be noted that "Initial Price" on contracts signed after 1954 was affected by Federal Power Commission regulation *to some extent*. This price was not *directly regulated* until 1959 (cf. *Atlantic Refining Co. et al., v. Public Service Commission,* 360 US 378), for the Commission earlier operated under the policy that initial price was not a rate-setting consideration. Initial price was allowed on all certified contracts (i.e. all in the sample) from 1956–58. There seem not to have been cases in which contracts were not certified because of initial price provisions before the 1959 Atlantic (or CATCO) case. The level of all initial prices and differences in initial prices on interstate-intrastate contracts do seem to have been affected by increased regulatory costs and the threat of regulation, however. These effects are the subject of a forthcoming study by Robert Gerwig of the University of Chicago; they do not seem to have changed pricing patterns to the extent of affecting "competitive" versus "noncompetitive" price formation.

The sample of contracts from the entire Gulf Coast-Louisiana area for 1956–58 is tested for alternative competition-monopoly hypotheses in the four rows of Table 6:14. Actual prices were such that P in the regression line was:

$$P = 13.527 + .1575V - .7129D + .1551T + .7169Y_{(1957)}$$
$$+ .9556Y_{(1958)} + .2601C_1 + 2.9847C_2$$

for the "small sales" of less than 24 billion cubic feet. Average contract price was:

$$P = 1.436 + .00613V - .5077D + .8748T + 2.2043Y_{(1957)}$$
$$+ .4173Y_{(1958)} - .7681C_1 + 1.925C_2$$

for the "larger contracts" of more than 24 billion cubic feet of reserves. Both computed equations follow the competitive pattern closely. The volume of reserves had a significant positive effect upon price in both calculated regressions (although the price differences from volume differences were distinctly greater on small contracts than on large contracts).[58] Prices were lower on contracts for reserves in farther locations (an amount from .51 to .71 cents per mcf less for each additional hundred miles to the end of transmission). Contracts for twenty years, rather than ten years, had an average initial price 1.55 cents per mcf higher in the sample of small contracts and 8.748 cents per mcf higher in large contracts.[59]

58. Given that $t > /1.96/$ for $\left\{ \dfrac{t = b_1{}' \text{ (large)} - b_1{}'' \text{ (small)}}{\sqrt{S_{b_{1+}}{}^{'2} S_{b_1}{}^2}} \right\}$ dis-
proves the hypothesis that $\beta_1{}'$ (larger) $= \beta_1{}''$ (small). The value of $t = 7.9399$ in this instance, so that the alternative hypothesis is accepted that $\beta_1{}''$ (on small contracts) is different from that $\beta_1{}'$ (on large contracts). The price difference between contracts for 50 billion cubic feet and 100 billion cubic feet was an average .305 cents per mcf, as compared to 1.57 cents per mcf for the difference between 20 billion cubic feet and 10 billion cubic feet. Larger price increases for additions to small volumes in "small contracts" is not unexpected because cost savings on transporting additions to small volumes are greater. Unit transmission costs for sizes of *large* volumes are approximately the same (as in Table 3:5) so that competitive prices on various-sized *large* contracts should be the same.

59. But the observed difference for longer term on large contracts was not sufficient indication of price offers for different term-lengths. The sample of 140 large contracts contained only two with 10-year terms and one with an 18-year term, while the rest had 20-year terms.

Price was higher in 1957 for both large and small sales. The increase for smaller-volume contracts was approximately .72 cents per mcf and for large-volume contracts was 2.20 cents per mcf. Price did not continue to rise in 1958, however: The small contracts had price only .16 cents per mcf higher (an amount not significantly different from 1957 price on a comparable contract) while the large contracts actually had price 1.88 cents per mcf lower than in 1957. In both samples,

TABLE 6:14. *Summary of Gulf Coast-Louisiana Prices, 1956–58*

Given that: $P = \alpha + \beta_1 V + \beta_2 D + \beta_3 T + \beta_4 Y + \beta_5 C_1 + \beta_6 C_2 + v$

P = initial contract price, cents per mcf.
V = volume of reserves, billions of cu. ft.
D = distance of trap, in hundreds of miles
T = term-length, in years
Y = either the first-year sample (zero) or the second year (one)
C_1 = presence of Favored Nations clause (= one)
C_2 = presence of Renegotiation (= one)
R^2 = coefficient of determination
S_u = standard error of estimate, cents per mcf.
S_p = standard deviation of price, cents per mcf.

A. *Small-Volume Contracts* ($V < 24$ *billion cu. ft.*)
    (*sample of 782 contracts*)

Regression equations

$P = \alpha + \beta_1 V + \beta_2 D + \beta_3 T + \beta_4 Y + \beta_5 C_1 + \beta_6 C_2 + v$

$P = 13.527 + .1575V - .7129D + .1551T + .7169Y_{57-56} + .9556Y_{58-56}$
$\quad\;\; (0.625) \;\; (.0194) \quad (.0305) \quad (.0295) \quad (.2669) \quad\quad (.2832)$

$\quad\;\; + .2601C_1 + 2.9847C_2$
$\quad\quad (.2479) \quad\; (0.2344)$

$R^2 = .551$
$S_u = 2.83$
$S_p = 4.20$

(Competitive) Predictions	(Monopoly) Predictions	Tests of computed equations
$\beta_1 > 0$	$\beta_1 \geqq 0$	If $t = b_i/S_{b_i} > \lvert 1.645 \rvert$ hypothesis $\beta_i = 0$
$\beta_2 < 0$	$\beta_2 \leqq 0$	is rejected.
$\beta_3 > 0$	$\beta_3 \geqq 0$	$\beta_1 > 0$ since $t_1 = \quad\; 8.1194$
$\beta_5 \leqq 0$	$\beta_5 \leqq 0$	$\beta_2 < 0$ since $t_2 = -23.3919$
$\beta_6 \leqq 0$	$\beta_6 \leqq 0$	$\beta_3 > 0$ since $t_3 = \quad\; 8.2556$
		$\beta_4 > 0$ since $t_4 = \quad\; 2.6858$
		$\beta_4' > 0$ since $t_4' = \quad\; 3.3747$ *
		$\beta_5 = 0$ since $t_5 = \quad\; 1.0489$
		$\beta_6 > 0$ since $t_6 = \; 12.7328$

* As compared to 1956.

TABLE 6:14. (*cont.*)

B. *Large-Volume Contracts* ($V > 24$ *billion cu. ft.*)
   (*sample of 140 contracts*)

Regression equations

$$P = \alpha + \beta_1 V + \beta_2 D + \beta_3 T + \beta_4 Y + \beta_5 C_1 + \beta_6 C_2 + v$$

$$P = 1.436 + .00613V - .5077D + .8748T + 2.2043Y_{57} + .4173Y_{58}$$
$$\quad\; (3.343)\;\; (.00316)\;\; (.0911)\;\;\; (.1620)\;\;\;\; (0.5308)\;\;\;\;\; (.6293)$$

$$\quad\; - .7681C_1 + 1.925C_2$$
$$\quad\;\;\; (.5223)\;\;\; (0.4287)$$

$R^2 = .566$
$S_u = 2.50$
$S_p = 3.69$

(Competitive) Predictions	(Monopsony) Predictions	Tests of computed equations
$\beta_1 > 0$	$\beta_1 \geqq 0$	$\beta_1 > 0$ since $t_1 = \quad 1.9362$
$\beta_2 < 0$	$\beta_2 \leqq 0$	$\beta_2 < 0$ since $t_2 = -5.5717$
$\beta_3 > 0$	$\beta_3 \geqq 0$	$\beta_3 > 0$ since $t_3 = \quad 5.4011$
$\beta_5 \leqq 0$	$\beta_5 \leqq 0$	$\beta_4 > 0$ since $t_4 = \quad 4.1528$
$\beta_6 \leqq 0$	$\beta_6 \leqq 0$	$\beta_4' = 0$ since $t_4' = \quad 0.6632$ *
		$\beta_5 = 0$ since $t_5 = -1.4708$
		$\beta_6 > 0$ since $t_6 = \quad 4.4899$

* As compared to 1956.

the presence of Favored Nations clauses had a negative, but insignificant, effect upon contract price. Curiously, the presence of Renegotiation clauses had a positive effect upon contract price on both large and small sales; the average addition to price was between 1.93 and 2.98 cents per mcf for those contracts with Renegotiation clauses.[60]

With similar patterns of price variation for both large and small contracts, it is not likely that the "large packages" were sold in a separate market at monopoly prices. There are more explicit tests for monopoly in large sales, however, than by comparison with the price pattern for small sales. The results from monopoly price formation would have included variation with volume, distance, and term but it would have been as important to set different prices for different buyers. There should have been an observable pattern of contrasting price levels for each buyer.

In the Gulf Coast, transporters with greater possibilities for

60. This is contrary to predictions of a negative clause-price relationship for both competition and noncompetition.

home resale, as compared to industrial resale, should have paid higher "monopoly prices," given that home resale demand was more price inelastic. United Gas Pipeline should have paid the lowest price because 53.2 per cent of its resales were to industrial users.[61] Southern Natural Gas and Texas Gas should have paid slightly higher prices because of relatively larger resale for home use (Southern sold 72.9 per cent while Texas Gas sold 88.4 per cent for home use). Transcontinental Gas Pipeline, Texas Eastern, Tennessee Gas Transmission, and Texas-Illinois should have paid significantly higher prices because their resales were to gas utilities (Transcontinental sold only 4.1 per cent to industry, Texas Eastern, and Tennessee less than 1 per cent to the industrial group, and Texas-Illinois none).

The monopoly pattern should have included price variation with volume, distance, and term. It should also have included higher prices for Transcontinental (and others) than for United Gas Pipeline. Price on a contract P should have equaled

$$P = \alpha + \beta_1 V + \beta_2 D + \beta_3 T + \beta_4 Y_{57} + \beta_5 Y_{58} + \beta_6 C_1 + \beta_7 C_2 + \beta_8 X_1 + \beta_9 X_2 + \beta_{10} X_3 + \beta_{11} X_4 + \beta_{12} X_5 + \beta_{13} X_6 + v$$

where $X_1, X_2, \ldots X_6$ denote the large six transporters other than United Gas and where $\beta_9, \beta_{10}, \ldots \beta_{13} > 0$ (i.e., prices paid by other lines should have been higher than those paid by United).[62] In order to maximize returns, a monopolist should have charged prices such that Texas-Illinois paid the

61. United should also have had the most elastic field demand, because the two other sources of resale demand should have been more price-elastic than for other pipelines. United's *Gulf Coast sales to home users* should have been *more* elastic than those of other transporters in northern population centers because there were fewer home purchasers (i.e., smaller population results in a demand curve *further to the left*, as shown in the Appendix). United's sales to other Southwest pipelines should have been highly elastic because most transport-buyers had a large (competitive) number of alternative sources of supply in producer's field markets.

62. The variable X_i, takes the value 1 when the contract is signed by transporter i, the value 0 when it is signed by United. For the monopoly prediction to be realized, each variable should have coefficient $\beta_i > 0$.

most (since $X_3 =$ Texas-Illinois, then $\beta_{10} > \beta_8$, β_9, β_{11}, β_{12}, β_{13}). Transcontinental, Texas Eastern, and Tennessee Gas should have paid more than Southern Natural or Texas Gas (with $X_2 =$ Transcontinental, $X_4 =$ Texas Eastern, and $X_6 =$ Tennessee Gas Transmission, then $\beta_{10} > \beta_9$, β_{11}, $\beta_{13} > \beta_8$, β_{12}).

Prices on large contracts did not follow this monopoly pattern, as shown in Table 6:11b. Rather than United Gas Pipeline having paid the lowest price, two transporters (Tennessee Gas Transmission and Transcontinental) had lower average prices. Rather than Texas-Illinois having the highest price, followed by the long-distance lines to the east, a local transporter (Southern Natural) paid the highest price. Only one firm paid a significantly higher price than United's.[63]

The pattern of prices was not in accord with specific monopoly predictions, but seems rather to have followed the competitive pattern. Four of the six transporters did not pay prices *different from those of United's*. The other two might have paid significantly different prices only for exceptional reasons. Southern Natural paid higher prices for reserves in those parts of North Louisiana where it was a new entrant, so the difference may have been due to temporary miscalculation of *market* prices at new locations.[64] Tennessee Gas paid significantly lower prices on what might have been the last contracts signed under monopsony conditions.[65] Given that

63. One firm, Tennessee Gas Transmission, paid a significantly lower price. This would not be expected from monopoly theory. Rather, it would seem to have followed from an ability to pay extraordinarily lower prices in Starr County, Texas. Tennessee purchases were the only ones there in these years (on the western fringe of the Gulf adjoining the Mexican border). They may have been the last monopsony prices in the Gulf Coast Basin.

64. They may also have resulted from miscalculation of marginal (competitive) "maximum offer price" at the time that monopsony in North Louisiana was still breaking down. The new competitive entrant would be expected to offer *his* maximum price when entering a supply area not completely competitive, rather than offering to purchase for the market clearing price (the marginal "maximum offer"). This may have been the case in the first years after the decline of buyer's power in North Louisiana.

65. Cf. note 63.

Summary of Gulf Coast-Louisiana Prices, 1956–58, Large-Volume Contracts (sample of 113 contracts)

Given that: $P = \alpha + \beta_1 V + \beta_2 D + \beta_3 T + \beta_4 Y_{57} + \beta_5 Y_{58} + \beta_6 C_1 + \beta_7 C_2 + \beta_8 X_1 + \beta_9 X_2 + \beta_{10} X_3 + \beta_{11} X_4 + \beta_{12} X_5 + \beta_{13} X_6 + v$

Where volume, distance, term,
et al. are as defined above and X_1 = sales to Southern Natural
X_2 = sales to Transcontinental
X_3 = sales to Texas-Illinois
X_4 = sales to Texas Eastern
X_5 = sales to Texas Gas Transmission
X_6 = sales to Tennessee Gas Transmission.

Regression equations

$P = .2346 + .00389V - .3582D + .9930T + .8993Y_{57} - .3152Y_{58}$
$\quad\quad\quad (.00294)\quad (.1367)\quad (.1661)\quad (.5272)\quad (.6017)$

$\quad - .6850C_1 + .8118C_2 + 2.0324X_1 + .4520X_2 - 1.5647X_3 - 1.6216X_4$
$\quad\quad (.5940)\quad (.5472)\quad (.6279)\quad (.7224)\quad (1.009)\quad (.8778)$

$\quad - 2.1281X_5 - 9.5683X_6$
$\quad\quad (.7220)\quad\quad (.8384)$

$R^2 = .692$
$S_u = 1.713$
$S_p = 3.086$

(Competitive) Predictions	(Monopoly) Predictions	Tests of computed equations
$\beta_1 > 0$	$\beta_1 > 0$	$\beta_1 = 0$ since $t_1 = 1.3221$
$\beta_2 < 0$	$\beta_2 < 0$	$\beta_2 < 0$ since $t_2 = -2.6203$
$\beta_3 > 0$	$\beta_3 > 0$	$\beta_3 > 0$ since $t_3 = 5.9723$
$\beta_6, \beta_7 \leqq 0$	$\beta_6, \beta_7 \leqq 0$	$\beta_6 = 0$ since $t_6 = 1.4832$
$\beta_8 = 0$	$\beta_8 > 0$	$\beta_7 = 0$ since $t_7 = -1.1532$
$\beta_9 = 0$	$\beta_9 > 0$	$\beta_8 > 0$ since $t_8 = 3.2368$
$\beta_{10} = 0$ (in a "perfect" market)	$\beta_{10} > 0$	$\beta_9 = 0$ since $t_9 = 0.6257$
$\beta_{11} = 0$	$\beta_{11} > 0$	$\beta_{10} = 0$ since $t_{10} = -1.5516$
$\beta_{12} = 0$	$\beta_{12} > 0$	$\beta_{11} = 0$ since $t_{11} = -1.8473$
$\beta_{13} = 0$	$\beta_{13} > 0$	$\beta_{12} = 0$ since $t_{12} = -2.4475$
	$\beta_{10} > \beta_9, B_{11}, \beta_{13} > \beta_8, \beta_{12}$	(for 10 contracts)
		$\beta_{13} = 0$ since $t_{13} = -11.4126$

Source. Expanded regression computations with the sample of contracts listed as "sales for resale in interstate commerce" (F.P.C. Docket G-9277 exhibit 2-LC, 3-LC) and listed as having estimated reserves of more than 24 billion cu. ft. Excluded were all sales to pipelines purchasing less than 5 contracts because of the lack of reliability of S_β from small samples (20 contracts were excluded in all). Note: the tests of the predictions are for $\beta_i = 0$ as compared to $\beta_i > 0$ when $i = 8, 9, \ldots, 13$. So that test values for t_i leading to rejection of the competitive hypothesis $\beta_i = 0$ in favor of the monopoly hypothesis $\beta_i > 0$ are equal to or greater than $+1.645$.

there was not perfect knowledge of all prices and consequently not an immediate uniform price for all comparable competitive contracts, the pattern of slight, but unpredicted, variation in prices between transporters seems close to the theoretical competitive pattern.

Price formation may have resulted in patterns closer to competitive theory than to monopoly theory, while still exhibiting behavior conforming *most* closely to the monopsony pattern. Since there had been significant loss of buyer's power to control price in most field markets, monopsony pricing was not likely. But if it were being practiced, then price formation should have followed the pattern of lack of variation with volume, distance, and term of contract observed in this region in 1946–47 (such that $\beta_1, \beta_2 = 0; \beta_3 \geq 0$).[66]

Actual patterns of prices on large and small contracts in 1956–57 producer's field markets were quite similar. The distance of the trap had a significant negative effect upon price, while the term and volume had a significant positive effect (with the tests of significance shown in Table 6:16). Price in the contract increased somewhat in 1957 for both large and small contracts. Contract clauses had little effect upon price with only Renegotiation clauses raising prices, however. Contract prices followed closely the pattern of the regression equation: The coefficient of determination R^2 was between .487 and .564 so that half of the variance in prices was "explained" by the regression factors.

The variation of prices with volume, distance, and term for both large and small contracts was expected from buyer's competition. The buyers of either large or small volumes were apparently not able to impose the uniform monopsony pattern that minimizes payments of rental returns. The increase in price levels and the increased variation with competitive demand conditions testify to the increased inability of the pipeline to set price.[67]

66. That is, prices should have been set in a monopsony manner in the various fields during a two-year producer's market period.

67. There is no complete explanation for observed variation of prices with the contingency clauses. Prices were (insignificantly) lower on

TABLE 6:16. *Summary of Gulf Coast-Louisiana Prices, 1956–57*

A. *Small-Volume Contracts*
   (*Sample of 504 contracts*)

Regression equations

$$P = \alpha + \beta_1 V + \beta_2 D + \beta_3 T + \beta_4 Y + \beta_5 C_1 + \beta_6 C_2 + v$$

$$P = 13.503 + .1699V - .7200D + .1619T + .7621Y_{57} + .3294C_1$$
$$\quad (0.778) \quad (.0245) \quad (.4661) \quad (.3579) \quad (.2707) \quad (.2903)$$

$$\quad + 2.6391C_2$$
$$\quad (0.2860)$$

$R^2 = .487$
$S_u = 2.83$
$S_p = 3.93$

(*Competitive*) Predictions	(*Monopsony*) Predictions	*Tests of computed equations*
$\beta_1 > 0$	$\beta_1 = 0$	$\beta_1 > 0$ since $t_1 = 6.5345$
$\beta_2 < 0$	$\beta_2 = 0$	$\beta_2 < 0$ since $t_2 = -15.4988$
$\beta_3 > 0$	$\beta_3 \geqq 0$	$\beta_3 > 0$ since $t_3 = 4.5257$
$\beta_5 \leqq 0$	$\beta_5 \leqq 0$	$\beta_4 > 0$ since $t_4 = 2.8149$
$\beta_6 \leqq 0$	$\beta_6 \leqq 0$	$\beta_5 = 0$ since $t_5 = 1.1348$
		$\beta_6 > 0$ since $t_6 = 9.2262$

B. *Large-Volume Contracts*
   (*sample of 108 contracts*)

Regression equations

$$P = \alpha + \beta_1 V + \beta_2 D + \beta_3 T + \beta_4 Y + \beta_5 C_1 + \beta_6 C_2 + v$$

$$P = 1.893 + .00580V - .4895D + .8435T + 2.2597Y_{57} - .6382C_1$$
$$\quad (3.622) \quad (.00350) \quad (.1209) \quad (0.1712) \quad (0.5554) \quad (.5871)$$

$$\quad + 1.7595C_2$$
$$\quad (.5067)$$

$R^2 = .564$
$S_u = 2.58$
$S_p = 3.78$

(*Competitive*) Predictions	(*Monopsony*) Predictions	*Tests of computed equations*
$\beta_1 > 0$	$\beta_1 = 0$	$\beta_1 > 0$ since $t_1 = 1.6573$
$\beta_2 < 0$	$\beta_2 = 0$	$\beta_2 < 0$ since $t_2 = -4.0467$
$\beta_3 > 0$	$\beta_3 \geqq 0$	$\beta_3 > 0$ since $t_3 = 4.9269$
$\beta_5 \leqq 0$	$\beta_5 \leqq 0$	$\beta_4 > 0$ since $t_4 = 4.0869$
$\beta_6 \leqq 0$	$\beta_6 \leqq 0$	$\beta_5 = 0$ since $t_5 = -0.9056$
		$\beta_6 > 0$ since $t_6 = 3.4724$

A REVIEW OF THE DECLINE OF MONOPSONY IN THE
GULF COAST-LOUISIANA REGION

In this extended history of interstate sales in the Gulf region, two tendencies seem predominant. The first was a trend toward discontinuous increases in price levels. The second was a radical change in both the structure of the demand side of markets and the pattern of prices.

Price in the regression equations increased over time in a discontinuous (and statistically unreliable) fashion, as can be seen from comparing Y for different samples in Summary Table 6:17. The sample of mid-1940 contracts showed little price change over time until the entry of one new independent purchaser. This purchaser did not continue the monopsony-type pricing policies of the established three buyers, but offered higher prices that raised the level of all prices. Samples of contracts in the early 1950s also indicated higher prices when new transporters entered old monopsony purchase regions. Prices rose in those years during which new buyers overlapped the previously exclusive supply areas of older transporters along the Gulf Coast. Prices rose substantially in South Louisiana during 1951–52 when there was no longer only one purchaser. In the late 1950s, the level of price fluctuated, with an increase in 1957 and a substantial decrease in 1958. The first year was marked by the expansion of the independent buyers throughout North Louisiana. There was a lack of both substantial expansion and buyer entry in 1958. In all, significantly higher prices followed after the entry of new transporters had "disrupting effects" upon previously noncompetitive buying practices.[68]

---

contracts with Favored Nations clauses as expected from competition (when the increased burden of risk imposed on the buyer is insignificant). But prices were higher on contracts with Renegotiation. This follows neither from competition nor from noncompetitive theory.

68. It is not possible to say that the change toward more competition *caused* rising prices in all cases, however. Extensive increases in demand from all transporters *may* have *caused* some of the larger price increases in the 1950s. Without data (on increments to demand over time at "end of transmission" price P) causality cannot be established.

The pattern of prices exhibited much change over time. There was a tendency toward variation of contract price with the volume of reserves, with the distance to the trap, and with the term of production in the early 1950s along the Texas and Louisiana Gulf, in the late 1950s throughout the Gulf Coast and Louisiana. This is indicated by the larger size (and statistical significance) of the coefficients in the regression equations for the Texas Gulf for 1950–54, and for all large and small contracts in 1956–58 (in Table 6:17). The coefficients came closer to those predicted from competitive pricing when a large number of pipeline buyers became established.

Entry by transporters did not lead to a common pattern of price variation. In some places, the level of prices increased and higher prices were offered first for larger volumes. In other supply markets, the first break in the previous uniform monopsony price took place on closer sales. The over-all results of new competition on the demand side of markets were similar, however; the relative prices for more desirable contracts increased sharply.

The ratio of the price of the "typical contract" to that on the "smallest contract," shown in column 3 of Table 6:18, points to buyers having had to offer higher prices for the "typical contract" when there was competition. This ratio was highest in the Texas Gulf region after the establishment of competition (1950–53) and throughout the Gulf Salt Basin (1956–58). It was lower in the Texas Gulf during 1945–46, when there were three buyers, and in Louisiana during 1950–53, a period in which there were exclusive North Louisiana buyer's markets.

Market structure and performance were undergoing significant change during 1945–60. A few buyers in the 1940s in Louisiana and Texas must have had power to set prices, given the stability and extent of their purchase shares. The similarity of the observed uniform pattern of prices to the theoretical monopsony pattern points to this power having been utilized by the few transporters. The entry and overlapping of new lines in the late 1940s-early 1950s throughout the coastal

TABLE 6:17. Summary of Price Behavior in the Gulf Coast Basin, 1945–58

$$P = \alpha + \beta_1 V + \beta_2 D + \beta_3 T + \beta_4 Y + \beta_5 C_1 + \beta_6 C_2 + v$$

R^2 = coefficient of determination
S_u = standard error of estimate, cents per mcf.
S_p = standard deviation of price, cents per mcf.

1945-46 (75 contracts)

$P = 4.861 + .0020V - .1465D - .0030T - .1127Y + 1.9569C_1 - .9417C_2$
　(.593)　(.0018)　(.0908)　(.0091)　(.2155)　(1.0609)　(.9176)
$R^2 = .121$
$S_u = .896$
$S_p = .916$

1946-47 (130 contracts)

$P = 5.321 + .0064V - .2187D - .0051T + .9946Y + .2951C_1 + .1089C_2$
　(.392)　(.0019)　(.0405)　(.0074)　(.1573)　(.3865)　(.4133)
$R^2 = .368$
$S_u = .804$
$S_p = .988$

1950-51 Texas Gulf Coast (91 contracts)

$P = 11.374 + .0035V - .7560D + .1614T - .5234Y - .3041C_1 - .4076C_2$
　(2.014)　(.0021)　(.2064)　(.0581)　(.4270)　(.4381)　(.4759)
$R^2 = .223$
$S_u = 1.80$
$S_p = 1.98$

1952-53 Texas Gulf Coast (285 contracts)

$P = 10.235 + .00394V - .4905D + .0780T + 1.7642Y + .3262C_1 + .8953C_2$
　(1.175)　(.00113)　(.1115)　(.0395)　(0.2549)　(.3717)　(.4257)
$R^2 = .195$
$S_u = 2.05$
$S_p = 2.34$

1953-54 Texas Gulf Coast (261 contracts)

$P = 11.3269 + .0227V - .4694D + .1261T + .3608Y + .5483C_1 - .1172C_2$
　(0.9369)　(.0050)　(.0932)　(.0308)　(.2137)　(.3022)　(.3606)
$R^2 = .274$
$S = 1.63$

$$P = 6.227 - .0001V - .2628D + .0191T + .2459Y + .5052C_1 - .2692C_2$$

1950–51 Louisiana (164 contracts)

$P = 6.227$ (1.532), $(.0009)$ $(.2027)$ $(.0346)$ $(.2802)$ $(.3113)$ $(.3653)$
$R^2 = .245$
$S_u = 2.47$
$S_p = 2.70$

$$P = 0.2566 + .00349V + .9631D + .0585T + 1.0982Y + 1.2460C_1 + 2.0804C_2$$

1952–53 Louisiana (196 contracts)

$P = 0.2566$ (1.8912), $(.00199)$ $(.2670)$ $(.0397)$ $(.3849)$ (0.4290) (0.4641)
$R^2 = .379$
$S_u = 2.61$
$S_p = 3.27$

$$P = 4.534 - .0023V + .5782D + .0594T + .0764Y + .7016C_1 + 1.7631C_2$$

1953–54 Louisiana (201 contracts)

$P = 4.534$ (1.815), $(.0028)$ $(.2540)$ $(.0352)$ $(.4004)$ $(.4418)$ $(.4566)$
$R^2 = .173$
$S_u = 2.80$
$S_p = 3.03$

$$P = 1.436 + .0061V - .5077D + .8748T + 2.2043Y_{57-58} + .4173Y_{58-56} - .7681C_1 + 1.925C_2$$

1956–58 Large contracts (140 contracts)

$P = 1.436$ (3.343), $(.0031)$ $(.0911)$ $(.1620)$ (0.5308) $(.6293)$ $(.5223)$ (0.4287)
$R^2 = .566$
$S_u = 2.50$
$S_p = 3.69$

$$P = 13.527 + .1575V - .7129D + .1551T + .7169Y_{57-58} + .9556Y_{55-58} + .2601C_1 + 2.9847C_2$$

1956–58 Small contracts (504 contracts)

$P = 13.527$ (0.625), $(.0194)$ $(.0305)$ $(.0295)$ $(.2669)$ $(.2832)$ $(.2479)$ (0.2344)
$R^2 = .551$
$S_u = 2.83$
$S_p = 4.20$

Source. Tables 6:3, 6:7, and 6:14.

region preceded a disruption of the monopsony pricing pattern. Monopsony power was "deteriorating," and prices displayed the results of new competition along with the last vestiges of buyer's control. Actual prices point to the deterioration of the uniform monopsony pattern first in the Texas Gulf, then in South Louisiana, and finally in North Louisiana. By the late 1950s, the overlap of transporters had become so complete that producers could count on at least six large sources of demand in each field. Each buyer also had more than a dozen extensive sources of uncommitted reserves. Prices should have followed competitive patterns in all extensive markets and, by and large, they seemed to have done so. Tests for both monopoly and monopsony during 1956–58

TABLE 6:18. *Regression Equation Prices for Two Types of Contracts*

	"Typical" contract price, cents per mcf	"Smallest" contract price, cents per mcf	Ratio of "typical" price to "smallest" price (1/2)
	1	2	3
1945–46 Gulf Coast–Louisiana	5.035	4.978	1.022
1946–47 Gulf Coast–Louisiana	3.667	3.397	1.079
1950–51 Texas Gulf Coast	6.682	3.380	1.977
1952–53 Texas Gulf Coast	8.452	6.707	1.260
1953–54 Texas Gulf Coast	11.208	7.283	1.541
1950–51 Louisiana	5.195	4.839	1.074
1952–53 Louisiana	11.011	9.664	1.139
1953–54 Louisiana	11.643	10.620	1.091
1956–58 Gulf Coast-Louisiana (for contracts at the Texas distance)	13.852	10.779	1.286

Source. "Typical" contract price is computed from the relevant regression equations in Table 6:17 for $V = 67.38$ billion cu. ft., $D = 6.35$ hundred miles in Louisiana, 9.85 hundred miles in Texas, $T =$ twenty years, and the contract including Favored Nations and Renegotiation clauses. "Smallest" contract price is computed for the same equations, with $V = 1.0$ billion cu. ft., $D = 6.35$ and 9.85 hundred miles, $T =$ one year, and the presence of the clauses. The values for these conditions in the "typical" contract were taken from average volume, distance, etc., for 1945–46.

provide no indication of pricing behavior other than the competitive.

Systematic competition had emerged, between 1955 and 1960, from what was once a series of buyer's monopsony markets.

7. The Sale of Reserves in the Mid-Continent Area

Price formation in the Mid-Continent fields of North Texas, Oklahoma, and Kansas exhibits similarity to *both* competitive and monopsonistic behavior. Sales of new reserves in fields having several buyers and sellers followed a pricing pattern like that predicted from perfect competition. These sales were clustered in the Panhandle and Hugoton fields. Sales in mid-Kansas-Oklahoma, in contrast, were from one-buyer supply markets and followed pricing patterns similar to the uniform monopsony pattern. Price behavior for the entire region was a composite of competition and monopsony, with monopsony characteristics becoming more predominant as time passed.

THE NATURE OF MARKETS

Differences in the extent of market control were, of course, due to the fact that fields were dispersed. Reserves were either concentrated in the adjoining Panhandle and Hugoton fields in North Texas and western Oklahoma-Kansas, or they were spread over all of central Kansas and Oklahoma in small fields. The Panhandle-Hugoton was a region of almost continuous traps in vertical and horizontal series on the western borders of Kansas and Oklahoma; the dispersed central Kansas and Oklahoma traps were at least 150–200 miles farther east. Each transporter concentrated transmission facilities in the Panhandle-Hugoton, and provided coverage only in those central fields close to his main transmission line. The supply areas of most of the transporters overlapped in the Panhandle-Hugoton but not elsewhere, because each pipeline traversed a different geographical portion of central Kansas or Oklahoma to reach separate points of resale.

With such a spread of field areas, producers found themselves in competitive or monopsonistic selling markets, depending upon the closeness of their reserves to the Panhandle-Hugoton. Each well-owner was limited to exchange within his field within two to three years after discovery was complete. The producer in the Panhandle probably could have offered his new reserves to a number of buyers and could have expected competitive bidding for these reserves. The producer selling new reserves in central Kansas, however, could have received bids from only a few pipelines.

The producers were finding large volumes of reserves in the Panhandle-Hugoton fields in the early 1950s, so that most buyers sought to extend lateral lines into these fields. Each of the interstate pipelines to the east [1] considered the two fields to be part of the relevant market area by 1950–53, since new reserves in this region were within reach of constructed lateral lines. But these fields were not the entire market area: each transporter was able to buy reserves along its main transmission system in central Kansas or Oklahoma as well (and in some cases to purchase gas in the Gulf region through a subsidiary). For the buyer, in effect, the supply area centered on the Panhandle-Hugoton, but included some fields along lateral lines beyond the limits of these two fields. Ownership of reserves in this supply area was not concentrated enough to allow for producer's control.

CONTROL OF SUPPLY IN RELEVANT BUYER'S MARKETS

Control would have followed from a few producers having had a majority of the uncommitted reserves in the entire

1. Some considerable amount of gas was sold throughout the 1950s to the Colorado Interstate Pipeline Company for resale in the Colorado-Wyoming area. The gas was from a separate supply area on the western fringes of the Panhandle-Hugoton, bordering on common supply with

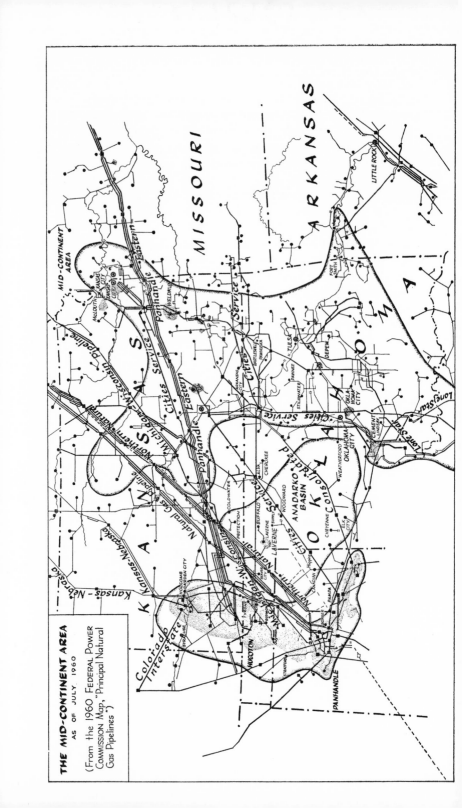

THE MID-CONTINENT AREA
AS OF JULY, 1960

(From the 1960 Federal Power Commission Map, "Principal Natural Gas Pipelines")

buyer's supply area. The buyers considered alternative volumes for sale over four-year periods in their supply territories, so that a monopoly producer would have had to control most new reserves for three to five years in at least the Panhandle-Hugoton. Indications are that no one or small group of producers owned most of the new reserves.

Sales of new reserves were highly concentrated in the Panhandle-Hugoton. In 1950–53 and 1951–54 any pipeline with gathering facilities throughout the Panhandle-Hugoton had access to 70 different sources of new reserves there (there were more than 70 sellers in each four-year period in these two fields). But four producers were responsible for a large share of total sales in each of these periods:

1950–53

Stanolind Oil and Gas:	36.121 %
Shamrock Oil and Gas:	19.997
Phillips Petroleum:	10.074
J. M. Huber Corporation:	6.027
	72.219 % of 3.691 trillion cubic feet [2]

1951–54

Shamrock Oil and Gas:	32.960 %
Phillips Petroleum:	16.839
J. M. Huber Corporation:	9.205
Shell Oil Company:	8.885
	67.889 % of 2.265 trillion cubic feet

The ten largest producers in the early period accounted for 89.914 per cent of the estimated total of new sales, and the

the eastern lines in any year. These sales were smaller than those to the east. They require a separate market study and will not be discussed here.

2. The estimated total of dedicated reserves under 1950–54 contracts is for gas to be delivered to the east only, since sales to Colorado transporters were in "a separate supply area."

ten largest in the 1951–54 period accounted for 81.070 per cent.[3]

Concentration in actual sales, while quite high, probably does not indicate that a few firms were able to control the volume of 1950–54 sales. The buyers had a number of other sources of supply almost as large as Stanolind, Shamrock, or Phillips. The largest buyers purchased reserves in the Gulf region (via the Texas-Illinois, American Louisiana, and Trunkline Pipeline Companies, each of which was affiliated with a Panhandle pipeline). To have controlled prices paid by these transporters, the Panhandle-Hugoton producers would have had to control all the uncommitted reserves in this region.[4] The interstate buyers without Gulf pipelines did have access, in the central counties of Kansas and Oklahoma, to other field areas where there were more than a dozen sources of new volumes of gas (some 30 or more contracts were signed for new volumes in the central regions each year, some in each separated supply area). At least three of these (signed by the Texas Company, Cities Service Producing Company, and Kerr-McGee Oil) could match half the volume in the big Stanolind contract. The transporter with an extended supply area encountered considerably lower producer

3. The larger firms all attained "largeness" in sales by dedicating an extensive "block of reserves": Stanolind provided its share of reserves in one contract in Marshall County, Kansas, while Shamrock committed one large volume in the Panhandle of Texas, etc.

4. This is to suggest that three of the largest buyers had supply regions including fields in both the Panhandle-Hugoton and the Gulf Coast of Texas. This is not to suggest that the Panhandle and the Gulf Coast should be considered one common supply area. For nine large lines in the Gulf, and all except three in the Panhandle-Hugoton, the limit of the supply region is the Gulf Salt Basin *or* the Mid-Continent Basin. The region relevant (for analysis) is in one basin or the other, unless perfect competition can be assumed to provide sources of arbitrage resulting in a uniform price level over the two basins (adding transport costs).

The three buyers with the consolidated Gulf-Panhandle supply region could have purchased in the first area if Panhandle sellers sought to restrict the supply of new reserves. Only by control of advance portion of total reserves in the two regions (requiring control of 100 per cent, at least, in the Panhandle-Hugoton) could these producers begin to consider setting price.

sales concentration than was to be found in the Panhandle-Hugoton area alone.

Changes in shares of sales (as opposed to concentration in sales alone) indicate a lack of control of reserves over the relevant market period. Stanolind experienced a 70 per cent decrease in its market share between 1950–53 and 1951–54. Shamrock, Phillips, and Huber had increases ranging 20 to 60 per cent of their respective 1950–53 shares of sales. Shell Oil Company completed sales that increased its share by 100 per cent. These changes seem to have followed from sales of new discoveries by entering or expanding producers. These firms did not obviously follow a sequence of sales prearranged to control market shares and restrict supply. Rather, the sequence of discoveries by *different* firms points to the continuous appearance of new sources.

The sources of supply seem to have been even more diverse in the later 1950s. Large volumes of new reserves were discovered in the Panhandle-Hugoton during 1953, 1954, and 1955 (as a result of deeper drilling in known producing regions). At the same time, the "run" of step-out gas drilling had begun in the central Kansas and upper-central Oklahoma fields. Promising wildcat discoveries during 1950–53 had led to some extensive development by 1955 throughout the Mid-Continent. As a result, a volume of 17.3 trillion cubic feet of uncommitted reserves had become available by 1956, and was widely owned for the most part (as is indicated by volumes of the largest six in Table 7:1). The six largest owners controlled only 15.60 per cent of total reserves in the area. The two pipelines controlled scarcely more through producing affiliates (16.18 per cent). Ownership in this two-year period would seem to have been diverse enough to prevent any one firm from controlling total commitments of new reserves.

Pipelines purchasing over longer periods than two years could have bid for these sources of reserves in 1954–56, or could have waited for newly discovered reserves to become available in 1957–58. Concentration in sales show that this wider market had as many sources of supply. In the sample of 1956–58 sales to interstate transporters in the Panhandle-

TABLE 7:1. *Ownership of Uncommitted Reserves in the Mid-Continent Region, 1954–56*

Company	Estimated total reserves (trillions of cu. ft.)	Estimated total uncommitted reserves (trillions of cu. ft.)	Estimated uncommitted reserves for sale to pipelines in the Mid-Continent area (trillions of cu. ft.)
Phillips Petroleum Co.	17.2	3.5	1.0
Texaco, Incorporated	11.5	4.8	0.5
Cities Service Oil Co.	4.9	0.5	0.3
Pan American Oil Co. (Standard Oil of Indiana)	9.9	4.8	0.3
Hugoton Production Co.	1.3	0.3	0.3
Magnolia Petroleum (Standard Oil of New York)	8.0	3.1	0.1
			Total 2.5

Pipeline Producing Affiliates	Estimated total reserves (trillions of cu. ft.)	Estimated total uncommitted reserves (trillions of cu. ft.)	Estimated uncommitted reserves for sale to pipelines in the Mid-Continent area (trillions of cu. ft.)
Panhandle Oil Corp.	3.1	0.9	2.2
Northern Producing Co.	2.2	1.5	0.7
			Total 2.9

Source. Total estimated and uncommitted reserves were obtained from annual reports and stock prospectus sources, or from surveys made by some of the above firms. Reserves in the Mid-Continent have been estimated by producers and buyers in the region in personal interviews. Worksheets on most of the company estimates are available upon request.

Hugoton, the four largest sellers provided only 28.384 per cent of 2.144 trillion cubic feet. Each of these four firms had almost identical shares: Humble Oil and Refining had 8.426 per cent; Shamrock Oil and Gas had 8.032 per cent; Pan American Oil Company had 6.151 per cent; Texas Company had 5.725 per cent for a total of 28.384 per cent. The ten largest sellers were responsible for 50.440 per cent of the total volume. In the sample of new contracts in the central Kansas and Oklahoma fields, the four largest sold 28.520 per cent of approximately 1.536 trillion cubic feet. The four largest sellers in these central fields (Jones and Pellow Oil, Magnolia, Sun, and Gulf) were different from those in the Panhandle, so that concentration in sales in the relevant supply area must have been lower than in the Panhandle-Hugoton alone.[5]

It is not likely that any producer with 5 to 8 per cent of sales could have set new contract prices. Even if the four largest were able strictly to limit their collective supply, they probably could not have set price effectively.[6] Rather, it is likely that each producer supplied reserves under competitive conditions. There seems to have been a sufficient number of producers and of large volumes of reserves to ensure the interstate buyers that no producer was able to control prices. Producers, in turn, were faced with competitive demand conditions in some fields. In other fields, however, they were faced with one purchaser.

CONTROL OF DEMAND IN RELEVANT PRODUCER'S MARKETS

There were at least three interstate pipeline buyers in the Panhandle-Hugoton from the beginning of the 1930s. The Natural Gas Pipeline Company of America purchased vol-

5. Of course the buyers with access to the Gulf Coast (in lines of subsidiaries) had opportunities to purchase in a "supply market" the size of the Mid-Continent and Gulf Coast Basins combined, and to operate in markets with even lower concentration.

6. To have set a higher than competitive price level while contributing only 30 per cent of sales would have required the "monopolists" to forego selling at least half of reserve holdings. This would not have been profitable compared to a policy of selling maximum reserves at the competitive price.

umes of gas in the central-southern Panhandle for resale in Chicago, and in 1931 had constructed a line able to transport 175 million cubic feet per day. Panhandle Eastern Pipeline Company constructed a comparable transmission pipeline to Detroit from the middle of the Hugoton field at the same time. The Northern Natural Gas Company purchased reserves in the northern sector of the Hugoton field before 1930 for transmission to cities in Minnesota. During the 1940s, each of these buyers expanded gathering lines through the entire Panhandle-Hugoton in search of more reserves. Northern built new lines to the Texas portion of the Panhandle field, as did the Panhandle Eastern Company, while Natural Gas Pipeline extended north into Kansas. Few traps in the entire Panhandle-Hugoton were not accessible to these three buyers.

Prior to 1950, at least three additional transporters entered portions of these two large fields. The Michigan-Wisconsin Pipeline Company constructed lines to Milwaukee and central Michigan communities in 1945, after purchasing reserves in the central region of the Panhandle-Hugoton.[7] The Cities Service Pipeline Company gathered reserves throughout the Panhandle and central Oklahoma for transmission to local industrial users and to Missouri cities.[8] Consolidated Gas

7. Michigan-Wisconsin actually purchased through an intermediary: the Phillips Petroleum Company purchased and gathered reserves from the central Panhandle-Hugoton, "stripped" these and its own reserves of liquids, then resold the entire volume under long-term contract. Strictly speaking, supply areas for the two companies would have been the same if Phillips were to act as Michigan-Wisconsin's agent. In any one to three-year market period, Phillips might have been able to control Michigan's purchases and prices if Phillips were to act "as a monopoly producer" of the reserves it purchased until Michigan could construct its own gathering lines. This is a possibility, and this is what was at issue in *Phillips Petroleum Company v. Wisconsin*, 247 U.S. 672. Short-run monopoly power of one (unregulated) pipeline over another is a unique case that, unfortunately, seems to have been mistaken as supposed-monopoly of all producers as a result of this decision.

8. Cities Service Pipeline was a large purchaser of reserves in the Panhandle-Hugoton prior to 1950, chiefly from the Cities Service Oil Company but also from a number of other producers. During the 1950s Cities Service became more of a transporter and less of a producer with transmission facilities as the amount of its purchases increased.

Utilities Company, an amalgamation of a number of separated local transporters from all parts of Texas, purchased for local use in the southern Panhandle, while Kansas-Nebraska Natural Gas Company provided a source of demand in the northern portion of the Hugoton field.[9]

There were, in effect, a half-dozen interstate pipelines able to purchase reserves in each of the traps in the Panhandle-Hugoton by 1950. Producers in the two large fields probably could have sought offers from any one of the six buyers. At least, there was little opportunity for any pipeline to bid for reserves on the basis that he was the only possible buyer.

In the newer fields of central Kansas and Oklahoma, transporters did not overlap to any great extent. Volumes of reserves were scattered over the central portion of the two states. Transporters directed main lines toward their respective areas of resale, so that each passed through only part of the region. It was as though the Panhandle-Hugoton fields formed the hub of a wheel while the pipelines were spokes going from the hub to surrounding resale locations.

The spokes running through the Kansas or Oklahoma central fields did not overlap.[10] The central counties of Kansas were, in fact, in the purchase areas only of Northern Natural and Natural Gas Pipeline Company. Northern had two lines, one from the Texas Panhandle and the other from the Kansas part of the Hugoton field, that merged in Ellsworth County in central Kansas.[11] Natural Gas Pipeline transmission equipment was in these same counties. The only other large interstate transporter in the vicinity, Michigan-Wisconsin Pipeline, did not purchase new reserves but relied upon volumes re-

9. Kansas-Nebraska purchased reserves there for resale to local gas utilities and to small industrial users in Kansas and Nebraska.

10. After 1955, new reserves in the central fields were so large that it was practicable for each to build larger-sized lateral lines, touching each other's transmission lines, but these lines were not constructed. This absence of encroachment may have been the result of agreement, or of lack of knowledge about relevant alternatives.

11. Both of these lines were adjacent to fields of new reserves, the northernmost in Pawnee and Barton Counties of Kansas, the southern in Meade, Clark, Edwards Counties of Kansas.

ceived on resale from the Phillips Petroleum Company Pipeline.[12]

The central counties of Oklahoma were in the purchase domain of Cities Service Gas Company throughout most of the 1950s. This transporter had three large lateral lines that, together, completely covered the central and northern Oklahoma fields. One transmission lateral ran west to east from the Oklahoma Panhandle field to Missouri, and was the only interstate line in Harper, Woods, Alfalfa, and Grant Counties. A second line ran due north through central Oklahoma and gathered most new reserves in Garvin, McClain, Oklahoma, Cleveland, and Logan Counties.[13] The third Cities Service line bisected the angle between the east-west and north-south lines, and allowed this company exclusive purchase opportunity in the non-Panhandle fields of southwest Oklahoma. Until entry of one other transporter in the late 1950s, the producers in central Oklahoma could count only on Cities Service Pipeline Company as an extensive purchaser of new reserves.

In southern Oklahoma there were only two large sources of demand. The Lone Star Gas Company purchased reserves in the counties along the Texas-Oklahoma border for transportation to Texas retail gas companies and overlapped at some locations with the small intrastate Oklahoma Natural Gas Company, or with local industrial firms. Prior to 1955 Lone Star was the only company able to purchase all new reserves. After 1955 the Natural Gas Pipeline Company of America obtained reserves for a new lateral line in the

12. There was a transporter farther north (Kansas-Nebraska Natural Gas) and one between the two sets of counties (Cities Service) but these two were not sources of demand in the particular counties containing the new reserve volumes. Also, Panhandle Eastern had a small purchase area to the south of these counties along with Cities Service. Consisting of Meade County (which was common to Northern and Natural Gas Pipeline as well) and the south-central Kansas counties of Reno and Pratt, this region was also highly productive of new reserves in 1950–56. It was a separate and distinct (exclusive) purchase region.

13. The only other sources of demand there were two state lines (Oklahoma Natural Gas and Consolidated Gas Utilities) that purchased from Cities Service.

southernmost fields, so that there was some opportunity for producers there to sell to one of two buyers.

Broadly speaking, there seem to have been contrasting demand conditions in the Panhandle-Hugoton and in the central fields. The Panhandle-Hugoton fields were the supply areas of a half-dozen overlapping transporters.[14] In contrast, fields in central Kansas and Oklahoma each had only one or two buyers. The northern Kansas-Oklahoma field areas had Northern and Natural Gas Pipeline, the central fields had only Cities Service, and the southern fields had only Lone Star Gas (and, later, Natural Gas Pipeline) as extensive sources of reserve demand.

Contrasting demand conditions are also indicated by actual purchases in producer's markets. In the Panhandle-Hugoton, concentration in the purchases of new reserves was high, but there was considerable turnover in individual pipeline purchase shares. During four market periods in the early 1950s (i.e., 1950–51, 1951–52, 1952–53, and 1953–54) there were never more than ten sources of demand of any size. As shown in Table 7:2, the four largest buyers in each market period together signed contracts for at least 90 per cent of the total volume of reserves in the sample. As shown in Table 7:3, levels of purchase concentration were similar in the 1956–58 selling periods, with the four largest pipeline buyers accounting for more than 96 per cent of the estimated total reserves.

During the 1950–54 market periods, the largest purchaser changed from Cities Service to Northern Natural Gas and the second largest changed from Panhandle Eastern to Phillips (i.e., Michigan-Wisconsin). Some of the smaller lines, such as the Kansas-Nebraska Pipeline and Consolidated Gas Utilities, purchased 7–8 per cent in one market period but a negligible amount thereafter. In general, two of the four largest purchasers differed in succeeding market periods.

In the later 1950s, there was not as much turnover in shares. Northern Natural Gas remained the largest purchaser during 1956–57 and during 1957–58; Panhandle Eastern remained the

14. That is, if the six had resale demand and main line capacity to transport the potential new contract volumes.

TABLE 7:2. *Concentration in the Purchase of Reserves in the Panhandle-Hugoton Field, 1950–54*

	1950–51	1951–52	1952–53	1953–54
Estimated volume of reserves (trillions of cu. ft.)	2.6101	1.3725	1.0813	.8927
Number of contracts	65	68	100	123
Number of buyers	14	11	10	11
Percentage of total new reserves purchased by the four largest buyers	Cities Service 53.834 Panhandle Eastern 16.978 Northern Natural 12.496 Kansas-Nebraska 7.273 90.581	Northern 56.943 Panhandle Eastern 26.894 Consolidated 8.857 Phillips 3.795 96.487	Northern 77.776 Phillips 7.532 Panhandle Eastern 4.413 Cities Service 3.588 93.309	Northern 58.589 Phillips 15.253 Kerr-McGee 10.979 Natural Gas Pipe-line 5.858 90.679
Percentage purchased by the ten largest buyers	99.981	99.998	100.000	99.916

224

Source. Compilation of contracts submitted by producers to the Federal Power Commission, Docket G-9277.

TABLE 7:3. *Concentration in the Purchase of Reserves in the Panhandle-Hugoton Field, 1956–58*

	1956–57	1957–58
Estimated volume of reserves (trillions of cu. ft.)	1.4733	1.5598
Number of contracts	248	263
Number of buyers	11	12
Percentage of total new reserves purchased by the four largest buyers	Northern Natural 46.707 Panhandle Eastern 28.428 Natural Gas Pipeline 10.073 Colorado Interstate 9.017 Kansas-Nebraska 2.846 97.071	Northern Natural 62.123 Panhandle Eastern 19.732 Natural Gas Pipeline 6.565 Colorado Interstate 5.109 El Paso Natural 2.635 96.164
Per cent of reserves purchased by the ten largest buyers	99.854	99.613

Source. As in Table 5:1.

second largest. The third largest buyer was the combined Colorado Interstate-Natural Gas Pipeline (Colorado had purchased new reserves in the eastern sector for resale to Natural Gas Pipeline [15] when the latter became a source of new demand for the first time in years). There was also one extensive new purchaser. In the last of the 1950s, the Transwestern Pipeline Company entered not only the West Texas-New Mexico area but also the Hugoton and fields immediately to the east in Oklahoma. This company began by obtaining more than .4934 trillion cubic feet in the area.[16] The "rebirth" of Natural Gas Pipeline and the entry of Transwestern resulted in more change in potential buyers shares than shown in Table 7:2.

Numbers of buyers, concentration in purchases, and changes in purchase shares provide insight into control of demand in the Panhandle fields. There were more than six possible buyers in each trap. The shares of purchases of the four largest were extensive and would have been sufficient for collusive buyer's power. But changes in shares during 1950–53 and extensive entry during 1956–58 were not likely to have been either the result of collusion or compatible with it. In the absence of collusion, price formation in the Panhandle-Hugoton during the 1950s should have followed a competitive rather than a monopsonistic pattern.

Buyer's concentration in the central Kansas-Oklahoma fields was much higher than in the Panhandle-Hugoton, and there was no change in purchase shares in most field areas. In the north-central fields, the Northern Natural Gas Company pur-

15. The result being that Natural Gas Pipeline obtained new reserves, at higher prices than in the 1930s, without triggering Favored Nations clauses in old contracts.

16. Cf. F.P.C. Opinion no. 328 in Docket G-14871, *Transwestern Pipeline Company, et al.* (1959). As a result of these purchases, "shares" are adjusted so that: Northern had 47.14 per cent, Transwestern had 24.03, Panhandle had 14.99 of 2.0532 trillion cubic feet in 1957–58. These are not all of Transwestern's purchases since 1958. Some contracts had not yet been listed, and one of three Panhandle contracts had no listed volume. Moreover, these shares are not indicative of alternative sources of demand in a common supply area; rather, since Transwestern came from the west, there was short-run overlapping of what should become two separated supply regions, east and west.

chased almost all of the new reserves sold in both 1950–54, and 1956–58.[17] The Cities Service Pipeline Company purchased almost all of the new reserves sold in central Oklahoma.[18] In the southernmost fields of Oklahoma, Lone Star Gas Company purchased almost all the listed new reserves.[19] These three transporters [20] each seem to have had exclusive purchase areas. From the producer's view, there were a num-

17. Along the first line running from the northern Hugoton to Ellsworth County, 100 per cent of new reserves in Pawnee and Barton Counties were sold to Northern. Along the second line from the Oklahoma Hugoton to Ellsworth County, Northern purchased 100 per cent of the new volumes in Clark and Edwards Counties, 90 per cent in Ford County (in all the market periods examined). Northern overlapped Natural Gas Pipeline in these counties, as mentioned, but Northern was the only buyer. This again was probably due to previous (1930–45) contracts of Natural Gas Pipeline having Favored Nations clauses that removed Natural from sharing purchases here at even monopsony prices. There was extensive multiple purchasing of reserves in Meade county only (adjoining the Hugoton field in Kansas) where Northern purchased 17.0 per cent in 1956–58, Colorado Interstate-Natural Gas Pipeline Company purchased 15.9 per cent, and Panhandle Eastern was responsible for 67.1 per cent.

18. Cities purchased 100 per cent of reserves in the sample of contracts, for 1950–54 and for 1956–58, from Barber and Cowley Counties in Kansas, and from Alfalfa and Woods Counties in Oklahoma along its east-west lateral lines. This pipeline took 100 per cent of the reserves sold in McClain, Cleveland, Oklahoma, Lincoln, Logan, and Noble Counties of central Oklahoma along its north-south lateral line. There was common purchasing of reserves with Consolidated Gas utilities in Kay County (where Cities' two lines cross). Consolidated purchased 10.0 per cent in 1953–54, 16.2 per cent in 1956–58 and Cities Service bought the remaining share. Since Cities Service was Consolidated's chief source of reserves there is no reason to doubt that purchases were "cooperative." Cities shared purchases in only one other central Oklahoma county: in Harper County, close to the Hugoton field, where Colorado Interstate took 5.9 per cent, Michigan-Wisconsin purchased 90.8 per cent of 1956–58 volumes, and Cities had the remaining. It appears from actual purchases that producers only in Harper County had access to more than one purchaser.

19. In Stephans, Garvin, and Murray Counties, on the Texas-South Oklahoma border, Lone Star was the only transporter to sign new reserve contracts. There were 18 new contracts in Garvin county in 1950–54, and as many in the other two counties in the 1950–54 and 1956–58 periods combined. There were other intrastate buyers in other counties, but only Oklahoma Natural purchased from more than one field and this buyer also bought from Lone Star.

20. Panhandle Eastern also purchased 10 per cent in Ford County, 67.1 per cent in Meade County, and 100 per cent in Reno, Kiowa

ber of field markets, each of which had only one of the three as a source of demand. From the buyer's view, there were alternative volumes available in a large number of fields. The pipelines must each have had control of prices in their separate fields.

Market structure in the central Kansas-Oklahoma region was distinctly monopsonistic, while market structure in the Hugoton-Panhandle fields was indicative of competition. Clearly there should have been monopsony pricing in the 1950s in the central Kansas-Oklahoma fields and there may have been competitive pricing in the Panhandle-Hugoton fields.

PRICE FORMATION IN THE PANHANDLE-HUGOTON AND THE
CENTRAL KANSAS-OKLAHOMA FIELDS

If the buyers did compete for reserves in the Panhandle-Hugoton, while controlling prices and sales in separate supply areas of central Kansas or Oklahoma, then there should have been contrasting patterns and levels of prices in the two sectors during the 1950s. In order to minimize transporter's purchase costs, monopsony price should have varied only with marginal production costs (not with field distance or with the available volume of reserves). In contrast, the prices following from competition in demand should have varied with the volume and the location of the reserves. Competitive or maximum offer prices should have varied with the term of contract, and with the presence-absence of a contingency clause.

With competition in the Panhandle-Hugoton, prices there should have conformed to the pattern $\{P = \alpha + \beta_1 V + \beta_2 D + \beta_3 T + \beta_4 Y + \beta_5 C_1 + \beta_6 C_2 + v\}$ where β_1, $\beta_3 > 0$ (prices higher on larger-volume, longer-term contracts) and where $\beta_2 < 0$, $\beta_5 < 0$, $\beta_6 < 0$ (prices lower on reserves at greater distances, and perhaps lower on sales in contracts with con-

Counties to the south of the Northern Natural gathering area. The percentages were similar for 1950–54 and 1956–58, and suggest that there was little overlap with Northern in other than Ford and Meade Counties.

tingency clauses). But the central Kansas-Oklahoma pricing pattern should not have included variation with these factors; rather prices should have been uniform so that $\{\beta_1, \beta_2, \beta_3, \beta_4, \beta_5, \beta_6 = 0\}$.[21] Price P should have been higher in the Panhandle-Hugoton than in the central fields.

Actual prices in the early 1950s followed a pattern consistently similar to that of competition in the Panhandle-Hugoton, but that of monopsony in the central Kansas-Oklahoma fields. The pricing patterns for Panhandle-Hugoton sales during producer's market periods in 1950–54 are summarized by the regression analyses in Table 7:4. The comparable central fields pricing pattern is derived from comparing the 1952–54 central Kansas-Oklahoma contracts with these regression analyses.[22]

For all market periods there was a positive relationship between contracted volume and initial price. For the 1951–52 and 1953–54 periods price was significantly higher on larger-

21. The only significant variation in monopsony prices might have been because of production cost differences between Anadarko and non-Anadarko reservoirs. The first had been a shallow, dry-gas basin with low pressure, so that it may have cost the producer less and the buyer more for compression to take reserves from this field area. Prices under complete monopsony should have been less in the Panhandle-Hugoton (Anadarko) fields than in the most easterly Kansas fields. Theoretically, there might have been some cost variation with longer term and without the contingency clauses, so that monopsony prices should have allowed $\beta_3 \geqq 0$, β_5, $\beta_6 \leqq 0$.

22. The contracts analyzed in Table 7:4 are all those for gas to be transported across state lines and listed with the Federal Power Commission (cf., exhibit 3-LC, 4-LC, *Champlin Oil and Refining, et al.*, F.P.C. Docket G-9277). Prices have been adjusted for gas pressure and B.T.U. differences according to F.P.C. practice. Data was available for the volume of 1955 delivery of gas, field location of the reserves, the term-length of production, the contract initial price, and the presence of any Favored Nations or Renegotiation clause in each contract. The volume of dedicated reserves was estimated for each contract by multiplying term-length by the amount of 1955 delivery. The relative location of each field was estimated by measuring distance from a common arc in Missouri and Iowa (through which all the relevant interstate pipelines travel) to the center of the county in which the field was located. As in the preceding chapters, the data is sufficient to calculate: $\{P = a + b_1V + b_2D + b_3T + b_4Y + b_5C_1 + b_6C_2 + U\}$ where b_i indicates the maximum likelihood estimate of β_i. The equation was calculated by the method of least squares.

TABLE 7:4. *Price Behavior in the Panhandle-Hugoton Fields*

Given that: $P = \alpha + \beta_1 V + \beta_2 D + \beta_3 T + \beta_4 Y + \beta_5 C_1 + \beta_6 C_2 + v$

P = initial contract price, cents per mcf.
V = volume of reserves, billions of cu. ft.
D = distance of trap, in hundreds of miles
T = term-length, in years
Y = either the first-year sample (zero) or the second year (one)
C_1 = presence of Favored Nations clause (= one)
C_2 = presence of Renegotiation (= one)
R^2 = coefficient of determination
S_u = standard error of estimate, cents per mcf.
S_p = standard deviation of price, cents per mcf.

A. *1950–51*
  (*sample of 64 contracts—2.6100 trillion cu. ft.*)

Regression equations

$P = \alpha + \beta_1 V + \beta_2 D + \beta_3 T + \beta_4 Y + \beta_5 C_1 + \beta_6 C_2 + v$

$P = 13.002 + .000381V - 1.1047D + .1187T + .4135Y + .2755C_1$
        $(.000946)\quad (.3994)\quad\ (.0320)\quad\ (.3269)\quad (.6753)$

    $+ .1923C_2$
      $(.3930)$

$R^2 = .504$
$S_u = 1.228$
$S_p = 1.659$

(Competitive) Predictions	(Monopsony) Predictions	Tests of computed equations
$\beta_1 > 0$	$\beta_1 = 0$	If $t_i = b_i / S_{b_i} > \mid 1.645 \mid$ the hypothesis
$\beta_2 < 0$	$\beta_2 = 0$	that $\beta_i = 0$ is rejected.
$\beta_3 > 0$	$\beta_3 \geqq 0$	$\beta_1 = 0$ since $t_1 = \quad 0.4028$
$\beta_5 < 0$	$\beta_5 \leqq 0$	$\beta_2 < 0$ since $t_2 = \ -2.7656$
$\beta_6 < 0$	$\beta_6 \leqq 0$	$\beta_3 > 0$ since $t_3 = \quad 3.7132$
		$\beta_4 = 0$ since $t_4 = \quad 1.2645$
		$\beta_5 = 0$ since $t_5 = \quad 0.4081$
		$\beta_6 = 0$ since $t_6 = \quad 0.4893$

B. *1951–52*
  (*sample of 67 contracts—1.3684 trillion cu. ft.*)

Regression equations

$P = \alpha + \beta_1 V + \beta_2 D + \beta_3 T + \beta_4 Y + \beta_5 C_1 + \beta_6 C_2 + v$

$P = 13.297 + .00505V - 1.0378D + .0673T + .7192Y + .1825C_1$
        $(.00248)\quad (.4300)\quad\ (.0319)\quad\ (.3722)\quad (.6369)$

    $+ .0933C_2$
      (4059)

$R^2 = .372$
$S_u = 1.436$
$S_p = 1.728$

(Competitive) Predictions	(Monopsony) Predictions	Tests of computed equations
$\beta_1 > 0$	$\beta_1 = 0$	$\beta_1 > 0$ since $t_1 = 2.0336$
$\beta_2 < 0$	$\beta_2 = 0$	$\beta_2 < 0$ since $t_2 = 2.4129$
$\beta_3 > 0$	$\beta_3 \geqq 0$	$\beta_3 > 0$ since $t_3 = 2.1060$
$\beta_5 < 0$	$\beta_5 \leqq 0$	$\beta_4 > 0$ since $t_4 = 1.9324$
$\beta_6 < 0$	$\beta_6 \leqq 0$	$\beta_5 = 0$ since $t_5 = 0.2865$
		$\beta_6 > 0$ since $t_6 = 2.2253$

C. *1952–53*

(*sample of 95 contracts—0.9001 trillion cu. ft.*)

Regression equations

$$P = \alpha + \beta_1 V + \beta_2 D + \beta_3 T + \beta_4 Y + \beta_5 C_1 + \beta_6 C_2 + v$$

$$P = 18.215 + .00634V - 1.5963D + .0648T + 1.3275Y - .1999C_1$$
$$\quad (.00438) \quad (.4678) \quad (.0362) \quad (.4436) \quad (.8917)$$

$$+ .8407C_2$$
$$\quad (.4729)$$

$R^2 = .322$
$S_u = 2.098$
$S_p = 2.464$

(Competitive) Predictions	(Monopsony) Predictions	Tests of computed equations
$\beta_1 > 0$	$\beta_1 = 0$	$\beta_1 = 0$ since $t_1 = 1.4496$
$\beta_2 < 0$	$\beta_2 = 0$	$\beta_2 < 0$ since $t_2 = -3.4126$
$\beta_3 > 0$	$\beta_3 \geqq 0$	$\beta_3 > 0$ since $t_3 = 1.7917$
$\beta_5 < 0$	$\beta_5 \leqq 0$	$\beta_4 > 0$ since $t_4 = 2.9924$
$\beta_6 < 0$	$\beta_6 \leqq 0$	$\beta_5 = 0$ since $t_5 = -0.2242$
		$\beta_6 > 0$ since $t_6 = 1.7779$

D. *1953–54*

(*sample of 105 contracts—.7489 trillion cu. ft.*)

Regression equations

$$P = \alpha + \beta_1 V + \beta_2 D + \beta_3 T + \beta_4 Y + \beta_5 C_1 + \beta_6 C_2 + v$$

$$P = 20.8448 + .0422V - 1.7397D + .0569T + .6231Y - 1.4743C_1$$
$$\quad (.0092) \quad (.4014) \quad (.3455) \quad (.3956) \quad (.9092)$$

$$+ .2802C_2$$
$$\quad (0.4583)$$

$R^2 = .361$
$S_u = 1.945$
$S_p = 2.362$

(Competitive) Predictions	(Monopsony) Predictions	Tests of computed equations
$\beta_1 > 0$	$\beta_1 = 0$	$\beta_1 > 0$ since $t_1 = 4.5713$
$\beta_2 < 0$	$\beta_2 = 0$	$\beta_2 < 0$ since $t_2 = -4.3338$
$\beta_3 > 0$	$\beta_3 \geqq 0$	$\beta_3 > 0$ since $t_3 = 1.6473$
$\beta_5 < 0$	$\beta_5 \leqq 0$	$\beta_4 = 0$ since $t_4 = 1.5752$
$\beta_6 < 0$	$\beta_6 \leqq 0$	$\beta_5 = 0$ since $t_5 = -1.6215$
		$\beta_6 = 0$ since $t_6 = 0.6114$

volume contracts.[23] There was a significant positive relationship between initial price and longer term-length in each of the chosen market periods.[24] There was a significant negative relationship between distance and price in each period; contracts in the Panhandle-Hugoton farther from the eastern resale centers had lower prices. Price for any year was higher than in the immediately preceding year, and it was higher by a statistically significant amount in 1952 and again in 1953. At the same time, there was no significant price difference for contracts having Favored Nations clauses, but in 1951–52 and 1952–53 contracts with Renegotiation clauses had significantly higher prices.[25]

This would seem to have been a pattern of price formation generally similar to that expected from competition. There were a number of obvious differences between the values of coefficients in the regression equations from market period to market period. Larger-volume contracts commanded an increasing premium, for example, and the level of prices increased by an increasing amount. But the general pattern was consistent: Tests of the computed equation point generally to $\beta_1 > 0$, $\beta_2 < 0$, $\beta_3 > 0$ in these markets (as is expected with competitive "maximum offer prices").

Prices in central Kansas and Oklahoma followed a different pattern. The 73 contracts signed in this region during 1950–54 had quite similar prices: 54 had a price of 10 cents per mcf and 10 of the remaining 19 had a price between 9 cents and

23. As concluded from testing the alternative hypotheses $\beta_1 > 0$; $\beta_1 = 0$ where $\dfrac{b_1 - \beta_1}{S_{b_1}}$ is distributed as "student's t" and where the hypothesis $\beta_1 = 0$ is rejected for values of t greater than 1.645.

24. That is, $t_3 = b_3/S_{b_3} > 1.645$ and it is concluded that the observed increase in b_2 did not likely follow from chance variation.

25. It should be noted that prices on the contracts in the sample were not affected by state minimum price laws in Oklahoma and Kansas. These laws ostensibly resulted in raising the price on old contracts to the level of initial prices in 1950–55. When initial price on one of the listed contracts was less than the minimum legal price, the two prices were listed and the lower was recorded as "suspended." This lower price was used in the sample as the indicator of market price. The minimum price laws themselves were declared invalid because of conflict with Federal Power Commission jurisdiction from the Phillips case. Cf. *Natural Gas Pipeline Co. v. Pomona Corp.* 349 U.S. 44 (1955), *Cities Service Gas Co. v. Kansas State Corp. Comm.* 355 U.S. 391 (1958).

12 cents. These contracts varied in term-length from one to twenty-five years, in distance from 4.5 to 6.8 hundred miles, and in volume from .04 billion to 340 billion cubic feet, while prices did not vary. Not only were prices uniform, but also the *level* of price was much lower than in the Panhandle. This can be seen from a comparison between "equivalent" prices for contracts comparable to these in the Panhandle-Hugoton, and actual central Kansas-Oklahoma prices.

Each contract for gas in central Kansas-Oklahoma, to have been signed under market conditions comparable to those in the Panhandle, should have had a price level the same as an "equivalent" Panhandle price. The equivalent Panhandle price can be calculated for a contract by inserting the volume, distance, term, etc., of that contract into the Panhandle regression equation. This equivalent price was higher than actual price in 71 of the 73 central field contracts. For some of the contracts, the difference between the equivalent price and the actual price was quite small and possibly due to chance variation. For a group of 16 contracts actual price was significantly lower than the equivalent price (these 16 are shown in Table 7:5).[26]

The sixteen low-price contracts indicate the contrast in price levels between the central Kansas-Oklahoma fields and the Panhandle-Hugoton fields. The equivalent prices ranged between 11.395 cents per mcf and 36.360 cents per mcf, while the actual prices ranged from 2.000 cents per mcf to 11.000 cents per mcf. The highest equivalent price levels were for volumes between 100 billion and 300 billion cubic feet, but

26. The test for the significance of the difference between actual and "equivalent price" involves comparison between the difference and $(0 \pm 1.96S_F)$, the confidence interval around "zero difference" that is expected from chance variation. S_F is the standard error of forecast that accounts for errors in calculating the true regression, and for errors in the actual price as an estimate of regression price (P) for such contracts. The standard error S_F is large for volume, distance, etc. because of greater chance of regression error. If actual price differences were within $(0 \pm 1.96S_F)$ for some 95 per cent of the contracts in *any* sample, then it can be assumed that the central Kansas-Oklahoma and Panhandle-Hugoton contracts were signed under the same market conditions (i.e., were from the same universe). If actual differences were not within this interval consistently, it can be assumed that actual prices were systematically lower than Panhandle equivalents.

TABLE 7:5. *Contracts in Central Kansas-Oklahoma*

Buyer	Seller	Rate schedule number	Actual price, cents per mcf	Equivalent (regression) price, cents per mcf	Standard error of forecast, S_{F}, confidence interval = $0 \pm 1.96\ S_{F}$	Computed minus actual price
Cities Service	Gas Trans. Co.	1	8.000	13.708	2.723 $0 \pm$ 5.337	5.708
Cities Service	Wunderlich Producing Co.	1	5.200	25.050	7.434 $0 \pm$ 14.571	19.850
Cities Service	Davidor and Davidor	1	5.200	12.330	2.696 $0 \pm$ 5.280	6.130
Cities Service	Aurora Gasoline Company	3	2.000	21.469	2.655 $0 \pm$ 5.225	19.469
Cities Service	Champlin Refining Company	1	12.000	34.605	10.542 $0 \pm$ 20.563	22.605
Cities Service	Briscoe Powell	1	10.000	15.292	2.622 $0 \pm$ 5.140	5.292
Cities Service	Cities Service Oil Company	42	9.830	24.700	4.391 $0 \pm$ 8.508	14.870
Northern Natural Gas	Alden E. Branine	1	11.000	16.160	2.629 $0 \pm$ 5.153	5.160

234

Kansas-Nebraska Natural Gas Co.	Graham-Rinehart Oil	1	7.000	21.680	$\dfrac{2.6617}{0 \pm 5.217}$ 4.086	14.680
Lone Star Gas	Carter Oil Co.	19	10.000	26.712	$\dfrac{0 \pm 8.008}{9.740}$	16.712
Lone Star Gas	Kerr-McGee Oil	17	10.000	36.360	0 ± 19.090	26.360
Lone Star Gas	G. C. Parker	1	10.000	15.728	$\dfrac{2.606}{0 \pm 5.108}$	5.728
Lone Star Gas	Superior Oil Co.	48	7.000	12.905	$\dfrac{2.541}{0 \pm 4.980}$	5.905
Lone Star Gas	Charlotte Barrett	6	10.000	18.299	$\dfrac{2.805}{0 \pm 5.498}$	8.299
Oklahoma Natural Gas	Anderson-Prichard Oil Company	11	10.000	15.207	$\dfrac{2.631}{0 \pm 5.157}$	5.257
Universal Gasoline Company	Carter Oil Co.	11	5.000	11.395	$\dfrac{2.515}{0 \pm 4.929}$	6.395

actual prices on these contracts were equal to those on
smaller-volume contracts. Actual prices were typically less
than half the "equivalent price," and the occurrence of 16 out
of 73 contracts with prices significantly less than expected
suggests that price behavior was quite different in the two
areas.[27] In effect, prices in the Panhandle were higher and
followed a strongly competitive pattern, while those in the
central Kansas-Oklahoma regions were lower and quite uniform.

The markets in the later 1950s seem to have emphasized
this contrast. The regression analyses of the 1956–58 Panhandle-Hugoton contracts indicate price formation similar to
that in 1950–54.[28] Again, prices were significantly higher for
larger-volume contracts and for contracts with longer term.[29]
For a contract with an additional 10 billion cubic feet of
reserves, price P was between .152 and .262 cents per mcf
greater. The contract with a twenty-year term had an average
price between 2.275 and 2.325 cents per mcf higher than that
with a fifteen-year term. Prices were lower for reserves of
gas located farther west: For each 100 miles of increased
distance, regression price was 1.595 to 1.790 cents per mcf
less.[30]

27. If the two regions experienced similar market results, then the
price differences should have been greater than $0 \pm 1.96 S_F$ in only 5
per cent of the cases. Central Kansas-Oklahoma prices were significantly
lower in 16 contracts out of 73. Testing to determine whether 16 was
not different from 5 per cent, $t = \dfrac{73(.05) - 16}{[(.05) \cdot (.95) \cdot 75]\,\frac{1}{2}}$ should not be
greater than 1.96. Here $t = 6.632$ so that the hypothesis is rejected.
There would seem to have been a significantly large number of lower
prices. In other words, there was a distinct contrast between price levels
in the central Kansas-Oklahoma fields and the Panhandle-Hugoton.

28. The data for each of 263 contracts are specified so as to be comparable: distance was estimated from the same end of transmission,
term-length and the presence of contingency clauses are reported in the
same manner as previously. But volume contracted was estimated from
the listed uniform monthly rate of production, rather than from any
realized production figures. This method of estimation is discussed in
the Appendix.

29. The tests for coefficients significantly different from zero are
shown in the last columns of Table 7:6.

30. Such variation is similar to that of "maximum offer prices" of
pipeline buyers competing for new reserves. Under ideal conditions, it
would cost approximately .70–1.00 cents per mcf to transport one thou-

Prices rose slightly in 1957 and in 1958. Price behavior with respect to Favored Nations and Renegotiation clauses continued to be ambivalent during the 1956–58 period. Contracts with a Favored Nations clause had significantly lower prices than those without one. But contracts with a Renegotiation clause had initial prices significantly higher than contracts without such a clause.[31]

The pattern of prices in central Kansas and Oklahoma again was uniform and generally lower than that in the Panhandle-Hugoton fields during the 1956–58 period (as shown in Table 7:6). Prices on these new contracts did not vary with the size of the volume of reserves (the hypothesis $\beta_1 = 0$ could not be disproved). Rather than price decreasing as distance from end of transmission increased, it was more than 2.0 cents per mcf greater in traps an additional hundred miles farther from points of resale. Prices were slightly higher on contracts with longer term (but the increase was not as great as in the Panhandle).[32] Prices on contracts with a Favored Nations clause were between 1.02 cents and 1.76 cents per mcf lower than on contracts without such a clause. Prices rose only slightly over time, with the 1957 regression price .4913 cents per mcf

---

sand cubic feet of gas an extra 100 miles, and approximately one-half cent per mcf less to gather a reserve volume 50 billion cubic feet larger (in a 2″–4″ gathering line, as in Chapter 3). Panhandle-Hugoton conditions were less than ideal: low well-head pressures made compression necessary, so that the level of additional costs were two to three times as great as in the ideal field. Prices should have been lower by 1.40–3.00 cents per mcf per hundred miles of extra transportation, and higher by 1.00–1.50 cents per mcf for each 50 billion cubic feet of larger reserves. Actual price variation was roughly of this order, as the regression equation indicates. The actual differences were −1.59 to −1.79 cents for distance, +0.75 to 1.10 for 50 billion cubic feet additional volume.

31. It is expected that competitive demand and supply conditions require lower prices for contracts containing these contingency clauses (*if* the buyer has to be compensated for "additional risk" of having to pay undetermined higher future prices). Expected behavior was realized only for Favored Nations in 1956–58. Actual behavior on contracts with Renegotiation cannot easily be explained. Perhaps the presence of Renegotiation did not impose cost burdens on the buyer.

32. Variation with the length of term was significant, with the 20-year contract having prices more than 1.0 cents per mcf higher than the 15-year contracts. This difference may have followed from the 14 contracts with term less than twenty years all being in central Oklahoma counties (where prices were significantly lower for *all* contracts).

TABLE 7:6. *Price Behavior throughout the Mid-Continent, 1956–58*

Given that: $P = \alpha + \beta_1 V + \beta_2 D + \beta_3 T + \beta_4 Y + \beta_5 C_1 + \beta_6 C_2 + v$

P = initial contract price, cents per mcf.
V = volume of reserves, billions of cu. ft.
D = distance of trap, in hundreds of miles
T = term-length, in years
Y = either the first-year sample (zero) or the second year (one)
C_1 = presence of Favored Nations clause (= one)
C_2 = presence of Renegotiation (= one)
R^2 = coefficient of determination
S_u = standard error of estimate, cents per mcf.
S_p = standard deviation of price, cents per mcf.

A. *Panhandle-Hugoton: 1956–57*
   (sample of 248 contracts—1.4733 trillion cu. ft.)

Regression equations

$P = \alpha + \beta_1 V + \beta_2 D + \beta_3 T + \beta_4 Y + \beta_5 C_1 + \beta_6 C_2 + v$

$P = 15.8925 + .02618V - 1.5946D + .4672T + .0886Y - 3.8061C_1$
$\qquad\qquad (.00843) \quad (.2014) \quad\quad (.0356) \quad (.0249) \quad (1.14119)$

$\qquad + .7340C_2$
$\qquad\quad (.2675)$

$R^2 = .572$
$S_u = 1.923$
$S_p = 2.904$

(Competitive) Predictions	(Monopsony) Predictions	Tests of computed equations
$\beta_1 > 0$	$\beta_1 = 0$	If $t_i = b_i/S_{b_i} > \mid 1.645 \mid$ the hypothesis
$\beta_2 < 0$	$\beta_2 = 0$	that $\beta_i = 0$ is rejected.
$\beta_3 > 0$	$\beta_3 \geqq 0$	$\beta_1 > 0$ since $t_1 =$ 3.1033
$\beta_5 < 0$	$\beta_5 \leqq 0$	$\beta_2 < 0$ since $t_2 = -$ 7.9150
$\beta_6 < 0$	$\beta_6 \leqq 0$	$\beta_3 > 0$ since $t_3 =$ 13.1160
		$\beta_4 = 0$ since $t_4 =$ 0.3548
		$\beta_5 < 0$ since $t_5 = -$ 2.6958
		$\beta_6 > 0$ since $t_6 =$ 2.7431

B. *Panhandle-Hugoton: 1957–58*
   (sample of 263 contracts—1.5598 trillion cu. ft.)

Regression equations

$P = \alpha + \beta_1 V + \beta_2 D + \beta_3 T + \beta_4 Y + \beta_5 C_1 + \beta_6 C_2 + v$

$P = 17.7979 + .01523V - 1.7900D + .4556T + .4913Y - 1.5706C_1$
$\qquad\qquad (.00711) \quad (.1859) \quad\quad (.0334) \quad (.2246) \quad (.6134)$

$\qquad + .5195C_2$
$\qquad\quad (.2270)$

$R^2 = .578$
$S_u = 1.759$
$S_p = 2.670$

(Competitive) Predictions	*(Monopsony)* Predictions	*Tests of computed equations*
$\beta_1 > 0$	$\beta_1 = 0$	$\beta_1 > 0$ since $t_1 =$ 2.1438
$\beta_2 < 0$	$\beta_2 = 0$	$\beta_2 < 0$ since $t_2 = -$ 9.6245
$\beta_3 > 0$	$\beta_3 \gtreqqless 0$	$\beta_3 > 0$ since $t_3 =$ 13.6552
$\beta_5 < 0$	$\beta_5 \lessgtr 0$	$\beta_4 > 0$ since $t_4 =$ 2.1872
$\beta_6 < 0$	$\beta_6 \lessgtr 0$	$\beta_5 < 0$ since $t_5 = -$ 2.5606
		$\beta_6 > 0$ since $t_6 =$ 2.2883

C. *Kansas-Oklahoma: 1956–57*
(*sample of 177 contracts—1.1807 trillion cu. ft.*)

Regression equations

$$P = \alpha + \beta_1 V + \beta_2 D + \beta_3 T + \beta_4 Y + \beta_5 C_1 + \beta_6 C_2 + v$$
$$P = -4.9131 + .04324V + 2.1991D + .2154T + .5146Y - 1.0173C_1 +$$
$$ (.03114) \quad (.3038) \quad (.0309) \quad (.2281) \quad (.2371)$$

$.7389C_2$
$(.2749)$

$R^2 = .727$
$S_u = 1.455$
$S_p = 2.730$

(Competitive) Predictions	*(Monopsony)* Predictions	*Tests of computed equations*
$\beta_1 > 0$	$\beta_1 = 0$	$\beta_1 = 0$ since $t_1 =$ 1.3826
$\beta_2 < 0$	$\beta_2 = 0$	$\beta_2 > 0$ since $t_2 =$ 7.2372
$\beta_3 > 0$	$\beta_3 \gtreqqless 0$	$\beta_3 > 0$ since $t_3 =$ 6.9719
$\beta_5 < 0$	$\beta_5 \lessgtr 0$	$\beta_4 > 0$ since $t_4 =$ 2.2565
$\beta_6 < 0$	$\beta_6 \lessgtr 0$	$\beta_5 < 0$ since $t_5 = -4.2911$
		$\beta_6 > 0$ since $t_6 =$ 2.6879

D. *Kansas-Oklahoma: 1957–58*
(*sample of 168 contracts—1.3923 trillion cu. ft.*)

Regression equations

$$P = \alpha + \beta_1 V + \beta_2 D + \beta_3 T + \beta_4 Y + \beta_5 C_1 + \beta_6 C_2 + v$$
$$P = -3.588 - .00776V + 2.1405D + .2324T + .000743Y -$$
$$ (.00816) \quad (0.3626) \quad (.0503) \quad (.02768)$$

$1.7612C_1 + .5000C_2$
$(.3196) \quad (.3135)$

$R^2 = .531$
$S_u = 1.745$
$S_p = 2.494$

(Competitive) Predictions	*(Monopsony)* Predictions	*Tests of computed equations*
$\beta_1 > 0$	$\beta_1 = 0$	$\beta_1 = 0$ since $t_1 = -$ .9390
$\beta_2 < 0$	$\beta_2 = 0$	$\beta_2 > 0$ since $t_2 =$ 5.9019
$\beta_3 > 0$	$\beta_3 \gtreqqless 0$	$\beta_3 > 0$ since $t_3 =$ 4.6281
$\beta_5 < 0$	$\beta_5 \lessgtr 0$	$\beta_4 = 0$ since $t_4 =$ 0.0264
$\beta_6 < 0$	$\beta_6 \lessgtr 0$	$\beta_5 < 0$ since $t_5 = -5.5111$
		$\beta_6 = 0$ since $t_6 =$ 1.5949

greater than that for 1956, and the 1958 price .0007 cents per mcf greater than that for 1957.[33]

The over-all contrast in patterns of price variation is striking.[34] Price formation with changes in volume, distance, and term indicate sharp differences in the Panhandle-Hugoton and the central Kansas-Oklahoma fields. Specific differences are also striking. The reason higher prices were offered farther west in central Kansas must have been because the more westerly fields were closer to the Panhandle or Hugoton. The

33. The only exceptions might have been the (unrecorded) changes in price levels in the central region brought about by the entry of Transwestern Pipeline Company. This line purchased reserves at new prices in the Panhandle field and in the adjacent northwest counties of Oklahoma. The prices in Transwestern's new Panhandle contracts, 23 cents and 21 cents per mcf, were comparable to those prevailing on large volume sales. Prices on the new dedications in central-west Oklahoma were supposed to have been between 3 cents and 8 cents per mcf greater (the figures have as yet not been officially reported in certification proceedings).

34. The two regression equations, for the Panhandle-Hugoton and for central Kansas-Oklahoma, were not similar. To test similarity, consider that the sets of coefficients were identical except for minor differences in the samples—that they both were estimates of one equation $\{P = \alpha + \beta_1 V + \beta_2 D + \beta_3 T + \beta_4 Y + \beta_5 C_1 + \beta_6 C_2 + v\}$. If this is the case, then the residuals between realized and predicted prices would not be further explained by two separate regression equations (rather than one consolidated regression line). That is

$$F_{P, N-P} = \left\{ \frac{\left(S_u^2 - \sum_{i=1}^{2} S_{ui}^2\right)/P}{\sum_{i=1}^{2} S_{ui}^2/(n_1 + n_2 - P)} \right\}$$

should be less than the tabulated value for the F distribution (ignoring probability $\leq .05$). Here, S_u^2 is total variance of residuals around the regression from the consolidated sample, S_{u1}^2, S_{u2}^2 from the Panhandle and central samples respectively. Cf. Gregory Chow, "Tests of Equality between Sets of Coefficients in Two Linear Regressions," 28 *Econometrica* 591–608 (1960). For the 1956–57 sample, the consolidated regression equation was:

$$\begin{bmatrix} P = .3627 + .0329V + .7860D + .3887T + .2333Y \\ \quad (.1479)\ (.00798)\ (.1991)\quad (.0276)\quad (.1991) \\ \quad\quad - 1.3866C_1 + .5506C_2 \\ \quad\quad (.3084)\quad (.2136) \end{bmatrix}$$

and $F_{7,418} = \dfrac{(1714.1525 - 542.5015)/7}{(545.5015)/418} = 128.2568$. Values of $F_{7,148} \geq$ 2.85 occur in only 1 per cent of the large number of such cases. The hy-

closer the reserves to those fields, the greater the number of independent sources of demand and the less the buyer's power to set price. In Meade and Clark Counties, Kansas, new fields were discovered within gathering distance of the Panhandle-Hugoton buyers and there were three buyers present. When there was this number of potential buyers, prices were at levels equal to those in the Panhandle (from 14 to 17 cents per mcf). But prices remained at 10 to 12 cents per mcf in the more easterly fields where each line continued to purchase exclusively.

Also, large sales close to the Panhandle had much higher prices than small sales, but large sales in the central counties had prices the same as on small sales. In 1956–57, there were seven contracts for more than 24.0 billion cubic feet. Only one of these contracts was for gas in the more central counties, while the other six were for reserves in the counties on the boundary of the Panhandle-Hugoton. These six had higher prices than contracts for smaller volumes in the same counties, and higher prices than all other contracts in the sample. In 1957–58, there were 10 contracts for 24.0 billion cubic feet or more, four of which were in central Kansas (in Grady, Oklahoma, and Barker Counties). These four had an initial price of 10.0 cents per mcf, the same as for smaller-volume sales there, while the six on the boundary again had the highest prices.

Higher prices on larger volumes closer to the Panhandle would indicate more extensive buyer's competition there. The consistent lack of price variation with volume, distance, and term-length in the central Kansas-Oklahoma fields also contrasts with the pattern of prices in the Panhandle-Hugoton.[35]

pothesis that the Panhandle and central field samples were from the same universe is rejected. It seems likely that market conditions and price behavior were not similar. For the 1957–58 sample, the consolidated regression equation was:

$$P = 9.357 + .0771V - .4223D + .3782T + .4217Y - 2.9213C_1 + .4076C_2$$
$$(1.153) \quad (.0612) \quad (.1373) \quad (.0316) \quad (.1977) \quad (0.2970) \quad (.2079)$$

and $F_{7,424} = \dfrac{(1759.5144 - 302.6858)/7}{(302.6858/424)} = 291.5307$. For value $F \geqq 2.85$ the hypothesis that the regressions were similar is rejected. They are assumed to be from different types of markets.

35. The contrast in over-all pattern of prices is apparent from relative

This contrast is expected, considering the small number of buyers in the more isolated central fields and the large number of buyers in the Panhandle. The regression equations exhibit strong similarity between actual prices and competitive price formation in the Panhandle-Hugoton and surrounding fields. They exhibit strong resemblance to monopsony pricing in the fields of central Oklahoma and Kansas.

In summary, it can be said that there was both monopsony and competition in pricing Mid-Continent reserves during the 1950s. The large fields, the Panhandle and the Hugoton, seem to have been competitive in both supply and purchase throughout 1950–54 and 1956–58. The small fields in the more central areas of Oklahoma and Kansas first appeared in the early 1950s, and were an important source of reserves only during 1956–58. Sales there were to buyers with power to set price, and the results of price formation were similar to the monopsony pattern. In the later 1950s, however, monopsony power was less securely established in fields closest to the Panhandle and prices were significantly higher at these points.

variations between "smallest" and "typical" contract prices. The "smallest" contract in the Panhandle-Hugoton might have involved dedication of 1.0 billion cubic feet, under a one-year contract, from a trap 7.3 hundred miles from the end of transmission (the average distance). The "typical" contract at the same location can be assumed to have involved the dedication of 40.155 billion cubic feet (the average size of contract) under a twenty-year term-length. Prices for "typical" contracts, "smallest" contracts, and the ratio of the two from the regression equations would have been the following (in cents per mcf):

	Smallest	Typical	Ratio of typical to smallest
1956	1.673	11.575	6.918
1957	4.151	13.402	3.228
1958	4.642	13.894	2.993

Typical and smallest contracts in the fields of central Kansas or Oklahoma might be assumed to have been the same size and for the same term-length, but for reserves at 5.93 hundred miles (the average distance). Prices would have been as follows (in cents per mcf):

	Typical	Smallest	Ratio of typical to smallest
1956	13.902	8.117	1.712
1957	12.187	8.077	1.508
1958	12.186	8.076	1.508

Even with considerable competition in purchasing reserves in the more western fields in this latter group of sales, the pattern of prices contained far less diversity in the central region than in the Panhandle-Hugoton (as can be seen from comparing Ratio of typical to smallest).

8. Competition, Monopsony, and Regulation

Price formation in the West Texas, Gulf Coast, and Mid-Continent regions would seem to have followed at times from monopsony, at times from competition in sales of new reserves. Monopsony prevailed in each of the three producing regions at some time, but pricing was generally becoming more competitive during the later 1950s.

MONOPSONY

Conditions in which one buyer controlled field purchases have been present in all the regions. One transporter controlled purchases (with some exceptions) in West Texas-New Mexico at least until 1958. The three original pipelines into the Gulf Coast had the opportunity to control prices there in the late 1940s, and remnants of this control were present in the 1950s at isolated inland fields. Each one of three transporters in the central Kansas-Oklahoma fields had control of prices in separate parts of this region in the late 1950s.

When there was control by the buyer, prices were set in the monopsony manner. Actual prices followed a pattern of preset uniformity (as can be seen from the regression equations in Table 8:1). There was remarkably little variation in price; the standard deviation of sample prices was between .916 cents and 1.97 cents per mcf. The volume of reserves, the

TABLE 8:1. *Price Formation Under Monopsony*

$$P = \alpha + \beta_1 V + \beta_2 D + \beta_3 T + \beta_4 Y + \beta_5 C_1 + \beta_6 C_2 + v$$

1951–52 West Texas–New Mexico (65 contracts)

$$P = 7.906 + .0129V - .1887D - .0847T + 1.198Y + .9218C_1 + .5023C_2$$
$$\qquad\quad (.0047) \quad (.0982) \quad (.1161) \quad (0.381) \quad (.9931) \quad (1.0185)$$

$R^2 = .307$
$S_u = 1.29$
$S_p = 1.47$

1953–54 West Texas–New Mexico (119 contracts)

$$P = 7.923 + .0041V + .0230D + .0804T + 1.444Y + .8938C_1 - 2.225C_2$$
$$\qquad\quad (.0034) \quad (.0558) \quad (.0329) \quad (0.215) \quad (.5431) \quad (0.598)$$

$R^2 = .426$
$S_u = 1.07$
$S_p = 1.38$

1945–46 Gulf Coast and Louisiana (75 contracts)

$$P = 4.861 + .0020V - .1465D - .0030T - .1127Y - 1.9569C_1 - .9417C_2$$
$$\qquad\quad (.0018) \quad (.0908) \quad (.0091) \quad (.2155) \quad (1.0609) \quad (.9176)$$

$R^2 = .121$
$S_u = .896$
$S_p = .916$

1950–51 Louisiana only (164 contracts)

$$P = 6.227 - .0001V - .2628D + .0191T + .2459Y + .5052C_1 - .2692C_2$$
$$\qquad\quad (.0009) \quad (.2027) \quad (.0346) \quad (.2802) \quad (.3113) \quad (.3653)$$

$R^2 = .247$
$S_u = 1.75$
$S_p = 1.97$

(Competitive) Predictions	*(Monopsony)* Predictions	*Tests for predictions*
$\beta_1 > 0$	$\beta_1 = 0$	If the computed coefficient divided by its standard error has a value greater than 1.645 then the competitive prediction $\beta_4 > 0$, $\beta_4 < 0$ is accepted over $\beta_4 = 0$.
$\beta_2 < 0$	$\beta_2 = 0$	
$\beta_3 > 0$	$\beta_3 \leqq 0$	
$\beta_5, \beta_6 \leqq 0$	$\beta_5, \beta_6 \leqq 0$	

Source. Relevant tables in Chapters 5, 6, 7.

term of the contract, and the distance to the trap, had little effect upon contract price.[1]

Uniform monopsony prices and low levels of average prices were found together. This is best indicated by differences in prices on contracts from the same general region, taking some contracts from fields in which there was one buyer, and others from fields containing a number of buyers. Sales prices were significantly greater in the fields where there was buyer's competition (as can be seen from inserting values in the regression equations in Table 8:2). In the farther Louisiana fields there were a number of buyers during 1951–54, while the closer fields in North Louisiana generally had one buyer each. Price levels were greater in the farther fields (since the regression price was between .578 and .674 cents per mcf greater for each additional 100 miles traveled by the buyer). A contract price in North Louisiana was on the average 1.50 cents per mcf less than the price on a similar sale in South Louisiana. Similarly, there were large numbers of buyers in the Mid-Continent fields near the Panhandle-Hugoton, while any field in central Kansas and Oklahoma had no more than one or two potential buyers. The first group of fields was farther away from points of resale than the second.[2] Prices were much higher in the farther fields: The regression price indicates that a contract on the border of the Panhandle had a price more than 4.20 cents per mcf higher than that for the same contract in the central Kansas-Oklahoma fields (200 miles closer).[3]

1. These separately did not have a statistically significant effect, and together they explained little more than 25 per cent of the variation in prices in the contracts. The coefficient of determination $R^2 = .121, .247, .307$, and $.426$. The last cannot be given much weight because it seems to depend upon the explanatory value of b_3, the coefficient of term, which was based upon a very small number of short-term contracts (as mentioned in Chapter 5).

2. Similar cases of higher prices at farther points were found in West Texas-New Mexico when a new pipeline entered the exclusive domain of El Paso Natural Gas Pipeline. (Cf. discussion of price offered by Transwestern Pipeline Company in Chapter 5.)

3. Competitive prices at farther points should have been *lower* than in closer fields because of additional transportation costs. Allowing for this, prices under competition should have been *lower* in South Louisiana and in fields closer to the Panhandle. The monopsony-competitive price difference in closer monopsony fields should have been the observed difference *plus* an amount for advantageous location.

TABLE 8:2. *Price Formation Under Partial Monopsony*

$$P = \alpha + \beta_1 V + \beta_2 D + \beta_3 T + \beta_4 Y + \beta_5 C_1 + \beta_6 C_2 + v$$

1951–52
Louisiana only
(168 contracts)

$P = 1.0808 + .00211V + .6744D + .1141T + .8157Y + .8181C_1 + 1.004C_2$
$\quad\quad\quad\quad (.00176)\quad (.3026)\quad (.0474)\quad (.4123)\quad (.4650)\quad (.5341)$

$R^2 = .234$
$S_u = 2.63$
$S_p = 2.95$

1953–54
Louisiana only
(201 contracts)

$P = 4.534 - .0024V + .5782D + .0594T + .0764Y + .7016C_1 + 1.7631C_2$
$\quad\quad\quad\quad (.0028)\quad (.2540)\quad (.0352)\quad (.4004)\quad (.4408)\quad (.4566)$

$R^2 = .173$
$S_u = 2.80$
$S_p = 3.03$

1956–57
Central Kansas
and Oklahoma
(177 contracts)

$P = 4.9131 + .0432V + 2.1991D + .2154T + .5164Y - 1.0173C_1 + .7389C_2$
$\quad\quad\quad\quad (.0311)\quad (.3038)\quad (.0309)\quad (.2281)\quad (.2371)\quad (.2749)$

$R^2 = .727$
$S_u = 1.46$
$S_p = 2.73$

1957–58
Central Kansas
and Oklahoma
(168 contracts)

$P = -3.588 - .0078V + 2.1405D + .2324T + .0007Y - 1.7612C_1 + .5000C_2$
$\quad\quad\quad\quad (.0082)\quad (0.3626)\quad (.0503)\quad (.0277)\quad (0.3196)\quad (.3135)$

$R^2 = .531$
$S_u = 1.75$
$S_p = 2.49$

(*Competitive*) Predictions	(*Monopsony*) Predictions	(*Partial Monopsony*) Predictions when there is competition in further fields	*Tests of predictions*
$\beta_1 > 0$	$\beta_1 = 0$	$\beta_1 \geqq 0$	If the computed coefficient divided by the standard error in parenthesis is greater than 1.645, the prediction $\beta_i = 0$ is rejected in favor of $B_i > 0$ or $\beta_i < 0$.
$\beta_2 < 0$	$\beta_2 = 0$	$\beta_2 \geqq 0$	
$\beta_3 > 0$	$\beta_3 \geqq 0$	$\beta_3 \geqq 0$	
$\beta_5, \beta_6 \leqq 0$	$\beta_5, \beta_6 \leqq 0$	$\beta_5, \beta_6 \leqq 0$	

COMPETITION

But monopsony was not pervasive, by any means. There had been a number of buyers in the Panhandle-Hugoton fields of the Mid-Continent since the beginning of development of this area. Shares of purchases and changes in shares of purchases indicate that these lines had not been able jointly to control demand. There were sufficient transporters along the Texas Gulf Coast by the early 1950s to have prevented any one of them, or a few of them, from controlling prices there. By the later 1950s, buyer's competition had broken out in West Texas-New Mexico with the entry of Transwestern Pipeline Company.

Price formation, where there were large numbers of buyers, was in contrast to price formation where there was one buyer. When pipelines sought the same reserves, superior contracts brought a price premium (as shown by the coefficients for volume, distance, term in the regression equations in Table 8:3). Reserves from traps closest to points of resale and reserves of larger size were preferred by the buyer, as were contracts of longer term. Contracts for reserves 100 miles closer had prices from .47 cents to 1.74 cents per mcf higher. Those for larger reserves had prices from .19 to 2.11 cents per mcf higher for each additional 50 billion cubic feet, while contracts for longer term had prices from .30 to 4.22 cents per mcf higher for each additional five years. Competition among pipelines seems to have forced the successful bidders to pay higher prices for the preferred new purchases. Prices were lower, in one of the competitive markets, for contracts with Favored Nations clauses, but prices were not lower in any of the markets for contracts with Renegotiation clauses. Prices increased each year for these sample groups of contracts.

All prices followed this pattern closely, as is indicated by large correlation coefficients (R^2) and relatively small standard errors of estimate (S_u).[4] The pattern was decidedly in

4. The percentage of "explained variation" R^2 was between 36.1 and 56.5 for markets other than the early Gulf Coast (where competition in

TABLE 8:3. *Price Formation Under Competition*

$$P = \alpha + \beta_1 V + \beta_2 D + \beta_3 T + \beta_4 Y + \beta_5 C_1 + \beta_6 C_2 + v$$

1951–52
Panhandle-Hugoton
fields only (67
contracts)

$$P = 13.2972 + .0050V - 1.038D + .0673T + .7192Y + .1825C_1 + .9033C_2$$
$$\qquad\qquad (.00248)\ \ (0.430)\ \ (.0319)\ \ (.3722)\ \ (.6369)\ \ (.4059)$$
$R^2 = .373$
$S_u = 1.435$
$S_p = 1.728$

1953–54
Panhandle-Hugoton
fields only (105
contracts)

$$P = 20.8448 + .0422V - 1.7397D + .0569T + .62306Y - 1.4743C_1 + .2802C_2$$
$$\qquad\qquad (.0092)\ \ (0.4014)\ \ (.0346)\ \ (.3956)\ \ (0.9092)\ \ (.4529)$$
$R^2 = .361$
$S_u = 1.944$
$S_p = 2.362$

1951–52
Texas Gulf only (151
contracts)

$$P = 10.280 + .0037V - .6048D + .1270T + 1.636Y - .3531C_1 - .4184C_2$$
$$\qquad\qquad (.0024)\ \ (.1810)\ \ (.0558)\ \ (0.539)\ \ (.5546)\ \ (.5736)$$
$R^2 = .196$
$S_u = 2.47$
$S_p = 2.70$

1953–54
Texas Gulf only (261
contracts)

$$P = 11.3269 + .0227V - .4694D + .1261T + .3608Y + .5483C_1 - .1172C_2$$
$$\qquad\qquad (.0050)\ \ (.0932)\ \ (.0308)\ \ (.2137)\ \ (.3022)\ \ (.3606)$$
$R^2 = .274$
$S_u = 1.63$
$S_p = 1.89$

1956–57 Gulf Coast-Louisiana "large" sales only (108 contracts)

$$P = 1.893 + .0058V - .4895D + .8435T + 2.2597Y - .6382C_1 + 1.7596C_2$$
$$\qquad\quad (.0035) \quad (.1200) \quad (.1712) \quad (0.5554) \quad (.5872) \quad (0.5067)$$

$R^2 = .565$
$S_u = 2.58$
$S_p = 3.78$

1956–57 Gulf Coast-Louisiana "small" sales only (504 contracts)

$$P = 13.503 + .1600V - .7200D + .1620T + .7621Y + .3295C_1 + 2.6391C_2$$
$$\qquad\quad (.0245) \quad (.0466) \quad (.0358) \quad (.2707) \quad (.2903) \quad (.2860)$$

$R^2 = .487$
$S_u = 2.83$
$S_p = 3.93$

(Competitive) Predictions	(Monopsony) Predictions
$\beta_1 > 0$	$\beta_1 = 0$
$\beta_2 < 0$	$\beta_2 = 0$
$\beta_3 > 0$	$\beta_3 \leqq 0$
$\beta_5, \beta_6 \leqq 0$	$\beta_5, \beta_6 \leqq 0$

Tests of predictions

If the computed coefficient (b_i) divided by its standard error (S_{b_i} shown in parenthesis under each b_i) is greater than 1.645, then the hypothesis $\beta_i = 0$ is rejected in favor of $\beta_i > 0$ or $\beta_i < 0$.

Source. Tables in Chapters 5, 6, 7.

contrast with uniform prices found in one-buyer markets (in Table 8:1).

In the last years of the 1950s, more of the new fields were in competitive markets. There was buyer's competition for new reserves throughout the Gulf Coast and Louisiana. The entry of Transwestern Pipeline into West Texas-New Mexico provided extensive potential competition in demand there. The Panhandle-Hugoton region of the Mid-Continent long had been competitive in supply and demand. Only the isolated central fields of Kansas and Oklahoma each had one pipeline buyer.

The effects of increasing competition upon pricing patterns in the most recent years are shown in Table 8:4. New prices in the Gulf Coast and in the Panhandle-Hugoton followed from competition in demand (including contract volume, term, and trap distance). There was considerable resemblance between the theoretical competitive pattern and the observed regression patterns in these two regions. Price formation in West Texas-New Mexico showed some similarity to that expected from competition: El Paso found it necessary to pay higher prices for larger volumes, and the level of price on all Transwestern contracts was considerably higher than in the regression equation (as noted in Chapter 5). But the absence of price variation with distance and term indicates a lack of systematic buyer's competition throughout West Texas. New prices in the central fields of Kansas and Oklahoma continued to vary with the extent of potential pipeline competition. Higher prices were paid only for reserves closer to the Panhandle and Hugoton fields where there were two or more buyers.

Extensive competition in the Gulf Coast and the Panhandle, emerging competition in West Texas, and a lack of buyer's competition in the central Kansas-Oklahoma fields are the legacy of market organization in the 1950s. The ques-

---

purchasing had just been established). The standard error of estimate was from .25 cents per mcf to 1.20 cents per mcf lower than the standard deviation of prices S_p.

$$P = \alpha + \beta_1 V + \beta_2 D + \beta_3 T + \beta_4 Y + \beta_5 C_1 + \beta_6 C_2 + v$$

1956–58
Gulf Coast "small"
sales (782 contracts)

$$P = 13.527 + .1575V - .7129D + .1551T + .7169Y_{56-57} + .9556Y_{56-58} + .2601C_1 + 2.9847C_2$$
$$ (.0194)\ \ (.0305)\ \ (.0295)\ \ (.2669)\ \ \ \ \ (.2832)\ \ \ \ \ (.2479)\ \ \ (0.2344)$$

$R^2 = .551$
$S_u = 2.83$
$S_p = 4.20$

1956–58
Gulf Coast "large"
sales (140 contracts)

$$P = 1.436 + .0061V - .5077D + .8748T + 2.2043Y_{56-57} + .4137Y_{56-58} - .7681C_1 - 1.9250C_2$$
$$ (.0032)\ \ (.0911)\ \ (.1620)\ \ (0.5308)\ \ \ \ \ (.6293)\ \ \ \ \ (.5223)\ \ \ (0.4287)$$

$R^2 = .566$
$S_u = 2.50$
$S_p = 3.69$

1957–58
West Texas-New Mexico
(69 contracts)

$$P = 6.830 + .0234V + .0682D + .1937T - .4891Y + 2.639C_1 - 1.0922C_2$$
$$ (.0066)\ \ (.1523)\ \ (.1974)\ \ (.5722)\ \ (0.9980)\ \ (0.9957)$$

$R^2 = .411$
$S_u = 2.14$
$S_p = 2.65$

1957–58
Panhandle-Hugoton
fields (263 contracts)

$$P = 17.798 + .0152V - 1.7900D + .4556T + .4913Y - 1.5706C_1 + .5195C_2$$
$$ (.0071)\ \ (.1859)\ \ (.0334)\ \ (.2246)\ \ (.6134)\ \ (.2270)$$

$R^2 = .578$
$S_u = 1.76$
$S_p = 2.67$

1957–58
Central Kansas and
Oklahoma (168 con-
tracts)

$$P = -3.588 - .0078V + 2.1405D + .2324T + .0007Y - 1.7612C_1 + .5000C_2$$
$$ (.0082)\ \ (0.3626)\ \ (.0503)\ \ (.0277)\ \ (0.3196)\ \ (.3135)$$

$R^2 = .531$
$S_u = 1.75$
$S_p = 2.49$

251

(*Competitive*)
Predictions

$\beta_1 > 0$
$\beta_2 < 0$
$\beta_3 > 0$
$\beta_5, \beta_6 \leqq 0$

(*Monopsony*)
Predictions

$\beta_1 = 0$
$\beta_2 = 0$
$\beta_3 \leqq 0$
$\beta_5, \beta_6 \leqq 0$

Test of predictions

If the computed coefficient b_i divided by its standard error (in parenthesis) is greater than 1.645, then the hypothesis $\beta_i = 0$ is rejected in favor of $\beta_i > 0$ or $\beta_i < 0$.

Source. Tables in Chapters 5, 6, 7.

tion remaining is what should be the nature of Federal Commission regulation in this diverse group of markets.

REGULATION

The Federal Power Commission received a mandate from the Supreme Court in 1954 to regulate field prices in order to prevent monopoly "extortion of consumers." [5] According to this mandate prices in the later 1950s should have been regulated to prevent realization by producers of monopoly profits. In the Gulf Coast, West Texas, or Mid-Continent regions the Commission need not have *set prices* in order to have prevented monopoly, given the predominant presence of competition or monopsony. Perhaps prices should have been regulated in some specific fields where there was one seller and where small buyers had no access to other fields. [6] But these would have been the exception to the rule, where the rule required no price control when there was no monopoly power.

The presence of an independent regulatory commission that regulates "best" (i.e., efficiently completes its assigned task) by *not* setting price is bound to give rise to some questions about the necessity for any regulation. Regulation is generally conceded to be of doubtful propriety if the reasons for imposition of control were fallacious. Regulation was advocated in the courts and Congress to prevent monopoly prices in the Southwest. Studies of most field and supply markets in Texas, Louisiana, Oklahoma, etc., indicate the presence of systematic competition or monopsony throughout the period in which regulation was proposed (as seen in Chapters 5, 6, 7). The problem to be solved by regulation seems not to have existed, so that the court mandate was given for "wrong" rea-

5. Cf. discussion of *Phillips Petroleum Company v. Wisconsin* 347 US 672 (1954) in Chapter 1 above.

6. This would no doubt have required regulation of a group of contracts for gas for resale within one state. The Federal Power Commission jurisdiction of "sales for resale in interstate commerce" would not have been applicable.

sons. The necessity for Federal Power Commission regulation is doubtful.

But perhaps it was the right policy that was followed, even if for the wrong reasons. The Federal Power Commission's newly established methods of regulation may yet have desirable net social effects not anticipated at the time of the *Phillips* decision. These results may warrant continuation of regulation, even in competitive and monopsonistic markets.

Current methods of regulation are the result of years spent searching for criteria to justify a "freeze" in the level of field prices. The Federal Power Commission refused to review initial price on a new contract (while issuing a "certificate of necessity and convenience" to a producer), but it did review price later, under section 4 of the Natural Gas Act, when a Favored Nations or Renegotiation increase was requested. This left producers and buyers free to sell new reserves for unregulated prices, since control of price increases could be avoided by paying a higher initial price. In 1959, the Power Commission review procedure was declared to be insufficient by the Supreme Court "where the proposed (initial) price is not in keeping with the public interest." Instead, it was suggested that "the Commission in the exercise of its discretion might attach such conditions (to the certificate) as it believes necessary." [7]

The Federal Power Commission, as a result, proposed the "establishment of price standards to be applied in determining the acceptability of initial price." [8] The price standards in 1960 were "area prices" for each of 23 producing regions, and each producer was left free to agree to a contract for a price less than or equal to the "area price" applicable to his region. Any producer seeking certification at a higher price would bear the burden of proving its "necessity and convenience," according to unspecified criteria.

7. *Atlantic Refining Company v. Public Service Commission,* 360 U.S. 328 (1959).

8. *Federal Power Commission Statement of General Policy No. 61-1* (Sept. 28, 1960).

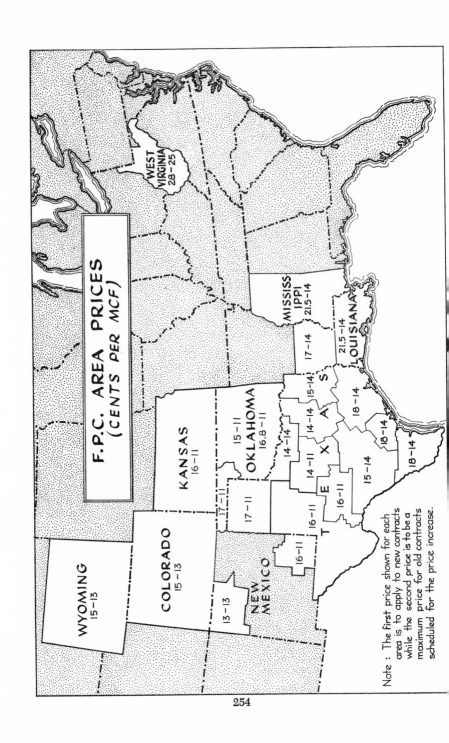

F.P.C. AREA PRICES
(CENTS PER MCF)

Note: The first price shown for each area is to apply to new contracts while the second price is to be a maximum price for old contracts scheduled for the price increase.

WYOMING
15-13

COLORADO
15-13

NEW MEXICO
13-13

KANSAS
16-11

OKLAHOMA
16.8-11

15-11

WEST VIRGINIA
28-25

MISSISSIPPI
21.5-14

LOUISIANA
21.5-14

TEXAS

17-11

17-11

16-11

16-11

16-11

14-11

14-14

14-14

14-14

15-14

15-14

17-14

18-14

18-14

18-14

Up to the present, maximum "area prices" have followed pricing patterns observed for 1956–58. The highest regulated "area prices" have been set where there had previously been buyer's competition; the lowest prices have been required where there had previously been one buyer. The level of "area prices" has been slightly higher than the regression price for 1958 on a contract for some 50 billion cu. ft.[9] But unregulated new contract prices in earlier markets had increased over time where there was buyer's competition, and particularly where monopsony was in decline. The presumed future effect of these "area prices" will be to prevent further price increases and to prevent the establishment of systematically competitive prices in West Texas-New Mexico or central Kansas-Oklahoma.

Are the effects of a price freeze beneficial? These effects include changes in rates of sale of reserves, in the distribution of production, and in returns to consumers (as opposed to producers). All such changes are not likely to increase general economic well-being. Holding down the level of price clearly benefits some consumers. Maintaining the 1958 price P_0 given regional (predicted) demand D and supply S of known reserves in 1960–65 [10] will result in excess demand as shown in Figure 8:1. The quantity Q_0 will have to be rationed among buyers seeking Q_0', probably by allowing sales to the established or closest transporter (given present Federal Power

9. Prices from the 1958 regression equations, for a contract of 50 billion cu. ft. of twenty-year term, were:

Gulf Coast =	16.75 ± 2.50 cents
West Texas =	13.43 ± 2.14
Panhandle-Hugoton =	13.69 ± 1.76
Central Kansas and Oklahoma =	12.25 ± 1.75

These estimates, computed from the regression equations in Table 8:4, can be compared with the initial prices on new contracts on the "area prices" map (shown as the first figure, while the second figure is maximum price on old contracts). They are more than the area prices (by more than the standard errors of estimates, shown as the amount after the regression price).

10. These curves are from Chapter 4 and are competitive demand and supply of uniform-quality sales at the "end of transmission." For purposes of this discussion, gathering costs and contract differences in term, volume, etc., are ignored.

Commission certification policies).[11] The exclusion of new pipelines or pipelines located farther from reserves will allow completion of actual sales to consumers included in demand D'. These consumers will receive an increased "consumer's

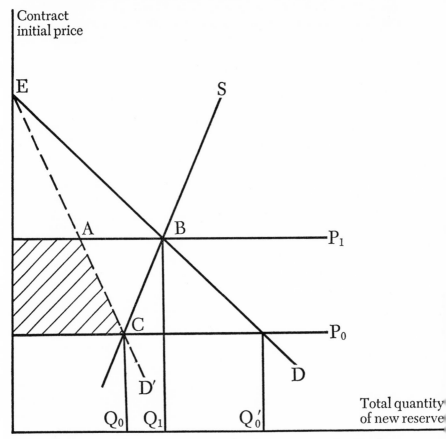

FIGURE 8:1   Maximum "Area Price" P_0 in a Competitive Market

11. During 1960 certain pipelines were not able to obtain sufficient volumes of new reserves to satisfy demand (at the prevailing resale price). The result was the placing of restrictions upon the installation of gas appliances in new dwellings or remodeled older dwellings in communities served by these pipelines. This was the case in: (1) Virden, Rockford, Peoria, and Quincy, Illinois; Muncie, Pendleton, Richmond, Greenfield, and Kokomo, Indiana; Battle Creek, Michigan;

surplus" equal to the shaded area in the diagram, by paying
P_0 rather than P_1.[12]

That this group of consumers will gain from the "area price"
is not enough to make regulation generally beneficial. Other
groups will lose by the imposition of price P_0. The producers
will lose economic rents in an amount equal to the shaded
area, plus the triangle ABC (rents composed of net returns
over and above short-run development costs for discovered
reserves, as shown in Chapter 4). Their loss will be greater
than the increase in the actual purchaser's surplus by the
amount ABC, so there will be a net social loss. Freezing price
at the level P_0 will have the effect of lowering earnings at
the margin of sales as well, so that production of new reserves
is decreased from Q_1 to Q_0.

Macon and Sedalia, Missouri; Paulding, Ohio, for Panhandle Eastern
Pipeline Company; (2) Nashville, Waukegan, and Chicago, Illinois, for
Natural Gas Pipeline Company of America; (3) Alton and East St.
Louis, Illinois; St. Louis, Missouri, for Mississippi River Fuel Company;
(4) Milwaukee, Wisconsin, for Michigan-Wisconsin Pipeline; (5) Evans-
ville, Indiana, for Texas Gas Transmission Corporation. Three of these
transporters were new purchasers in the most active source-region for
new volumes. Panhandle Eastern, Natural Gas Pipeline, and Michigan-
Wisconsin all sought to buy new reserves in the last few years in sectors
of the Panhandle-Hugoton where they had not previously had gathering
lines. Mississippi River Fuel and Texas Gas purchased in a small North
Louisiana region characterized by almost no new discoveries after 1960.
They would have had to go elsewhere to purchase any reserves as a new
entrant. Their excess demand, as last entering buyers, may be a first indication of the problems to follow from price control in the 1960s.

12. "Consumer's surplus" is the excess satisfaction gained from paying
a price for all units equal only to the utility of the marginal unit (or to
the marginal rate of substitution between this and other goods). In
money terms, consumer's surplus is the amount buyers would pay for
Q_0 over and above $(P_0 \cdot Q_0)$ rather than be deprived of purchases alto-
gether. The shaded area indicates this gain, given a number of extremely
limited assumptions:

1. There must be no "income effect" from price P_0 rather than P_1
that results in appreciably larger demand for other goods (if there is,
consumer's surplus is larger than the shaded area).

2. Price must be equal to marginal cost in all other industries and
marginal costs should be constant (if this does not hold, losses elsewhere have to be counted). Cf. I. M. D. Little, *A Critique of Welfare
Economics* (Paperback, London, Oxford University Press, 1958)
chap. 10.

These predicted effects may or may not be beneficial. Quantity of output Q_0 is clearly less than optimal, since an increment to output costs less than consumers would be willing to pay (as indicated by the difference between supply and demand prices for any output between Q_0 and Q_1). Yet redistribution of income to consumers from producers has long been a central goal of regulation, from the Granger endeavors toward state railroad regulation in the 1860s and 1870s to Professor Kahn's statement: "When changes in (gas field) demand are so great, and supply so apparently inelastic, as to double the basic real price . . . conferring large economic rents and possibly monopoly profits on those who have managed to appropriate a part of our national resources, I am skeptical that economics can be said to dictate a policy of laissez-faire." [13]

But the excluded potential consumers incur a considerable loss of "consumer's surplus" as well. This loss of surplus, represented by the area AEB in Figure 8:1, has to be regarded as a direct effect of the actual purchasers' gain in surplus.[14] For there to be an improvement for all consumers, through regulation, the excluded buyers must be compensated for their loss by the actual buyers and the latter left with a net gain.[15] A net gain is not likely, given that the surplus from the

13. A. E. Kahn, "Economic Issues in Regulating the Field Price of Natural Gas," 50 *American Economic Review* 507 (May 1960).

14. If consumer's surplus analysis were to be applied in a thoroughgoing fashion, some attempt should be made to determine whether the limiting assumptions hold and to measure area AEB. Then a comparison could follow of area AEB with the shaded section to determine *net* social gain (i.e., whether AEB is less than the shaded area ignoring the producer's net loss ABC). But "there is the obvious fact that areas under demand curves cannot be measured" as noted by Little, p. 179. Rather than using consumer's surplus analysis to compare utility gained and lost, however, the framework of the theory can be formulated to present only the types of comparisons that have to be made in any attempt to maximize social welfare by regulation. Consumer's surplus framework is convenient because it involves no introduction of further diagrammatical devices than those used throughout the preceding chapters. But operational procedures of decision-making can be formulated in the discussion in terms of the more insightful "new welfare economics" concern for interpersonal compensation.

15. "Before we can say that 'welfare' increases . . . we must know

first units of consumption for excluded purchasers is likely to be quite large. It is yet to be acknowledged that such compensation is necessary, so that this recently established regulation is not a rationalized system of control.

Over the next few years, these matters pertinent for justifying regulation should become more apparent. The choice between low-priced gas for some consumers while others have none, as contrasted with sufficient gas to serve all at a higher price, will be made in a most striking fashion in regions served by new reserves from fields in newly competitive supply areas. "Area prices" in fields emerging from monopsony will involve a differential of at least 35 per cent between competitive and regulated price (if the regulated price is set at the monopsony level after the new pipelines have entered, as seems likely in West Texas and in central Kansas and Oklahoma). Excess demand at this low "area price" is likely to be apparent both to consumers and the Commission. The consumers necessarily excluded from gas service will be the customers of the entering lines creating the competition.[16] With a large number of unsatisfied customers in one consuming state, there is likely to be demand for "equitable" distribution of reserves.

Even more important will be the effects of "area prices" upon the amount of new reserves. Not only will there be some effect, such as $Q_1 - Q_0$, upon the sales of *known* reserves in any given supply market, but also there should be an effect upon the discovery of new reserves. In simplest terms, the expectation of higher future prices provides incentives for larger exploration investments. Given a priori probabilities of success in finding dry-gas reserves, the larger investment results in larger discovery.[17] The more intensive exploration

(whether) the gainer by the change can profitably compensate the loser, or bribe him into accepting it; and the loser cannot bribe the gainer into rejecting it." J. DeV. Graaf, *Theoretical Welfare Economics* (Cambridge, Cambridge University Press, 1957), p. 87.

16. The buyer will be much more willing to sell to the established transporter able to begin taking gas immediately, *given* the uniform area price.

17. It is difficult, of course, to point to probabilities for finding various volumes of undiscovered reserves of gas at different locations. But there

accompanying higher prices might be related to the supply of new reserves S, the less intensive exploration to supply S′

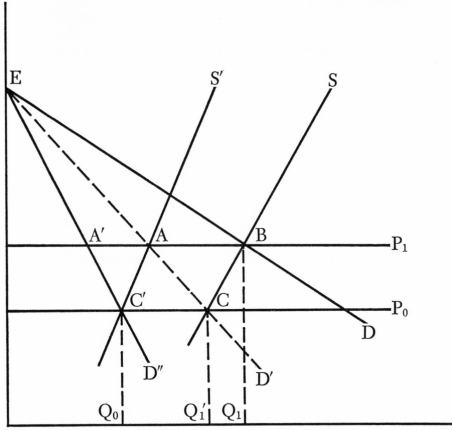

FIGURE 8:2   Maximum "Area Price" P_0 and Long-Run Market Condition

in Figure 8:2.[18] In the long run, the surplus for actual buyers would be less and the loss of surplus of excluded buyers would be greater (the area $A′EB$ rather than AEB). Producer's

is proof of their existence in the validation of the theory that follows. This proof has been extensively provided by M. A. Adelman in "The Supply and Price of Natural Gas" (available from the author).

18. It is interesting to note that the monopsony buyers setting prices similar to P_0 from all appearances solve the "long-run" problem by

economic rents for new reserves would have been decreased, and rates of sale of reserves would have fallen by the additional amount $Q'_1 - Q_0$.

The decrease in output is likely to be large. To begin with, "if we compare new gas reserves with new contract prices . . . same-year prices would indicate that for every cent of increase in price, about 750 billion cubic feet of additional reserves are found per year; previous-year prices would make it about an even trillion." [19] That is, experience during the 1950s points to the long-run supply of known reserves being represented by the straight lines:

$$Q_T = 1,672 + 767P_T$$
$$Q_{T+1} = \ \ \ 230 + 965P_T$$

where $P_T =$ average initial price on new contracts in cents per mcf, $Q_T =$ billions of cubic feet of newly discovered reserves in year T.[20] If this experience continues, while market price rises 1.0 cents per mcf per year, then actual sales some five years hence might well be five trillion cubic feet less as a result of maintaining area prices.[21] Consumers as a group may end up with 20 per cent "fewer reserves" for purchase.[22]

---

doing their own exploration. The share of discovered reserves coming from El Paso Natural Gas exploration department was quite large by 1955 (as shown in Chapter 5). The large lines in the Mid-Continent also carried out extensive exploration (as seen from the figures on uncommitted reserves in Chapter 7) but in the Gulf Coast, where competition was pervasive, pipelines did not carry out exploration to any great extent.

19. Adelman, pp. 69, 71. Professor Adelman discusses all due limitations of the estimation procedure utilized in reaching this conclusion in pages 69–80. These limitations would not seem to be nearly extensive enough to require abandonment of these quoted rules-of-thumb.

20. Adelman, p. 75a. The long-run supply curve is the locus of the intersection points of supply S and demand D (such as points B and C' in Figure 8:2) and is computed by the least-squares regression technique with time-series data.

21. Professor Adelman also expects the long-run supply curve to shift to the left in the future because of increases in the real costs of finding gas (cf. Adelman, pp. 77–78). If this is the case, the foregone annual volumes of new reserves would be smaller than five trillion cubic feet.

22. Given that 1957–58 actual sales in the Southwest were 16.3 trillion cubic feet, future sales might be $(16.3 - 5.0)$ trillion each two years, when they could be 16.3 trillion. This is assuming that 50 per cent

Demands for "distributive justice," and for more intensive exploration of dry-gas reserves, may make these results from price control obvious. At that point, an attempt to justify the presence of regulation should be made. It has been argued heretofore that the original reason for regulation—i.e., that producer's monopolizing activities need be prevented—has no substance in general. Regulation of competitive and monopsonistic markets can be considered "right," for this "wrong" reason, only if it can be shown that some consumers gain more than is lost by others, excluded potential consumers, and only if it can be further shown that the loss in discovery of new reserves should be ignored. Otherwise, control of gas field prices by the Federal Power Commission cannot be justified.[23]

POLICY FOR MORE EFFICIENT NONREGULATED MARKETS

But this is not to suggest that policy should entirely be directed toward removing intervention in gas field markets. Control of other aspects than price can be investigated with hopes of some gain in consumer welfare.

In particular, some control of income from production may be justified. Differential rents earned on some sales from

---

of undiscovered reserves would be in the Gulf Coast, West Texas-New Mexico, and the Mid-Continent.

23. Pervasive regulation could be justified if it follows a particular course of action:

    1. A system of "shadow prices" is so constructed that each consumer's demand is calculated for a uniform gas supply at a particular location. Gas then is *rationed* on the basis of "shadow prices" so that the marginal value ("price") of a cubic foot is the same for each consumer.

    2. Gas is sold at actual price P_0, but marginal rewards are paid to producers sufficient to shift supply from S' to S. This would result in the optimal conditions of production and exchange, but with redistribution of income from producer's rents to consumer's surplus. But such a scheme of "ideal regulation" does no more than reproduce the conditions of a competitive exchange (when income has been redistributed). And the impositions of rationing and subsidization can be avoided by recourse to the original conditions of the market—which would seem to be an advantage.

prices greater than unit development and long-run exploration costs could be considered income for potential taxation. There may be political preference for giving higher real incomes to consumers and lower incomes to producers (or to those investing in oil companies) that can be realized by specific "rent taxes." Taxes that affect rental returns only, as opposed to taxes affecting marginal exploration, remain to be formulated.[24] It is fair to say, however, that "rent taxes" involve no greater problems than does a policy of direct price control for the purposes of income redistribution, and may involve considerably less.[25]

For similar reasons, investigations of monopsony may be in order. Pipelines long able to purchase gas reserves at monopsony price levels (similar to P_0 in Figure 8:1) have taken it upon themselves to ration gas among consumers. This rationing has come about, of course, because the quantity demanded at the resale price is greater than the quantity purchased by the transporter (by an amount similar to $Q_0' - Q_0$, in Figure 8:1, assuming that demand D is resale demand minus transportation costs). The specific basis on which pipelines have rationed consumption in the past is not known. That is a study in itself. Perhaps lags in regulation of transporters have allowed them to utilize prices to allocate quantity Q_0 among buyers. In this case, extra-normal profits should have followed for the transporter.[26] Perhaps regulation has set resale price equal to P_0 plus the costs of transport, so that the quantity has been allocated on the basis of first come, first served.[27] In this case, output and distribution effects are the

24. The returns over and above long-run unit costs (including the expected value of exploration expense) should be the only source for taxation, if the continued scarcity problem is to be avoided. These excess returns, after further research, may prove to be negligible.

25. The tax would not necessarily exclude some consumers from purchasing so that other consumers can experience a gain in surplus at the same time.

26. Monopsony excess returns are likely to complement monopoly returns from sales to industrial users (since these are unregulated and the industrial demand curve is not generally highly elastic, as has been seen in Chapter 3).

27. This is not as likely as the first possibility. There do not seem to be restrictions on gas use in areas served by El Paso Gas, for example,

same as those resulting from "area price." Either situation could be improved upon by introducing competition in field demand.[28]

A policy toward contingency clauses in contracts could be most important to increased efficiency of nonregulated markets past and present. These Favored Nations and/or Renegotiation clauses have been presumed to transfer, from producer to pipeline, the *risk* of "too low" a price during the contract term. If this had happened, both competitive and monopsonistic prices would have been lower for those clauses with contracts. But actual contract prices did not indicate any clear tendency to be lower for contracts containing clauses, than for those without clauses during the 1950s.[29] This can only mean the clauses recently have not been providing any protection for the producer or any expected cost to the buyer. Contingency clause contracts have, however, resulted in some relocation of buyers. Older buyers (like Transcontinental Gas Pipeline and Natural Gas Pipeline Company) have found themselves unable to purchase in their established supply areas when new purchases required raising price on all old contracts. Instead, the older lines have constructed extensive, sometimes-circular lateral systems elsewhere, to gain entry into regions where they have no old contracts outstanding. It is doubtful that this resulted in a net saving to the economy: the costs avoided were rent payments on old reserves, while the costs incurred were for construction resources. Moreover, the rents were payments in compensation to those not taking

but the search for alternative sources of supply by the large California companies has been intensive. And they have found that gas is available only at higher prices, because of higher field prices paid by Transwestern and others after field buyers competition has been established. Cf. *Transwestern Pipeline,* F.P.C. Docket G-1487.

28. The income redistribution would be from pipeline to consumer, in the first case, and from consumer to producer in the second. The second case *might* be improved by "rent taxation" and gains in consumer's surplus from removing regulation—as when area prices are removed. The first case would seem more likely.

29. Cf. coefficients for C_1, C_2 in Tables 8:1, 8:2, 8:3. The theory suggests that the coefficients should be negative. They are not in most regression equations, and there is no "pattern" of consistency as to area, the state of competition, etc.

part in a current market.[30] With the clauses having little "contingency" value in current markets and resulting in the economic cost of pipeline relocation, there would seem to be some advantage from voiding them.[31]

A FINAL REVIEW

As has been suggested by this long analysis of price formation in the 1950s, gas markets were diverse in structure and behavior, and were generally competitive or were changing from monopsony toward competition. It would seem possible that this could result in price level changes and in a revolution of pricing patterns in contrast with those associated with monopoly. Markets with such characteristics need not be regulated by the Federal Power Commission to prevent monopoly pricing. Nor, at present, is it easy to justify regulation on other grounds, given the undesirable effects on excluded consumers and the rate of discovery and sale of reserves. But it is easy to suggest that an interesting—and potentially rewarding—investigation could be made into the effects of taxes on producer's rents, and into the consequences of voiding contingency clauses. But, by and large, the strongest suggestion arising from this study of competition, monopsony, and regulation in the 1950s is that there should be more of the first.

30. 1956 deliveries of reserves sold in 1946 from jointly held fields bear no relation to 1956 sales of new reserves, since 1946 *reserves* could not have been "saved" for commitment in 1956. These windfall returns have the most tenuous connection to present exploration for new reserves.

31. This is to suggest that established pipelines were mistaken in signing 1945 contracts with clauses. The mistakes should not be repeated (that is, expected cost of the clause, to the buyer, should be close to realized cost). Voiding clauses in old contracts would interfere with payments of rents under the old errors, and would prevent mislocation of the transporters. Omission of clauses in new contracts should have an insignificant effect upon prices in new reserve markets (as seen by the regression equations).

An Appendix on Statistical Analysis

ESTIMATION OF CITY-WIDE HOME DEMAND FOR GAS

A cross-section analysis of home use of gas can provide an approximation to long-period demand in one city if certain conditions are met. The data concerning prices and quantities in different cities have to be indicative of demand at various prices at one location. For this to be the case, groups of consumers in various cities have to be highly similar—to have the same requirements for heat, the same incomes, and to be equal in number. Given that there are differences from city to city, then differences in tastes or "income effects" must be accounted for and separated from the demand function $Q = f(P)$.

Intercity price differences for gas and differences between consumers can be assumed to have at least a linear effect upon consumption. That is, $[Q = \alpha + \beta_1 P + \beta_2 P_0 + \beta_3 T + \beta_4 N + \beta_5 Y + v]$ where Q = millions of cubic feet consumed per annum in one city; P = price of gas for the *marginal* thousand cubic feet consumed per capita, cents per mcf; P_0 = price of fuel oil for the average consumption per capita, cents per gallon; T = "temperature degree days," the cumulative number of degrees below 60° in the year in that city (as an indication of heating requirements, at different locations); N = population in that city; Y = median income per resident in that city. An estimate of this equation from a sample of pertinent data for 1959 in 52 United States cities,[1] is as follows:

1. Source: *Brown's Directory of Natural Gas Companies, 1959* (New York, Moore Publishing Company, 1960). These cities were chosen because data for each was complete, and because there had been no price change in the previous 18 months at each such location. The latter requirement was designed to prevent including in the sample *short-run* changes in quantity demanded because of a price change.

$$Q = -53521.327 - 66.359P + 806.597P_0 + 2.242T + .0307N$$
$$\quad\quad\quad (54.792) \quad (1431.140) \quad (1.308) \quad (.0121)$$
$$+ 19.613Y.$$
$$(3.843)$$

The standard deviations of regression coefficients are given in parentheses, and relative magnitudes indicate that the coefficients β_3, β_4, β_5 are significantly different from zero. The coefficient of determination R^2 is .5215, so that 52.15 per cent of the variance in quantities purchased is "explained" by changes in values of these factors. The standard error of estimate S_u is 11,406.304 mmcf. The demand relation $Q = f(P)$ in a "typical city" is shown in Table 3:1, and is derived by inserting *mean* values for P_0, T, N, and Y in this equation.

ESTIMATES OF INDUSTRIAL DEMAND SCHEDULES

The demand for industrial gas in a particular industry in any one-state market can be indicated by analysis of demand in that industry at a number of different locations. If firms purchasing gas at different locations each have the same demand schedule, and if there are equal numbers of firms at all locations, then price and quantity at each point may represent values for the common demand function $Q = f(P)$.

For each industry considered, the number of firms at any location has to be "held constant," as does the size of any particular firm (since economies or diseconomies of scale should affect industrial demand for gas). The prices of substitute fuels have to be the same for all firms, so that the quantities purchased of gas at some price are in accordance with similar opportunities for substitution of fuel oil or coal. An attempt to determine (and eliminate) differences in substitution and output effects at different locations follows from calculating the coefficients for P_2, P_3, S, F in the equation:

$$[Q = \alpha + \beta_1 P_{gas} + \beta_2 P_2 + \beta_3 P_3 + \beta_4 P_4 + \beta_5 S + \beta_6 F + v]$$

where: Q = millions of cubic feet of gas consumed by the industry in one state; P_{gas} = average price of gas in that state, cents per thousand cubic feet; P_2 = average price of fuel oil in that state, cents per gallon; P_3 = average price of coal in that state, dollars per ton; P_4 = average price of electricity in that state, cents per thousand kilowatt hours; S = average size of the firm in that state (as indicated by average value added to output); F = number of firms in that state. Once values for the coefficients of the independent variables are calculated by the method of least squares then the

TABLE A:1. *Regression Equations For Demand in Six Industries*

$$Q = \alpha + \beta_1 P_{gas} + \beta_2 P_2 + \beta_3 P_3 + \beta_4 P_4 + \beta_5 S + \beta_5 F + v$$

Meat Processing

$$Q = 1123.238 - 16.4961P_{gas} - 385.125P_2 + 46.784P_3 + 173.197P_4 + 3.173S - 1.4049F$$
$$(12.90) \qquad (331.6) \qquad (171.5) \qquad (166.4) \qquad (1.223) \quad (3.324)$$

$R^2 = .4411$
$S_u = 1276$
N (number of items in sample) = 25

Bakery Products

$$Q = 1090.427 - 9.348P_{gas} - 43.323P_2 - 33.762P_3 - 18.873P_4 + 1.1938S + 1.015F$$
$$(4.657) \qquad (134.9) \qquad (60.97) \qquad (24.24) \qquad (1.789) \quad (.4005)$$

$R^2 = .4006$
$S_u = 438.6$
$N = 29$

Structural Clay Products

$$Q = -2641.7096 - 43.1546P_{gas} - 265.079P_2 + 634.459P_3 + 69.314P_4 + 5.4765S + 10.9735F$$
$$(27.81) \qquad (545.1) \qquad (599.7) \qquad (216.1) \qquad (4.273) \quad (13.63)$$

$R^2 = .3604$
$S_u = 2041$
$N = 18$

Motor Vehicles and Equipment

$$Q = -3736.665 - 30.6845P_{gas} + 21.484P_2 + 139.482P_3 + 460.592P_4 + .8606S + 12.266F$$
$$(17.29) \qquad (162.6) \qquad (57.85) \qquad (61.50) \qquad (.1703) \quad (2.792)$$

$R^2 = .9526$
$S_u = 578.5$
$N = 13$

Beverage Manufacturing

$$Q = 363.368 - 8.711P_{gas} - 16.749P_2 + 22.308P_3 - 7.921P_4 - .0132S + .7760F$$
$$(3.062) \qquad (32.83) \qquad (22.56) \qquad (7.096) \qquad (.1952) \quad (.4072)$$

$R^2 = .3913$
$S_u = 234.1$
$N = 30$

Iron and Steel Foundries

$$Q = -1834.963 - 14.639P_{gas} - 114.670P_2 - 11.734P_3 + 169.712P_4 + 1.3639S + 11.8308F$$
$$(7.219) \qquad (185.1) \qquad (30.05) \qquad (68.91) \qquad (.3929) \quad (1.841)$$

$R^2 = .9398$
$S_u = 326.0$
$N = 16$

Source. All listed states for which there was complete information on all variables in *Census of Manufacturers 1947: Fuels and Electric Energy Consumed,* U.S. Department of Commerce, Bureau of the Census, Washington, 1949.

269

effect of gas price on quantity can be examined in $\{Q = \alpha + \beta_1 P_{gas} + \alpha'\}$ (with α' obtained by inserting average values for P_2, P_3, S, F, in the original equation).

The computed equations are shown in Table A:1. From these are derived the (condensed) demand curves in Table 3:2, indicating quantities and prices for "typical" conditions of average price of fuel oil, etc., at one location.

REGRESSION ANALYSES OF PRICE FORMATION

A number of issues with respect to calculation of

$$P = \alpha + \beta_1 V + \beta_2 D + \beta_3 T + \beta_4 Y + \beta_5 C_1 + \beta_8 C_2 + v \text{ in Chap-}$$
ters 5, 6, and 7 have not been discussed in these chapters, so as not to distract attention from the extended discussion of the actual pricing patterns. The most serious problems of calculation include estimates of values of the variables for specified contracts, and the characteristics of the sample in relation to prerequisites for calculating a regression equation. These can be reviewed in turn.

Estimating contract data. As mentioned in Chapter 3, some items pertinent for price formation are not set down in the contract, but rather are estimated by the pipeline and seller.

The distance to points of resale is not specified in the contract because there is no need to do so. The location of the new reserves is specified by field, county, and state. The only available estimate of distance D is that from measuring the shortest distance between the pertinent main transmission lines and the middle of the county containing the new field. Public maps of gas fields do not indicate the exact location of most new fields until some years after sale of reserves, so that measurement to the center of the county has to be tolerated.

The volume of recoverable reserves is estimated by buyer and seller but is not listed in the contract (for reasons mentioned in Chapter 3). The estimate for volume for each contract in the regression analysis is 1955 production multiplied by term-length (for contracts signed before 1955) or the listed "expected monthly rate of production" multiplied by term in months (for contracts after 1955). These estimates may not be accurate. There is no test for accuracy of the estimates on contracts before 1955 given present data; contracts for 1955–60 can be compared with a partial listing of reserves by buyers, however.

Pipelines are required to list field contracts and volumes of reserves dedicated in each contract in the "Form 2" annual reports to the Federal Power Commission. These listings of reserves are far from complete. The list seldom consists of estimates of reserves made at the time of contract signing, but rather indicates revised estimates of reserves consistent with volume and pressure changes during production. The only estimates of "new reserves" at the time of the contract are those in new contracts. The 1958 new contract reserves shown in Form 2 can be compared to the estimate of volume (from multiplying monthly production by term) used in the regression analysis. If the latter estimate V_E is a completely accurate appraisal of reserves, and if the Form 2 listing V_L is that volume to which buyer and seller agree (and is not inflated to justify pipeline excess capacity in the present), then estimate V_E equals listing V_L In the linear equation $\{V_L = \alpha + \beta V_E\}$, $\alpha = 0$ and $\beta = 1$. If the estimate systematically appraises reserves to be less than shown in Form 2, then in $(V_L = \alpha + \beta V_E)$, $\beta > 1$. Or if the estimate "exaggerates" the amount of reserves, then $\beta < 1$. For the sample of 37 contracts for 1958 (all that were found in the Federal Power Commission Form 2's for the operating pipelines) the least squares equation is:

$V_L = 6419.8 + .87\ V_E$ [with the standard error of β calculated as $S_b = .17$ and the coefficient of correlation $R^2 = .566$].

This equation suggests that the estimate is "too large," particularly for large volume contracts, but that the difference between estimated and listed volumes is not great (it is not possible to disprove the hypothesis that $\beta = 1$, given that $t = \dfrac{b - \beta}{S_b} = .76$, a difference that could occur by chance more than 50 per cent of the time). In general the estimate appears to provide an accurate prediction of "volume of reserves" in the only known listing of reserves in new contracts.

Samples of Contracts and the Theory of Regression. Reliable tests for hypotheses concerning coefficients β_i

in $\{P = \alpha + \beta_1 V + \beta_2 D + \beta_3 T + \beta_4 Y + \beta_5 C_1 + \beta_6 C_2 + v\}$

require that the conditional frequency distributions $f(P \mid V)$, $f(P \mid D)$, etc., be normal distributions with the expected value of P on a straight line in each dimension and with the variance independent of values of V, D, T, et al. Furthermore, it must be possible to assume that sample values of P are independent and that sample values of the variables V, D, T are independent of each other. Random sampling from such a universe and calculations by least squares result in values of $t = \dfrac{\beta_i - b_i}{S_{b_i}}$ that are normally distributed about zero mean and that have unit variance. With data consisting of information on all known contracts and with incomplete knowledge as to particular values of variables it is doubtful that these preconditions strictly hold.

These conditions may be roughly approximated by existing samples, however. At least one sample of contracts indicate approximate conditions of "normality." The sample of 1956–58 large-sized Gulf Coast contracts was subject to examination of residuals during the analysis of monopoly discrimination in Chapter 6. The Univac regression program at the Operations Analysis Laboratory of the University of Chicago allowed calculation of the residual u between actual and predicted regression price for each contract. These approximations for v should be normally distributed in accordance with the assumptions for the theoretical conditional frequency function. The distribution of residuals on the 113 contracts closely approximates a normal distribution. A normal distribution of a sample of 113 items would include class-values e as shown in column 2 of Table A:2. The differences between observed values o in column 1 and e are insignificant (as concluded from comparing computed $\chi^2 = \Sigma \dfrac{(o - e)^2}{e} = 20.428$ with $\chi^2 = 22.362$ for the 5 per cent level of significance; a value for computed χ^2 greater than 22.362 would disprove the hypothesis that the distribution was normal).

The sample of 359 Panhandle-Hugoton contracts for 1956–58 indicates a similar distribution. An exceptionally large number of contracts with low relative prices in the second sample results in skewness, however ($\chi^2 > 22.362$ so that normality is disproved). These lower-priced sales may well belong in monopsony markets, and do not detract from indications of approximate normality for contracts in the same market.

The two samples also indicate that values of the independent variables may not be interrelated. The simple correlation coefficient between contract volume and term r_{VT} equals ($-.272$) in the Gulf Coast sample; correlation between volume-distance r_{VD} equals ($+.027$) and distance-term r_{DT} equals ($+.230$). Correlation between Favored Nations and Renegotiation $r_{c_1 c_2}$ equals ($-.243$), so that there does not seem to be an unduly large number of contracts in which both occurred or both did not occur. Correlations were lower in the Panhandle sample: $r_{VT} = -.023$, $r_{VD} = -.036$, $r_{DT} = .124$, $r_{c_1 c_2} = .106$. Such low correlations would seem to suggest that bias in estimation of β_i because of lack of independence of values of the variables is not an important problem.

TABLE A:2. *Distribution of Residuals*

$$\text{``}u\text{''} = [P - (a + b_1V + b_2D + b_3T + b_4Y + b_5C_1 + b_6C_2)]$$

Class boundaries (in units of standard deviations of residuals)	(1) 1956–58 Gulf Coast sample of 113 contracts	(2) A normal distribution of a sample of 113 contracts	(3) 1956–58 Panhandle-Hugoton sample of 359 contracts	(4) A normal distribution of a sample of 359 contracts
−4.0 to −3.6	0	0.02	0	0.07
−3.5 to −3.1	0	0.12	3	0.40
−3.0 to −2.6	2	0.55	8	7.74
−2.5 to −2.1	4	1.86	6	5.92
−2.0 to −1.6	4	4.98	6	15.83
−1.5 to −1.1	5	10.38	14	38.24
−1.0 to −0.6	14	16.94	52	53.81
−0.5 to −0.1	22	21.63	91	68.73
+0.0 to 0.4	33	21.63	90	68.73
+0.5 to 0.9	18	16.94	52	53.81
+1.0 to 1.4	9	10.38	28	35.24
+1.5 to 1.9	1	4.98	4	15.83
+2.0 to 2.4	1	1.86	4	5.92
+2.5 to 2.9	0	0.55	0	1.74
+3.0 to 3.4	0	0.12	1	0.40
+3.5 to 3.9	0	0.02	0	0.07

Index

North Houston Field, Texas, 147 n.

Panhandle Field, Oklahoma and Texas, 212 ff.
Partial monopsony in the Southwest fields: Louisiana, 245–46; central Kansas and Oklahoma, 245–46
Pawnee County, Kansas, 221, 227 n.
Permian Basin, Texas, 94, 97
Permian Basin Pipeline Company, 98, 110, 122, 127, 136
Phillips Petroleum Company, 99, 130, 136, 192, 215, 220
Phillips Petroleum Co. v. Wisconsin, 1, 2, 102, 220, 252
Pictured Cliffs Field, San Juan Basin, New Mexico, 128
Pioneer Natural Gas Company, 98, 135, 136
Pipeline demand for gas reserves. *See* Demand conditions
Plaquemines Parish, Louisiana, 162
Poran, H. B., 66 n.
Pratt County, Kansas, 222
Price discrimination: of the monopoly seller, 67–73; tests for, in the Gulf Coast, 200–05
Price formation during the late 1950s: summary evaluation, 250–52
Production costs. *See* Costs of supplying natural gas reserves
Prospectus, El Paso Natural Gas Company, 94
Puckett formation, Permian Basin, 129
Pure Oil Company, 174, 192
Pure Oil Co. et al., F.P.C. Docket G-17930, 66 n.

Refugio County, Texas, 149
Regression equation estimation, 115, 116 n.

Regulation of gas field prices: monopoly as the rationale, 4–7. *See also* Federal Power Commission regulation since 1954
Relative prices, "typical" and "smallest" contracts, 143–45, 209–10, 241–42
"Renegotiation" clause, 31, 50–51
Reno County, Kansas, 222, 227 n.
Republic Natural Gas Company, 102, 105, 192
Required initial capacity, 13–14
Richardson and Bass Company, 134, 142 n.
Robinson, Joan, *The Economics of Imperfect Competition*, 68 n.
Rodessa Field, Louisiana, 147 n.
Rostow, E. V., *A National Policy for the Oil Industry*, 16 n.
Roswell, New Mexico, 98

St. Landry Parish, Louisiana, 172
San Juan Basin, New Mexico, 94, 127
San Salvador Field, Texas, 147 n.
Scitovsky, Tibor, *Welfare and Competition*, 14 n., 76 n.
Seaboard Oil Company, 175
Shamrock Oil and Gas Company, 215, 219
Shell Oil Company, 175, 215
Shepard, G. S., *Marketing Farm Products*, 54 n.
Simkin, C. G. F., "Aspects of Discrimination," 80 n.
Sinclair Oil Company, 99, 105
Skelly Oil Company, 105, 154, 173, 174, 175
"Smallest" contract. *See* Relative prices, "typical" and "smallest" contracts
Smith, R. V. et al., "Flow of Gas through Transmission Lines," 39 n.

Yale Studies in Economics